Huddersfield Drill Hall War Memorials 1899-1902 and 1939-1945

The Duke of Wellington's Regiment

2nd Volunteer Battalion
BOER WAR

5th Battalion
SECOND WORLD WAR

7th Battalion
SECOND WORLD WAR

Drill Hall
Roll of Honour
1899-1902

2nd Volunteer Battalion
The Duke of Wellington's
(West Riding Regiment)

Drill Hall
War Memorials
1939-1945

5th and 7th Battalions
The Duke of Wellington's
Regiment (West Riding)

Compiled by
Scott Flaving

A
VALENCE HOUSE
Publication

First published in Great Britain in 2023
By Valence House Publications
Valence House, Becontree Avenue,
Dagenham, Essex RM8 3HT

www.valencehousecollections.co.uk

The text has been compiled by the authors as an educational, non-profit making publication to inform relatives and researchers of the 'Dukes' soldiers commemorated on the War Memorials in Huddersfield Drill Hall.

Images courtesy of the Trustees of the DWR Museum and Archive, unless otherwise annotated.

Maps © Richard Harvey, DWR Volunteer Archivist.

The publisher is not responsible for the accuracy or continued existence of any websites referenced.

ISBN - 978-1-911391-96-8

All proceeds will be shared between Valence House Volunteers and the Huddersfield Drill Hall and Trust, Charity Number 224671.

Previous Publications

Milnsbridge Drill Hall War Memorial 1914 to 1921:
7th Battalion The Duke of Wellington's (West Riding Regiment) (978-1-911391-97-5)

Huddersfield Drill Hall War Memorial 1914 to 1921:
5th Battalion The Duke of Wellington's (West Riding Regiment) (978-1-911391-98-2)

The Death of the 'Dukes': A Story of Valour & the Sacrifices
Made by a Battalion of the Old Contemptibles (978-1-911391-99-9)

All rights reserved. No part of this publication may be reproduced, stored in a retrieval system, or transmitted, in any form or by any means, electronic, mechanical, photocopying, recording or otherwise, without the prior permission of the copyright owner.

VALENCE HOUSE
a place of discovery

CONTENTS

List of Plates, Illustrations and Maps	2
Foreword	3
Dedication	4
Introduction	5
Glossary	7
Abbreviations	8
Volunteer Service Companies, Boer War 1899-1902	9
5th Battalion, WW2 Normandy Campaign 1944-45	16
7th Battalion WW2 - the Fallen	34
2/7th Battalion, WW2 France and Belgium Campaign 1939-40	78
1/7th Battalion, WW2 Normandy Campaign, 1944-1945	90
115 Regiment Royal Armoured Corps (2/7th DWR)	118
Addenda	122
Heritage and Legacy	125
Acknowledgements	127
Bibliography	128

LIST OF PLATES, ILLUSTRATIONS AND MAPS

PLATES:

Front Cover:

Image © Richard Harvey.

Back Cover:

Images from Major (Retired) Hervé Savary, France.

All other images – courtesy of the Trustees of the Huddersfield Drill Hall, the Trustees of the Museum and Archives of The Duke of Wellington's Regiment or the author.

MAPS:

© Richard Harvey (2018-2019).

FOREWORD

Again I am honoured to have been asked to write a forward to another book compiled by Mr Flaving and his fellow archivist volunteers. Having created a book (2019) giving information about those listed on the 5th Battalion DWR War Memorial boards, the team decided to complete a similar exercise (2021) for the 7th Bn DWR War Memorial tablets which are displayed below those of the 5th Bn DWR memorial boards and which form the front of the balcony in St Paul's Street Drill Hall.

This sequel to their previous book brings to life those whose names are listed on the wooden panel mounted on the wall, and the smaller stone tablet on the floor, below the balcony at the southern end of the main hall.

It is difficult to imagine the amount of research that must be undertaken to establish the identity and background information relating to each individual remembered on these boards. I would not even know where to start. However, once again Mr Flaving and his team have done just that, through endless hours of painstaking work. In so doing they have not only given us a superb reference book relating to those who served and died as members of 7th Bn, but have honoured the memory of those brave soldiers of the Great War.

Again, there appear to be some anomalies and some names missed off which perhaps should have been inscribed when the tablets were commissioned. The Trustees of Huddersfield Drill Hall hope to be able to rectify this by adding the missing names at an appropriate date in the future.

I can recommend this book to anyone with an interest in the 7th Bn DWR, the Huddersfield Drill Hall or a more general interest in the Great War and the part played by men of the local area.

Major (Retired) S M Armitage TD
Chairman of the Drill Hall Trustees
May, 2022.

DEDICATION

This book is dedicated to the men recorded on these memorials who suffered so much,
and their families, who grieved so much,
during and after the Second World War.

May they be ever remembered by future generations.

LEST WE FORGET

INTRODUCTION

**2nd Volunteer Battalion The Duke of Wellington's (West Riding Regiment)
Boer War Roll of Honour
5th and 7th Battalions Duke of Wellington's Regiment (West Riding)
World War Two War Memorials**

housed in Huddersfield Drill Hall

The origins of this book.

This book is the sequel to the previous two books dedicated to the commemoration of the men of the 5th and 7th Battalions of The Duke of Wellington's Regiment (West Riding), who are listed on the two major War Memorials dedicated to those who fell in the Great War, now displayed in Huddersfield Drill Hall. In addition to these imposing memorials are four smaller memorials to the local men who served alongside their Regular counterparts in other conflicts: the Boer War Commemoration Roll of Honour, on the wall above the Stores, lists all those men from the 2nd Volunteer Battalion who were selected from those serving in the Huddersfield Drill Hall to join the Volunteer Service Companies for overseas service, highlighting the three men of the first contingent who died in South Africa. The 5th Battalion WW2 Memorial, situated on the Balcony facing the WW1 Memorials, commemorates the participation of the Unit, at that time titled 600 Regiment Royal Artillery, in the Normandy Campaign. There are also two WW2 Memorials to the units formed by the 7th Battalion (1/7th and 2/7th), the main memorial board was moved from the Milnsbridge HQ when the 7th Battalion was merged with the 5th Battalion, briefly becoming the 5/7th Battalion, in one of the frequent reorganizations of the Territorial Army. The second Memorial is a small stone plinth, which is dedicated to the fallen of D Company of the 1/7th Battalion. This memorial has recently been relocated to be united with the main memorials.

A note on sources:

The major source of information for this work has been the Commonwealth War Graves Commission website. Unlike records for the First World War, which have already been released into the public domain, the records of soldiers from conflicts since then are not due to be released for another twenty years, or so. I am indebted to Mr Richard MacFarlane, who has diligently researched the men of the 1/7th Battalion in Normandy and made his information available to the Regimental Archives.

The Regimental Archives was fortunate in being able to obtain the Inter War Enlistment Books, which were about to be destroyed by a major national museum, which contain some details of those who enlisted, and re-enlisted, following the First World War. These books have been indexed and the relevant book and page numbers have been included where appropriate.

For a more comprehensive list of other sources, please see the bibliography.

Layout:

This book has been split into three sections, by Campaigns, in chronological order. Each section is laid out in following order: The Memorials; The Fallen; The Unit; The Campaign; Honours and Awards; Plates (where available).

The layout of each entry follows as closely as possible to the following sequence:

1. Names are listed alphabetically, for ease of reference, although they are not in strict alphabetical order on the War Memorial boards. Note that not all the men listed have been traced and fifteen men who have been identified in the 7 DWR units are not recorded on the Memorials.

2. Regimental Numbers. Following the formation of the Territorial Army in the early 1920s the Duke of Wellington's Regiment was issued with the block of numbers starting 4601001 but at some stage during the war these numbers were superseded by an eight figure numbering system. However, not all the Regimental numbers belong to the 'Dukes', particularly those who joined the units after the initial transfer of the local infantry units to specialist employments, such as Anti Aircraft, in the case of the 5th Battalion, and Royal Armoured Corps, in the case of the $2/7^{th}$ Battalion.

3. Ranks are shown abbreviated, see the glossary.

4. Family details or residence, if known, are included.

5. Battalion, Company (if known); date of death; the Battle or Sector in which he fell and age (where known), where appropriate.

6. Burial, where applicable. Fewer men from the Second World War than the Great War have no known grave; their names are recorded on a number of Memorials close to the battle sites, such as Dunkirk.

7. Commemorations: we have included as many commemorations as can be traced. The Drill Hall Memorials include the column, for ease of identification. A large number of national and local War Memorials are yet to be fully researched and the names of 'Dukes' who can be identified are being added to a growing database, which the Regimental Archives Team has been working on for many years. The Rotherham WW2 War Memorial has been fully researched and details of this are held in the Archives.

8. Details of mentions in other publications are listed, chiefly the Barclay History Roll of Honour.

9. Finally, epitaphs which were submitted by families after the war, to be carved at the base of the CWGC headstones, are also included.

Example of a full entry:

OVERTON, Jack Forster, 2Lt, 5th DWR (43 AA Bn RE - later 47571 Flt Lt, 613 Sqn RAF).
Awarded Distinguished Flying Cross, *LG 29 Dec 1944,* and French Croix de Guerre.
Son of Ernest and Gertrude Mabel Overton, Lindley, Huddersfield, Yorks, husband of Margaret Overton, Huddersfield, Yorks.

Killed in Action:	Normandy Campaign, France, aged 26.
Buried:	Cambrai (Route de Solesmes) Communal Cemetery, 2, B, 1.
Commemorated:	RAAF Memorial, National Memorial Arboretum, Alrewas, Staffs.
	5 DWR WW2 War Memorial, Col 3.
Commissioned:	6 Jan 1939; transferred to RAF, as Pilot Officer, 29 Nov 1941.

"WERE THEY IMMORTAL WINGS THAT BORE HIM ON HIS FINAL FLIGHT?"

Legacy

We hope that this book will help the relatives of those men who are commemorated on the Drill Hall War Memorials to find out more about their forebears who sacrificed their lives for King and Country. It is also intended to reassure readers that these men, and others, from the Regiment are not forgotten by their comrades who have followed them into the ranks of the Duke of Wellington's Regiment, as well as the friends and supporters working to sustain the history and heritage of the Regiment into the future.

GLOSSARY

Common Military terms used:

Cenotaph	Stone monument erected in a local community to commemorate the men from that community who fell in war and whose remains are elsewhere.
DWR	The Duke of Wellington's Regiment. The Regiment was raised as Huntingdon's Regiment in 1702 and numbered 33rd from 1751. Named The Duke of Wellington's Regiment (DWR) on 18th June, 1853. Amalgamated with the 76th (Hindoostan) Regiment in 1881, forming the 1st and 2nd Battalions of the Regiment. Was known as the West Riding Regiment (W Rid R) in the Boer War and Great War. Its soldiers have been proud to bear the nickname 'Dukes' for many years. The title Duke of Wellington's (West Riding Regiment) became The Duke of Wellington's Regiment (West Riding) in 1922.
First Line	The original Territorial Army battalions, renamed 1/5th, etc, on the raising of the second line units in September 1939.
Formation	A grouping of a number of units, a number of Brigades or a number of Divisions.
Ranks	Private (Pte), Lance Corporal (LCpl), Corporal (Cpl), Lance Sergeant (LSgt), Sergeant/Serjeant (Sgt), Company/Regimental Quarter Master Sergeant (CQMS/RQMS), Company/Regimental Sergeant Major (CSM/RSM), 2nd Lieutenant (2Lt), Lieutenant (Lt), Captain (Capt), Major (Maj), Lieutenant Colonel (Lt Col), Brigadier (Brig), Major General (Maj Gen).
Regiment	Originally raised as a single battalion size unit, named after the Colonels who had been commissioned to raise them. From 1751 the regiments were numbered in order of precedence in the Army List; DWR was numbered 33rd. From 1881, as part of the amalgamations of the Cardwell Reforms, Regiments were grouped in two regular battalions, one for home service, and one for overseas service, usually with a Militia Battalion. In 1883, the Volunteer Battalions were formally linked to their local Recruiting District regular units. In 1908 the Volunteers were re-organised into the Territorial Force. In August, 1914, Regiments were ordered to double the number of their Territorial Force battalions as well as raise further Service (Kitchener) Battalions. For the Second World War the Regiment mobilized 6 Infantry Battalions (two later converted to Armour), 2 Anti Tank Regiments, 1 Searchlight Regiment (later converted to infantry), 2 Royal Armoured Corps Regiments and a Holding Battalion (training and drafting).
Roll of Honour	A list of men who fell, who served, or a combination of both, usually on scrolls, in books or on plaques.
Second Line	The newly raised Territorial Army battalions, named 2/7th, etc, on the splitting of the first line units in September, 1939, in order to double their strength.
Unit	A battalion size grouping, approx 1,000 men in the Infantry.
War Memorial	Normally a stone structure, usually carved or bearing a plaque, with the names of the fallen. However, in many places wooden or metal plaques, lychgates, stained glass windows and even village halls have been erected as war memorials.

ABBREVIATIONS

Abbreviations have been kept to the minimum:

AA	Anti Aircraft
ADR	Armoured Delivery Regiment
ADS	Army Delivery Squadron
Bn	Battalion.
Cons	Consecrated ground
CWGC	Commonwealth War Graves Commission, publications and website.
DEMS	Defensively Equipped Merchant Ships
DWR	*See Glossary.*
EB	Enlistment Books (incl TED; OVER & UNDER Nos - unable to determine meaning)
FDS	Forward Delivery Squadron
HAA	Heavy Anti Aircraft
LG	London Gazette
Mil	Military
RA	Royal Artillery
RAC	Royal Armoured Corps
RAF	Royal Air Force (RAF).
Ranks	*See Glossary.*
RE	Royal Engineers
Regt	Regiment
RoH	Roll of Honour.
S/L	Search Light
TED	EB: Transferred, Enlisted, Discharged
Uncons	Unconsecrated ground
Vol	Volunteer
VSC	Volunteer Service Company (1st, 2nd & 3rd Companies)
WM	War Memorial.

Huddersfield Drill Hall

THE WAR MEMORIALS

INTRODUCTION:

The entries below are in Unit (2nd Volunteer Battalion, 5th and then 7th Battalions) and then alphabetical name order for ease of looking up the names, which is not actually the case on all the War Memorials. There are a few spelling errors, which have been corrected using contemporary sources, wherever possible.

Part 1

THE BOER WAR

2nd Volunteer Battalion The Duke of Wellington's Regiment (Volunteer Service Companies) 1900-1902

THE MEMORIAL

THE FALLEN
of the 2nd Volunteer Battalion

HEMINGWAY, Harry Hirst, 6142 Pte, 2 Vol Bn DWR (1 VSC) [Plaque shows Hemmingway H H].
Son of Allan and Emily Hemingway, Stocksbank, Mirfield, enlisted on 18 Jan 1900 at Huddersfield.
    Died of Enteric Fever: 9 Jul 1900, South Africa, aged 24.
    Buried: South Africa.
    Commemorated: **Drill Hall Boer War Commemorative Roll of Honour, Col 2.**
    South Africa Memorial, Greenhead Park, Huddersfield.
    South Africa Memorial, York Minster.

MELLOR, Joshua Charlesworth, 6119 Pte 2nd Vol Bn DWR (1 VSC).
Son of Sarah Mellor, 22 Mount Road, Marsden, Huddersfield, enlisted on 16 Jan 1900 at Huddersfield.
    Died of Enteric Fever: 22 Jun 1900, Bloemfontein, South Africa, aged 24.
    Buried: South Africa.
    Commemorated: **Drill Hall Boer War Commemorative Roll of Honour, Col 3.**
    South Africa Memorial, Greenhead Park, Huddersfield.
    South Africa Memorial, York Minster.

WALKER, Ernest, 6126 Pte, 2nd Vol Bn DWR (2 VSC).
Resided 19 Whitehead Lane, Fagley, Bradford, enlisted on 16 Jan 1900 at Huddersfield, Yorks.
    Died of Enteric Fever: 27 May 1900, Cape Town, South Africa.
    Buried: South Africa.
    Commemorated: **Drill Hall Boer War Commemorative Roll of Honour, Col 4.**
    South Africa Memorial, Greenhead Park, Huddersfield.
    South Africa Memorial, York Minster.

THE UNIT

6th West Yorkshire Rifle Volunteer Corps
2nd Volunteer Battalion (Duke of Wellington's Regiment) West Riding Regiment

The transition of the 6th Rifle Volunteer Corps, through 2nd Volunteer Battalion and then 5th Battalion (Territorial Force/Territorial Army) between 1859 and 1921 exemplifies the traditions of the ever changing volunteer movement in the country. The Rifle Volunteer Corps had been raised for local defence in 1859/60 during an invasion scare, when it was thought France was once more planning to land an army on English soil. The rapid expansion in the country's defences at that time was obviously sufficient to put them off. It appears that annual training camps were held locally.

In 1862 the Riding School, which was opened on 21st February, 1848, as a dual purpose theatrical venue and riding school, and home to the Yorkshire Yeomanry Cavalry, was sold to the 6th West Yorkshire Rifle Volunteer Corps for use as their Armoury.

In 1883 three Volunteer Battalions were officially associated with the Duke of Wellington's Regiment, the 1st (Halifax), the 2nd (Huddersfield) and the 3rd (Skipton). Unlike the Rifle Volunteer Corps units, the new Battalions were organised and equipped along the lines of the Regular Army, with eight Companies and the Battalion recruiting area then extended from Mirfield, through Huddersfield and the Colne and Holme Valleys, taking in Holmfirth and Meltham, then crossed the Pennines between Marsden and Diggle to Mossley.

From 1883 the 2nd Volunteer Battalion travelled further afield for its annual camps, including Pensarn (Wales), Scarborough, Blackpool, Bridlington, Aldershot, Strensall and even the Isle of Man on two occasions. After 1889 the training camps were conducted at Brigade level (the 1902 Camp was declared a provisional camp and only 31 soldiers attended).

In 1899 the Foundation Stone of the new Drill Hall at St Paul's Street had been laid by Field Marshal Lord Roberts of Kandahar VC KP GCB GCSL GCIE on 4 May, 1899. The money being raised by holding a Military Bazaar and by public subscriptions. Later a board of Trustees was formed to look after the Drill Hall on behalf of the Volunteers and the citizens of Huddersfield. The Drill Hall was completed in 1901 at the same time that some of the Volunteers from the Battalion were serving alongside the 1st Battalion of the Regiment in South Africa and, in 1902, the Armoury was sold to the Northern Theatre Company and turned into the Hippodrome Theatre.

Holmfirth Company detachment selected for service in South Africa.

THE CAMPAIGN

*Transvaal, showing Blockhouse Line from Pretoria to Pietersburg,
1 DWR and the VSC Coys manned the sector north of Watervaal, 1902*

The Boer War in South Africa began on 12 October, 1899, with the invasion of the British Natal and Cape Colony by the Boers, from the Orange Free State and Transvaal, who feared British expansionist policies which threatened their sovereignty. British forces in South Africa at this time were a mere 12,000 men and in December of 1899 the British Regular Army was defeated at Stormberg, Magersfontein and Colenso in what became known as 'Black Week'. Ladysmith, Kimberley and Mafeking were all besieged by strong Boer forces.

In Britain, as part of the mobilisation of the British Empire's power, the Volunteer Battalions in the United Kingdom were called upon to raise Active Service Companies of 116 men under Special Army Order Number 2, dated January 1900. To get round the Home Defence clause of the Volunteer Act, each volunteer was to enlist into the Regular Army for one year. These volunteers were required to be aged between 20 and 35 years, be physically fit, first class shots, of good character and graded as 'efficient' during their previous two years of service. To be selected for service there was much competition between the volunteers:

"Close on 60 men were selected out of about 80 who went through the preliminary inspection, but it was known that the number would have to be considerably reduced still further, and last night the total was brought down to 36 with one placed on the reserve list." Reported in the Keighley Herald, 19th January 1900.

The Volunteer Companies were to serve as formed bodies alongside their Regular counterparts, earning regular rates of pay and a discharge bounty of £5.00. Cotton khaki drill uniforms were issued, although the foreign service helmet was soon replaced by the 'slouch hat'. The full personal kit issue, as listed by the Keighley Herald of 19 January, 1900, was:

"2 prs boots, pr canvas shoes, 2 shirts, 2 pr socks, woolen cap, 3 prs each boot & shoe laces, kit bag, holdall, housewife, towel, razor in case and shaving brush, button brush, cloth brush, 2 pr puttees, comb, clasp knife with lanyard, field dressing, pint mug, tin of grease and a tin of dubbin."

At the beginning of the 20th Century the West Riding Regiment had the following Volunteer Battalions: (**HQs** and Companies)

1st Volunteer Battalion The Duke of Wellington's Regiment (West Riding) - **Halifax**, Brighouse and Hebden Bridge.

2nd Volunteer Battalion The Duke of Wellington's Regiment (West Riding) - **Huddersfield**, Holmfirth, Saddleworth district and Mirfield.

3rd Volunteer Battalion The Duke of Wellington's Regiment (West Riding) - **Skipton**, Settle, Burley, Keighley and Bingley.

Members of these three battalions, assembling at the depot from every corner of the recruiting area, formed three Volunteer Service Companies for service in South Africa. The 1st Volunteer Service Company was attested on 15th January, 1900, with the Regimental Numbers in the series 6071 to 6199, with a strength of 3 Officers and 131 Other Ranks. The Company was mobilised on 21st January, 1900, and sailed from Liverpool on 16th February, landing in South Africa in April, 1900.

The 2nd Volunteer Service Company was attested between 13th March 1900 - with these members being held in a Waiting Company, with pay, until the following year - and 26th February 1901 with Regimental Numbers in the series 7000 to 7131, with a strength of 2 Officers and 122 Other Ranks. This Company was mobilised on 8th March, 1901, and sailed on 16th March, landing in South Africa in April 1901.

A third 'Volunteer Service Company', comprising 26 men, enlisted in February, 1902, with Regimental Numbers in the series 7132 - 7157. This group reached South Africa in March, 1902.

On arrival in South Africa each of the first two Companies, in turn, joined the 1st Battalion and took part in the operations of the Battalion, coming under fire for the first time at Pienaars River. The third Company, on arrival, reinforced the second Company on Blockhouse Line duties.

The major actions of the 1st Battalion were:

Relief of Kimberley: (relieved 3rd Mar 1900)
Klip Drift	15 Feb 00	51 casualties
Drieput Drift	16 Feb 00	30 casualties
Paarderberg	18 Feb 00	184 casualties
Driefontain	12 Mar 00	many casualties
Bloemfontein	4 Mar 00 (occupation)	73 died

Colesberg & Plewman's Farm   24 Feb 00   30 casualties, 1 VC
(F - Mounted Infantry - Coy)

Pienaars River   18 Aug 00   no casualties
(A, B, G & Volunteer Service Coys)

The Great Sweep
Wagons Drift	Sep 00	captured 22 Boers and 35,000 cattle
Rhenoster Kop	29 Nov 00	49 casualties
Northern Railway Blockhouses (between Pretoria & Pietersberg)	19 Jan 01 - Jun 02	1 DWR few casualties
The Train Ambush (close to Watervaal North blockhouse)	31 Aug 01	1 DWR, 6 men killed, 2 Offrs and 17 ORs wounded
Blockhouse Line (Beaufort West to Victoria Road Section)	27 Nov 01 - Mar 02	3rd Militia Bn. Pte J Broadbent killed, 13th Feb.

The 3rd Militia Battalion had initially been employed at Simonstown in Prisoner of War duties but during the second phase of the war they had been deployed on Blockhouse Line duties in the area of Beaufort.

The Blockhouses along the lines of communication (the railways, in effect) reduced the mobility of the Boer Commandos considerably and, as their families were placed into camps, their cattle rounded up and their farms burnt in numerous 'sweeps', they were unable to continue their operations effectively. On 15th May, 1902, the Boer republics' representatives met at Vereeniging, where, on 31 May, 1902, a third proposal of surrender was accepted, with a vote of 54 to 6. The war was finally over.

In 1910 the Boers were given full sovereignty of the Republic of South Africa.

Volunteer Service Company volunteers selected for active service in South Africa, Keighley Drill Hall, 1899.

'Dukes' Bivouac Site, South Africa, 1900.

Sketch of Blockhouse by Cpl Gilley, DWR, South Africa, 1902.

Completed Blockhouse with DWR Band, South Africa, 1902.

Part 2

SECOND WORLD WAR

5th Battalion The Duke of Wellington's Regiment (600 Regiment RA) 1944-1945

THE MEMORIAL

5 DWR WW2 Memorial Boards in Huddersfield Drill Hall being refurbished, 2018.

THE FALLEN
of the 5th Battalion

BENNETT, Roger Arthur, 2044058 Gnr, 5th DWR, later 115 HAA Regt RA.
Son of Alfred and Agnes Bennett, Holmbridge, Yorks.
    Killed in Action: 3 Oct 1944, Normandy Campaign, Netherlands, aged 24.
    Buried: Bergen op Zoom Canadian War Cemetery, 6, D, 7.
    Commemorated: **5 DWR WW2 War Memorial, Col 1.**
    DWR Enlistment Books: No trace.
"A MEMORY FOND AND TRUE FROM THOSE WHO THINK OF YOU. DAD, MUM, BROTHERS AND SISTERS"

BROOKER, CHARLES GEORGE, Bdr, 5th DWR (600 Regt RA).
Son of William and Harriett Brooker, husband of Lillian Brooker, Gravesend, Kent.
    Killed in Action: 16 May 1945, Normandy Campaign, Dunkirk Investment, aged 40.
    Buried: Coxyde Military Cemetery, 1, B, 25.
    Commemorated: **5 DWR WW2 War Memorial, Col 1.**
    DWR Enlistment Books: No trace.

BROWN, W, 5th DWR.   Unable to identify.
    Killed in Action: 4 x Gnrs but no Bdr W Browns listed in CWGC records.
    Buried: No known grave.
    Commemorated: **5 DWR WW2 War Memorial, Col 1.**
    DWR Enlistment Books: No trace.

BROWNLESS, John George, 1606366 Gnr, 5th DWR (600 Regt RA).
Son of George and Margaret Brownless, Evenwood, Co Durham.
    Killed in Action: 14 Apr 1945, Normandy Campaign, Dunkirk Investment, aged 36.
    Buried: Cassell Communal Cemetery Extension, E, 14.
    Commemorated: **5 DWR WW2 War Memorial, Col 1.**
        5 DWR Album, volume 3, Page 119, Col 3
    DWR Enlistment Books: No trace.
"RESTING WHERE NO SHADOWS FALL, IN PERFECT PEACE, YOU AWAIT US ALL"

CHAPPELL, R, Pte, 5th DWR.   Unable to identify.
    Killed in Action: Only one R Chappell in CWGC records, 1 Para, kia 8 Mar 1943.
    Buried: No known grave.
    Commemorated: **5 DWR WW2 War Memorial, Col 1.**
    DWR Enlistment Books: OVER 37, page 46, lists 19094105 Reginald Chappell.

CHARLESWORTH, Frank, 4607633 Sgt, 5th DWR (43 S/L Regt RA).
    Died: 18 Sep 1939, Home Duties.
    Buried: Holmfirth (Holy Trinity) Burial Ground, S, 56.
    Commemorated: **5 DWR WW2 War Memorial, Col 1.**
    DWR Enlistment Books: EB 7, page 127, enlisted 18 Aug 1924, Holmfirth.

DAVIES, John Arthur, 14680197 Gnr, 5th DWR (600 Regt RA).
Son of Ebenezer and Sarah Davies, Llanelly, Wales.
    Killed in Action: Normandy Campaign, Dunkirk Investment.
    Buried: Cassell Communal Cemetery Extension, E, 16, aged 35.
    Commemorated: **5 DWR WW2 War Memorial, Col 1.**

DWR Enlistment Books: No trace.
"HEDD, PERFAITH HEDD"

DAVIES, Walter John, 1078723 Gnr, 5th DWR (600 Regt RA)
Killed in Action:	15 Apr 1945, Normandy Campaign, Dunkirk Investment.
Buried:	No known grave.
Commemorated:	**5 DWR WW2 War Memorial, Col 1.**
DWR Enlistment Books:	No trace.

DAWSON, Leslie, 228159 Lt, 5th DWR, att R Norfolk Regt.
Son of John William and Elsie Dawson, Halifax, Yorks.
Killed in Action:	1 Mar 1945, Normandy Campaign, Germany, aged 27.
Buried:	Reichswald Forest Cemetery, 62, E, 13.
Commemorated:	**5 DWR WW2 War Memorial, Col 1.**
Commissioned:	

"THEY NEVER FAIL WHO DIE IN A GREAT CAUSE"

DODSON, Harold, 1659649 Gnr, 5th DWR (later 415 Bty, 126 Regt RA).
Son of Thomas Herbert and Beatrice Dodson, Huddersfield, husband of Alice Dodson, Huddersfield, Yorks.
Died:	12 Mar 1943, aged 29.
Buried:	Huddersfield (Lockwood) Cemetery, Sec 2, Grave 92.
Commemorated:	**5 DWR WW2 War Memorial, Col 1.**
DWR Enlistment Books:	3 x H Dodsons listed.

"WE CANNOT, LORD THY PURPOSE SEE BUT ALL IS WELL THAT'S DONE BY THEE"

ELLIS, Clifford. 161194 Gnr, 5th DWR 43rd Garrison Regt RA).
Son of Fred Thorpe and May Ann Ellis, Mossley, Lancs.
Died:	26 Oct 1944, aged 31.
Buried:	Mossley Cemetery, 2677.
Commemorated:	**5 DWR WW2 War Memorial, Col 1.**
DWR Enlistment Books:	TED 24 lists a 4624105 Clifford Ellis.

"HE GAVE HIS LIFE THAT WE MIGHT BE ASSURED OF PEACE AND LIBERTY"

ELLIS, Gaybriel, 14586039 Gnr, 5th DWR (600 Regt RA).
Killed in Action:	15 Apr 1945, Normandy Campaign, Dunkirk Investment, aged 44.
Buried:	Cassell Communal Cemetery Extension, E 10.
Commemorated:	**5 DWR WW2 War Memorial, Col 1.**
DWR Enlistment Books:	No trace.

EMBLETON, Frank, 11005140 Gnr, 5th DWR (600 Regt RA).
Son of Fran and Mary Jane Embelton, Leeds, husband of Ivy Embleton, Leeds, Yorks.
Killed in Action:	20 Apr 1945, Normandy Campaign, Dunkirk Investment, aged 27.
Buried:	Longuenesse (St Omer) Souvenir Cemetery, 4, AA, 27.
Commemorated:	**5 DWR WW2 War Memorial, Col 1.**
DWR Enlistment Books:	No trace.

"YOUR LOVE LINGERS STILL, SLEEP IN PEACE, DEAR, 'TIS GOD'S WILL. SADLY MISSED BY LOVING WIFE"

GENT, John, 1521014 Gnr, 5th DWR (371 Bty, 43 S/L Regt RA).
Died:	14 Nov 1940, Home Duties.
Buried:	Huddersfield (Edgerton) Cemetery, Cons Sec 7, grave 183.

Commemorated:	**5 DWR WW2 War Memorial, Col 1.**
DWR Enlistment Books:	No trace.

GRAHAM, George Reed, 1761520 Gnr, 5th DWR (600 Regt RA).
Son of Fairlamb Reed and Deborah Graham, husband of Elizabeth Graham, Northumberland.

Killed in Action:	17 Mar 1945, Normandy Campaign, Dunkirk Investment, aged 34.
Buried:	Coxyde Military Cemetery, 1, B, 16.
Commemorated:	**5 DWR WW2 War Memorial, Col 1.**
DWR Enlistment Books:	No trace.

"HE DID THAT WE MIGHT LIVE. MAY GOD GIVE PEACE AND REST TO HIS SOUL. LOVED BY ALL"

HACKWELL, Arthur Everitt, 1698212 Bdr, 5th DWR (600 Regt RA).
Husband of Zillah Emily May Hackwell, Battersea, London.

Killed in Action:	15 Apr 1945, Normandy Campaign, Dunkirk Investment, aged 33.
Buried:	Cassell Communal Cemetery Extension, B, 12.
Commemorated:	**5 DWR WW2 War Memorial, Col 2.**
DWR Enlistment Books:	No trace.

"ONLY GOOD NIGHT BELOVED, NOT FAREWELL"

HALLAS, J, Rfn, 5th DWR.   Unable to identify.

Killed in Action:	No J Hallas listed in CWGC records.
Buried:	No known grave.
Commemorated:	**5 DWR WW2 War Memorial, Col 2.**
DWR Enlistment Books:	No trace.

HARPER, Witold Ralph, 6017302 Bdr, 5th DWR (600 Regt RA).
Son of Ernest and Maria Harper.

Killed in Action:	15 Apr 1945, Normandy Campaign, Dunkirk Investment, aged 28.
Buried:	Cassell Communal Cemetery Extension, E, 21.
Commemorated:	**5 DWR WW2 War Memorial, Col 2.**
DWR Enlistment Books:	No trace.

"HE FOUGHT FOR PEACE ON EARTH, AND HAVING WON ETERNAL PEACE, RESTS HERE"

HASELL, Frank, 1493014 Gnr, 5th DWR (373 Bty, 43 S/L Regt RA), memorial shows Hassell.
Son of Albert James and Alice Maud Beatrice Hasell, Splott Cardiff, Wales.

Died:	2 Jun 1941, Home Duties, aged 22..
Buried:	Cardiff (Cathays) Cemetery, Sec EP, 110.
Commemorated:	**5 DWR WW2 War Memorial, Col 2.**
DWR Enlistment Books:	No trace.

"A MEMORY THAT WILL NOT FADE A LOVE THAT CANNOT DIE"

HAYHURST, Fred, 1760870 Gnr, 5th DWR (600 Regt RA).
Son of William and Elizabeth Hayhurst, Blackburn, husband of Annie Hayhurst, Blackburn, Lancs.

Killed in Action:	15 Apr 1945, Normandy Campaign, Dunkirk Investment, aged 36.
Buried:	Cassell Communal Cemetery Extension, E, 9.
Commemorated:	**5 DWR WW2 War Memorial, Col 2.**
DWR Enlistment Books:	No trace.

"PEACEFULLY SLEEPING, FREE FROM PAIN, IN GOD'S OWN TIME WE SHALL MEET AGAIN"

HEYS, Harry, 2049957 Bdr, 5th DWR (506 Bty 80 S/L Regt) - only Bdr H Heys listed by CWGC.
Son of Harry and Hannah Heys, husband of Eileen Heys, Stanford Bishop, Herts.
Died:	2 Sep 1942, aged 22.
Buried:	Stanford Bishop (St James) Churchyard, North of Church.
Commemorated:	**5 DWR WW2 War Memorial, Col 2.**
DWR Enlistment Books:	No trace.

"IN LOVING MEMORY"

HITCHEN, Albert Lans, Pte, 5th DWR (later 3 PARA?) - only A L Hitchen listed by CWGC
Killed in Action:	24 Sep 1944, Normandy Campaign, Arnhem, Netherlands, aged 28.
Buried:	Arnhem Oosterbeek War Cemetery, 24, B, 10.
Commemorated:	**5 DWR WW2 War Memorial, Col 2.**
DWR Enlistment Books:	No trace.

HOBSON, William John, 1642163 Gnr, 5th DWR (600 Regt RA).
Died of Wounds:	20 Apr 1945, Normandy Campaign, Dunkirk Investment, aged 34.
Buried:	Coxyde Military Cemetery, 1, B, 19.
Commemorated:	**5 DWR WW2 War Memorial, Col 1.**
DWR Enlistment Books:	No trace.

HUNTER, Robert Cousins, 2043868 Spr, 5th DWR (43 AA Bn RE).
Died:	8 Dec 1939, Home Duties.
Buried:	Barnsley Cemetery, Sec 13, grave 213.
Commemorated:	**5 DWR WW2 War Memorial, Col 2.**
DWR Enlistment Books:	No trace.

JOHNSON, Leonard. 1689795 Gnr, 5th DWR (600 Regt RA).
Killed in Action:	15 Apr 1945, Normandy Campaign, Dunkirk Investment, aged 34.
Buried:	Cassel Communal Cemetery Extension, E, 13.
Commemorated:	**5 DWR WW2 War Memorial, Col 2.**
DWR Enlistment Books:	TED 27, page 57 lists a 4627560 Pte Leonard Johnson.

KAY, John William, 16599878 Gnr, 5th DWR (372 Bty, 43 S/L Regt RA).
Killed in Action:	25 Jun 1942, Home Duties. Aged 35.
Buried:	Leeds (Hunslet New) Cemetery, Sec 4, Cons, Grave 219.
Commemorated:	**5 DWR WW2 War Memorial, Col 2.**
DWR Enlistment Books:	No trace.

KERSHAW, Norman, 1589242 Bdr, 5th DWR (600 Regt RA).
Son of Samuel and Annie Kershaw, husband of Phyllis Bertha Kershaw, Great Horton, Bradford, Yorks.
Killed in Action:	14 Apr 1945, Normandy Campaign, aged 27.
Buried:	Beckingen War Cemetery, 18, C, 1.
Commemorated:	**5 DWR WW2 War Memorial, Col 2.**
DWR Enlistment Books:	No trace.

"IN HEAVENLY LOVE ABIDING"

LOCKYEAR, Francis Ernest, 11060164 Gnr, 5th DWR (600 Regt RA).
Son of Thomas Augustus and Mary Lockyear, husband of Kathleen Edith Lockyear, Worcester.
Killed in Action:	15 Apr 1945, Normandy Campaign, Dunkirk Investment, aged 40.
Buried:	Cassel Communal Cemetery Extension, E, 11.
Commemorated:	**5 DWR WW2 War Memorial, Col 2.**
DWR Enlistment Books:	No trace.

"HE BRAVELY ANSWERED DUTY'S CALL AND GAVE HIS LIFE FOR ONE AND ALL"

MILLS, FRANK EDWARD, 4614028 BQMS, 5th DWR (43 AA Bn RE).
    Killed in Action: 31 Jul 1944, aged 39.
    Buried: Dover (St James's) Cemetery, B, joint grave 16.
    Commemorated: **5 DWR WW2 War Memorial, Col 2.**
    DWR Enlistment Books: TED 14, page 4 (transferred 9 Dec 1936).

MORELAND, Alfred Thomas, 1652000 Gnr, 5th DWR (600 Regt RA).
Son of Alfred John and Florence Maria Moreland, husband of Doris May Moreland, Hornchurch, Essex.
    Killed in Action: 15 Apr 1945, Normandy Campaign, Dunkirk Investment, aged 31.
    Buried: Cassel Communal Cemetery Extension, E, 18.
    Commemorated: **5 DWR WW2 War Memorial, Col 2.**
    DWR Enlistment Books: No trace.
"WE LOVED HIM WELL, GOD LOVED HIM BEST, AND TOOK HIM HOME TO HEAVENLY REST"

MURPHY, Michael, 1714109 Gnr, 5th DWR (600 Regt RA).
    Killed in Action: 15 Apr 1945, Normandy Campaign, Dunkirk Investment, aged 34.
    Buried: Cassel Communal Cemetery Extension, E, 20.
    Commemorated: **5 DWR WW2 War Memorial, Col 3.**
    DWR Enlistment Books: No trace.
"MOST SACRED HEART OF JESUS, HAVE MERCY ON US"

MURRAY, John William, 140622 Gnr, 5th DWR (601 Regt RA) - the only Gnr J W Murray listed by CWGC.
    Killed in Action: 19 Apr 1945, Normandy Campaign, France.
    Buried: Pihen les Guines War Cemetery, 2, C, 7.
    Commemorated: **5 DWR WW2 War Memorial, Col 3.**
    DWR Enlistment Books: No trace.

McBURNEY, William Henry, 4440071 Sgt, 5th DWR (43 S/L Regt RA).
Son of William and Mary Elizabeth McBurney, husband of Mary Jane McBurney, Penistone, Yorks.
    Killed in Action: 21 Jul 1942, Home Service, aged 42.
    Buried: Penistone (Stottercliffe) Cemetery, Sec 4, Cons, grave 109.
    Commemorated: **5 DWR WW2 War Memorial, Col 3.**
    DWR Enlistment Books: No trace.
"HE GAVE HIS LIFE THAT WE MIGHT LIVE IN FREEDOM"

NEWBERRY, William Henry, 1761526 Gnr, 5th DWR (600 Regt RA).
    Killed in Action: 17 Apr 1945, Normandy Campaign, Dunkirk Investment.
    Buried: Longeunesse (St Omer) Souvenir Cemetery, 4, AA, 26.
    Commemorated: **5 DWR WW2 War Memorial, Col 3.**
    DWR Enlistment Books: No trace.

NUTTALL, Percy, 2044892 Pte, 5th DWR (later York and Lancaster Regt).
Son of Richard Farr and Marie Nuttall, Holmfirth, husband of Emma Nuttall, Holmfirth, Yorks.
    Killed in Action: Normandy Campaign, France, aged 26.
    Buried: Banneville la Campagne War Cemetery, 6, E, 7.
    Commemorated: **5 DWR WW2 War Memorial, Col 3.**
    DWR Enlistment Books: UNDER 24, page 25.
"RESTING WHERE NO SHADOWS FALL"

OVERTON, Jack Forster, 2Lt, 5th DWR (43 AA Bn RE - later 47571 Flt Lt, 613 Sqn RAF).
Awarded Distinguished Flying Cross, *LG 29 Dec 1944,* and French Croix de Guerre.
Son of Ernest and Gertrude Mabel Overton, Lindley, Huddersfield, Yorks, husband of Margaret Overton, Huddersfield, Yorks.
    Killed in Action: Normandy Campaign, France, aged 26.
    Buried: Cambrai (Route de Solesmes) Communal Cemetery, 2, B, 1.
    Commemorated: RAAF Memorial, National Memorial Arboretum, Alrewas, Staffs.
    5 DWR WW2 War Memorial, Col 3.
    Commissioned: 6 Jan 1939; transferred to RAF, as Pilot Officer, 29 Nov 1941.
"WERE THEY IMMORTAL WINGS THAT BORE HIM ON HIS FINAL FLIGHT?"

OWERS, Tom Jobson, 1076293 Gnr, 5th DWR (372 Bty, 43 AA S/L Regt RA).
Son of John and Ada Owers, West Pelton, Chester le Street, Co Durham.
    Killed in Action: 25 Jun 1942, Home Duties, aged 29.
    Buried: Pelton Cemetery, Sec B, New ground, grave 450.
    Commemorated: **5 DWR WW2 War Memorial, Col 3.**
    DWR Enlistment Books: No trace.
"HE GAVE HIS LIFE THAT OTHERS MIGHT LIVE"

OXLEY, Arthur, 1589263 Gnr, 5th DWR (126 Bty, 9 Middlesex Lt AA Regt RA) - only A Oxley serving in RA listed by CWGC, shown as LBdr. Son of Norman and Alice Oxley, husband of Margaret Oxley, Skipton, Yorks.
    Killed in Action: 13 Apr 1942, Home Duties, aged 28.
    Buried: Skipton (Waltonwrays) Cemetery, 7, K, 14.
    Commemorated: **5 DWR WW2 War Memorial, Col 3.**
    DWR Enlistment Books: No trace.
"IN LOVING MEMORY OF ARTHUR BELOVED HUSBAND OF MARGARET. TENDER MEMORIES OF OUR LOVED ONE"

PATE, Tom, 1825511 Gnr, 5th DWR (600 Regt RA).
    Killed in Action: 15 Apr 1945, Normandy Campaign, Dunkirk Investment, aged 32.
    Buried: Cassel Communal Cemetery Extension, E, 8.
    Commemorated: **5 DWR WW2 War Memorial, Col 3.**
    DWR Enlistment Books: No trace.

PEGG, William Henry, 4609589 Gnr, 5th DWR (371Bty, 43 S/L Regt RA).
Son of Samuel and Annie Pegg, and stepson of Albert Perry, Dalton, Huddersfield, Yorks, husband of Doris Pegg, Great Houghton, Yorks.
    Killed in Action: 25 Mar 1941, Home Duties, aged 30.
    Buried: Kirkheaton Cemetery, 2017.
    Commemorated: **5 DWR WW2 War Memorial, Col 3.**
    DWR Enlistment Books: EB 9, page 118, disch 9 Dec 1936, shown as later Transferred.
"HE THAT FOLLOWTH ME SHALL NOT WALK IN DARKNESS, BUT SHALL HAVE THE LIGHT OF LIFE"

PENROSE, Joseph, 4612462 Spr, 5th DWR (43 AA Bn RE).
Son of Mr and Mrs Arthur Penrose, husband of Marion Penrose, Lockwood, Huddersfield, Yorks.
    Killed in Action: 26 Jul 1945, aged 38.
    Buried: Huddersfield (Edgerton) Cemetery, Cons Sec 14, grave 40.
    Commemorated: **5 DWR WW2 War Memorial, Col 3.**
    DWR Enlistment Books: EB 12, page 78 disch 9 Dec 1936, shown as later Transferred.
"GOD KNOWS BEST"

PHILLIPS William, 1718619 Gnr, 5th DWR (600 Regt RA).
Son of Walter James and Laura Phillips, husband of Lilian Nellie Phillips, Bisterne, Hants.
    Killed in Action: 15 Apr 1945, Normandy Campaign, Dunkirk Investment, aged 37.
    Buried: Cassel Communal Cemetery Extension, E, 17.
    Commemorated: **5 DWR WW2 War Memorial, Col 3.**
    DWR Enlistment Books: No trace.
"ALL YOU HAD HOPED FOR, ALL YOU HAD, YOU GAVE TO SAVE MANKIND"

RICHARDSON, Edward E, 268693 Lt, 5th DWR (600 Regt RA) Awarded MID, *LG 13 Jan 1944, p 260*. Son of Edward and Winifred Richardson, husband of Iris Clare Richardson, Taplow, Bucks.
    Died of Wounds: 15 Apr 1945, Normandy Campaign, Dunkirk Investment, aged 25.
    Buried: Etaples Military Cemetery, 46, C, 20.
    Commemorated: **5 DWR WW2 War Memorial, Col 3.**
    Commissioned: Mar 1943.
"UNTIL WE MET AGAIN"

ROEBUCK, Amos, Sgt, 5th DWR (43 S/L Bn RA).
Son of Amos and Emily I Roebuck, husband of Nora Roebuck, Penistone, Yorks.
    Killed in Action: 21 Jul 1942, Home Duties, aged 32.
    Buried: Netherfield Congregational Chapelyard, 14, 28.
    Commemorated: **5 DWR WW2 War Memorial, Col 3.**
    DWR Enlistment Books: No trace.
"DEARLY LOVED HUSBAND OF NORA BELEOVED OF EMILY AND AMOS ROEBUCK"

ROPER, Ernest, 2087450 Gnr, 5th DWR (371 Coy 43 S/L Regt RA).
Son of James and Ada Roper, Huddersfield, husband of Annie Roper, Lockwood, Huddersfield, Yorks.
    Killed in Action: 9 Jul 1940, Home Duties, aged 23.
    Buried: Huddersfield (Lockwood) Cemetery, Cons Sec C, grave 84.
    Commemorated: **5 DWR WW2 War Memorial, Col 3.**
    DWR Enlistment Books: No trace.
"AT THE GOING DOWN OF THE SUN AND IN THE MORNING WE WILL REMEMBER THEM"

SAMMONS, David Nicholls, 1654435 Bdr, 5th DWR (600 Regt RA).
Son of Williamd and Ellen Sammons, husband of Violet S Sammons, Burntwood, Staffs.
    Killed in Action: 15 Apr 1945, Normandy Campaign, Dunkirk Investment, aged 32.
    Buried: Cassel Communal Cemetery Extension, E, 15.
    Commemorated: **5 DWR WW2 War Memorial, Col 4.**
    DWR Enlistment Books: No trace.
"PROUD AND BEAUTIFUL MEMORIES OF MY DARLING HUSBAND. GOD BLESS 'JIM'"

SHORROCKS, J, Pte, 5th DWR. Unable to identify.
    Killed in Action: CWGC - 2086114 Pte W J C Shorrocks, 7 DWR, kia 10 Aug 1944.
    Buried: No known grave.
    Commemorated: **5 DWR WW2 War Memorial, Col 4.**
    DWR Enlistment Books: EB 6, page 86 shows a 2086114 J L Shorrocks, disch 10 May 1923.

SNEESBY, Charles Ernest, 1554957 Gnr, 5th DWR (600 Regt RA).
Son of William Henry and Mary Ann Sneesby, Sheffield, Yorks, husband of Edith Holberry Sneesby, Sheffield, Yorks.
    Killed in Action: 15 Apr 1945, Normandy Campaign, Dunkirk Investment.
    Buried: Cassel Communal Cemetery Extension, E, 19.
    Commemorated: **5 DWR WW2 War Memorial, Col 4.**

        DWR Enlistment Books: No trace.
"HOLD HIM LORD NOW HE IS THINE, LOVE HIM AS WE LOVED HIM, WITH LOVE DIVINE"

STEELE, James William, 2056996 LBdr, 5th DWR (373 Bty, 43 S/L Regt RA).
Killed in Action:	9 Aug 1940, Home Duties.
Buried:	Barnsley Cemetery, Sec 9, Grave 573.
Commemorated:	**5 DWR WW2 War Memorial, Col 4.**
DWR Enlistment Books:	No trace.

THORPE, E, Sgt, 5th DWR.   Unable to identify.
Killed in Action:	4 x F Thorpe listed by CWGC, none of them Sgt.
Buried:	No known grave.
Commemorated:	**5 DWR WW2 War Memorial, Col 4.**
DWR Enlistment Books:	No trace.

TIBBOTT, Charles Edward, 2053144 Gnr, 5th DWR (415 Bty, 9 Middlesex Lt AA Regt RA).
Killed in Action:	3 Oct 1942, Home Duties.
Buried:	Kirkheaton Cemetery, grave 2568.
Commemorated:	**5 DWR WW2 War Memorial, Col 4.**
DWR Enlistment Books:	No trace.

WESTHEAD, Thomas Maurice, 143081 Maj, 5th DWR (600 Regt RA).
Son of William and Mary Westhead, Librarian.
Killed in Action:	16 Apr 1945, Normandy Campaign, Dunkirk Investment, aged 35.
Buried:	Cassel Communal Cemetery Extension, E, 7.
Commemorated:	**5 DWR WW2 War Memorial, Col 4.**
Commissioned:	

"IN LOVING MEMORY OF A DEVOTED SON AND BROTHER, REST IN PEACE"

WHITE, John Henry, 4613605 Gnr, 5th DWR (373 Coy, 43 AA Bn RE).
Son of Arthur and Emma White, Dewsbury, husband of Gladys White, Dewsbury, Yorks.
Killed in Action:	21 Nov 1939, Home Duties.
Buried:	Dewsbury Cemetery, Uncons Sec, grave 536.
Commemorated:	**5 DWR WW2 War Memorial, Col 4.**
DWR Enlistment Books:	TED 13, page 61, transferred to RE 9 Dec 1936.

"REST IN PEACE, YOUR LOVING WIFE GLADYS AND CHILDREN PEGGY AND JUNE"

WILLIAMS, Roger Anthony, 78426 Lt, 5th DWR (80 S/L Regt RA).
Son of Capt Cecil Athelstan Wynn [formerly 2/5th DWR] and Ann Myfawnwy Williams, Honley, Yorks.
Killed in Action:	17 Sep 1942, Home Duties.
Buried:	Huddersfield (Lockwood) Cemetery, Sec E, grave 3.
Commemorated:	**5 DWR WW2 War Memorial, Col 4.**
Commissioned:	22 Nov 1938, 43 AA Bn RE.

WORSLEY, Joseph Henry, 4604775 Sgt, 5th DWR (371 Coy, 43 AA Bn RE , later RA).
Son of Frederick and Annie William Worsley, Huddersfield, Yorks, husband of Mabel Worsley, Sheepridge, Huddersfield, Yorks.
Killed in Action:	29 Oct 1939, aged 37.
Buried:	Brighouse Cemetery, Sec F Cons, grave 546.
Commemorated:	**5 DWR WW2 War Memorial, Col 4.**
DWR Enlistment Books:	EB 4, page 130. Enlisted 14 Jul 1921, disch 9 Dec 1936, later CQMS 43 Bn RE.

YARKER, Francis William, 1689827 Gnr, 5th DWR (600 Regt RA).
    Died of Wounds: 22 Apr 1945, Normandy Campaign, Dunkirk Investment, aged 30.
    Buried: Harrogate (Stonefall) Cemetery, Sec 8E, grave 172.
    Commemorated: **5 DWR WW2 War Memorial, Col 4.**
    DWR Enlistment Books: No trace.

THE UNIT

5th Battalion

Title Changes - 1860 to 1945

6th West Yorkshire Rifle Volunteer Corps
2nd Volunteer Battalion (Duke of Wellington's Regiment) West Riding Regiment
5th Battalion Duke of Wellington's (West Riding Regiment) (Territorial Force)
5th Battalion Duke of Wellington's Regiment (West Riding) (Territorial Army)
43rd (5 DWR) Anti Aircraft (Search/Light) Battalion Royal Engineers
43rd (5 DWR) Anti Aircraft Regiment Royal Artillery
43rd (5 DWR) Heavy Anti Aircraft Regiment Royal Artillery
43rd (5 DWR) Garrison Regiment Royal Artillery
600 (5 DWR) Regiment Royal Artillery

The titles of the Huddersfield Volunteers were changed with great regularity after becoming the 5th Battalion of the Duke of Wellington's Regiment in 1908. Initially part of the Territorial Force, until the end of the First World War, and then Territorial Army on the re-formation of the volunteers in 1920. Before, during and after the Second World War came a stream of changes in affiliation, Royal Engineers and Royal Artillery, and roles, Anti Aircraft, Searchlight and Garrison Regiment. After the war it remained a Royal Artillery unit until converting back to the Infantry role in 1957.

In the lead up to the Second World War the Army became aware that there were not enough Anti Aircraft, Anti Tank or Armoured units in the Order of Battle and many infantry units were converted to these roles from about 1936, which involved no less than seven 'Dukes' Battalions.

On 10th December, 1936, the 5th Battalion was re-titled 43rd (5 DWR) AA Bn RE and placed under command of 31st North Midland Group, 2nd AA Division (TA),. It was equipped with searchlights and sound ranging equipment, for picking up German bombers, in the event of their attacking Britain. On 1st August, 1940, the unit was transferred to the Royal Artillery and given the title 43rd (5DWR) Heavy Anti Aircraft (Search Light) Regiment RA. On 16th October, 1943, it became 43rd Garrison Regiment (5 DWR) (TA), becoming 43rd (5 DWR) Garrison Regiment RA on 1st November, 1944. It embarked for France shortly afterwards, becoming, about February 1945, 600 (5 DWR) Garrison Regiment RA.

Many changes of role and titles followed after 1945, until becoming infantry once more in May, 1957. Even then, another eight changes of title followed, culminating in being amalgamated into the 4th Battalion of the Yorkshire Regiment in 2006.

THE CAMPAIGN
5 DWR

The Normandy Campaign, 1944-1945.

*Czech Independent Armoured Brigade HQ map,
showing the Allied perimeter line, the German defensive lines and the flooded area.*

In May, 1944, the 43rd Searchlight Regiment, under the command of Lt Col F A Carlile, was mobilised for active service and transferred to 21st Army Group from AA Command. After some AA training as a mobile searchlight Regiment, it was realized that this type of unit would not be required on the continent and, in September, 1944, was re-mobilized as 43rd Garrison Regiment RA and, in October 1944, the Battalion was converted to infantry, less Support Company, and reduced from 1,500 men to 750.

In November, 1944, after a period of intensive training, the unit embarked for France, and during December and January it was engaged in guarding ammunition dumps and stores, as well as further training, in the vicinity of La Panne.

On 11th February the Regiment was placed under command of the Czechoslovak Independent Armoured Brigade Group, which had been tasked with the investment and reduction of the German occupied port of Dunkirk.

The German Garrison at that time comprised about 11,000 men, of various nationalities, with about 500 French civilians still living there after a withdrawal of 15,000 civilians in September, along with about 100 Allied Prisoners of War. The Garrison Commander, Admiral Frisius, had a mixed force of Naval and Wehrmacht officers and men, from Germany and Alsace, with Poles Austrians and Russians who had volunteered or been conscripted into the German Forces.

The Admiral's Chief of Staff, Hauptman Turke, ran a Battle School and students qualified by successfully conducting patrols behind enemy lines, a perimeter of some 45 miles long enclosing the beaches from where British and French troops had been evacuated in June, 1940. The area was still littered with the debris of that operation, but had been fortified since then as part of the powerful Atlantic Wall.

The Germans controlled the lock gates of the many canals in the region and had flooded portions of the area to the south in order to reduce the perimeter of land defences.

The Allied front line ran from Bray Dune Plage, through Bray Dunes, Ghyvelde (close to the flooded area) and, to the west, northwards towards Loon Plage. The western portion of the line was held by the 2nd Czech Armoured Regiment (fighting dismounted but using tanks as close support artillery) and the Czech Mortorised Battalion. The eastern line was held by the 1st and 3rd Czech Armoured Regiments. In support was a Czech Field Artillery Regiment, a heavy AA Regt RA and two Light AA Regts RA, all firing in the ground role, and a S/L Battery deployed in the AA role and for ground illumination (commonly known as 'Monty's Moonlight').

The Regiment initially took over a part of the western sector, close to Loon Plage, with a Company of French troops under command, who failed to maintain their positions during a large German raid some time afterwards. The line in this area consisted of a succession of strong points, isolated and ruined farm houses and a few bunkers, one of which became Battalion HQ, A, B and C Companies took up positions in the front line, D Coy being in reserve. The enemy was active in this area, being able to infiltrate at low tide across a very wide expanse of sand, necessitating frequent patrolling between the spread out posts.

During this period the unit was once more retitled, to 600 (DWR) Regt RA and, in early March the Battalion was relieved at Loon Plage and moved into the eastern sector, close to Ghyvelde, where the defences were more substantial, a succession of mutually supporting defended localities, although the patrolling continued unabated. The Germans used the flooded area to infiltrate the defences in this sector and on one occasion Major J C Shaw of B Echelon, a fluent German speaker, impersonated a member of a patrol which had been captured a few days earlier, in an attempt to capture the German naval party which was due to pick up the patrol, without success.

On 24th February a prisoner was captured who gave information concerning his Battalion positions and the food situation in Dunkirk. As a result of some earlier desertions at this time, the following order was issued by Admiral Fresius:

OC DUNKIRK FORTRESS   20 Feb 45
SOLDIERS OF DUNKIRK FORTRESS

> Another swine has deserted. By doing so he brought unmentionable misery to his family. In such cases we can expect they will be liquidated.
> What we owe to these deserters can always be immediately noticed, as enemy arty switches fire on targets not fired at hitherto. But, of course, such creatures without any conscience do not mind. In my disappointment about the existence of such creatures within the fortress, only the fact that quite a number of them have perished gives me some consolation. Apart from the one we caught in time and who will hang from the Town Hall tower, I found out by bearers of a flag of truce and by PW interrogation that at least 7 of them were either shot in no-man's-land or killed by mines. 2 of the latter were recently offered to me by the enemy for burial which, naturally, I refused. According to PW statements 3 more remained in the minefields and are still there as nobody wants to bring them in owing to the danger of such an attempt. 2 were shot by enemy outposts as only too late was it found out they were not carrying any weapons. But we hope that even more have perished in such a way.

> Soldiers of DUNKIRK.
> Remember that it is everyone's duty to support weak men in moments of their weakness. Then some may be saved from treachery. When you notice that somebody weakens and you are not sure you will succeed in putting them straight again, report to your superior. Anything suspicious may be important. It is much better that you should report such a case and by doing so spare your comrades and yourself greater misfortune than to think – by a wrong sentiment of comradeship – that you are obliged to remain silent.
> In addition, don't forget even for a single instant what you owe to your fatherland, to your family and to your own honour as Germans.
> FRISIUS Vice-Admiral.

Even so, the Psy Ops propaganda unit operating in the area was largely unsuccessful in bringing more than a handful of deserters, having been regarded as successfully persuading 10,000 soldiers to give themselves up at Cherbourg but the small unit did provide much amusement to the besieging troops.

Lacking a Support Company, LSgt S Barclay improvised a number of weapons, including modifying French and German mortars to fire the standard British 3" mortar shells, and the use of captured German weapons gave the unit some increased firepower.

The Unit War Diary noted a reinforcement of the perimeter in the Battalion's locality by three Flights from 2765 RAF Regiment until 25th March when they returned to their unit, other Flights were sent by 2861 and 2862 Squadrons in April.

On 3rd/4th April, 1945, a strong German attack was launched on the north west sector of the line, possibly a precursor to an attempted break out, but the attack broke down under artillery, tank and small arms fire. As a consequence, on 14th April, a Company of the Czech Motorised Battalion and 600 Regt RA were transferred to the western sector in order to carry out a counter attack to regain some positions lost by the French. The attack went in at first light on 15th April. The German resistance was strong, especially its artillery response, and the Battalion lost two Officers and 15 Other Ranks killed and three Officers and sixty Other Ranks wounded. The enemy lost 100 men and 75 prisoners. The unit was relieved by 601 Regt RA and returned to the eastern sector. On 18th April Bn HQ moved to La Panne and, by 4th May, the whole Battalion was concentrated at La Panne to rest and refit.

The German garrison surrendered on 9th May, 1945, although Admiral Frisius was planning to fight on, having lost his family in a British air raid on Hamburg, but was persuaded to capitulate by his Second in Command, who did not survive the confrontation. The Battalion took over two sectors of the perimeter to prevent the enemy moving out and civilians into the town. By 11th May the Battalion was involved in the disarming of the enemy and marched a large portion of the 21,000 prisoners to a Prisoner of War cage about forty miles away, at Zedelghem, despite the attitudes of the local French and Belgian populace along the way, ranging from violence to fraternization.

On 30th May, 1945, the unit received orders to move to Germany in early June, reaching Bad Oyenhausen on 3rd June, 28 Officers and 722 Other Ranks on strength. On 4th June the unit took over the responsibility of perimeter guards for 21st Army Group HQ.

A number of decorations were awarded for this campaign, notably to Major J C Shaw, who received the MBE, Capt C P Robinson, who received an immediate award of the MC, and Private Pont, who received an immediate MM. There were also some Mentions and Certificates. Extracts from the Regimental Gallantry Medals and Civil Honours Roll show the following awards were recorded for this campaign in the Regimental Archives:

HONOURS AND AWARDS
5 DWR

CARLINE, Francis Allen, 30975 Lt Col, 600 Regt RA (5 DWR).
Territorial Decoration.
"The King has been graciously pleased to confer the Efficiency Decoration upon the following Officers of the Territorial Army who have been duly recommended for the same under the terms of the Royal Warrant dated 17th August, 1908 - Major (Temp Lt Col) F A Carline (30975)."
LG: 23 Jun 1942, page 2746.
Officer, the Most Excellent Order of the British Empire. WW2.
"The King has been graciously pleased to give orders for the following promotions in, and appointments to, the Most Excellent Order of the British Empire, in recognition of meritorious service. To be additional Officers of the Military Division of the said Most Excellent Order."
LG: 6 Apr 1945, page 1901.

EMBLETON, Frank, 11005140 Gnr, 5 DWR (600 Regt RA).
Mentioned in Despatches, Dunkirk, Normandy Campaign, NW Europe, 1945.
"The King has been graciously pleased to approve that the following be mentioned in recognition of gallant and distinguished services in North West Europe - 11005140 Gnr F Embleton RA."
LG: 23 Aug 1945, page 4265.

HIGGINS, Sidney William, 93127 Capt QM (later Maj), 5 DWR (600 Regt RA)
(later 7 DWR), r. Huddersfield.
Member, the Most Excellent Order of the British Empire, WW2.
"The King has been graciously pleased to give orders for the following promotions in, and appointments to, the Most Excellent Order of the British Empire in recognition of gallant and distinguished services in North West Europe. To be additional Members of the Military Division of the said Most Excellent Order."
LG: 21 Jun 1945, page 3220.
Efficiency Decoration (Territorial).
"The King has been graciously pleased to confer the Territorial Efficiency Decoration upon the following Officers."
LG: 21 Apr 1950, p 1934.
Efficiency Decoration (Territorial).
"The King has been graciously pleased to confer the 1st Clasp to the Territorial Efficiency Decoration upon the following Officers of the Territorial Army."
LG: 13 Jul 1951, p 3799.

KENYON, Peter Whorlow, 68981 Capt, 600 Regt RA (5 DWR)
(from Rossall School Contingent jnr Div OTC, to 43 S/L Regt RA, 22 Oct 1940).
Member, the Most Excellent Order of the British Empire, WW2.
"The King has been graciously pleased on the occasion of His Majesty's Birthday to give orders for the following appointments to the Most Excellent Order of the British Empire. To be additional Members of the Military Division of the said Most Excellent Order."
LG: 8 Jun 1944, page 2579.

MALLINSON, Ralph, 4614208 Bdr, 5 DWR (600 Regt RA).
Mentioned in Despatches, for Normandy campaign, NW Europe, WW2.
"The King has been graciously pleased to approve that the following be mentioned in recognition of gallant and distinguished services in North West Europe - 4614208 Bdr R Mallinson."
LG: 22 Mar 1945, page 1553.

PONT, Ernest Stanley, 48445 Sgt, RFA
(later 6621 Capt, 5 DWR, 43rd AA Bn RE, 600 Regt RA (5 DWR), r. Swindon.
Military Medal, WW1.
"The King has been graciously pleased to award the Military Medal for Bravery in the Field to the undermentioned Non-Commissioned Officers and Men - 48445 Sgt E S Pont RFA."
LG: 27 Feb 1916, page 10483.
Member, the Most Excellent Order of the British Empire.
"The King has been graciously pleased to give orders for the following appointments to the Most Excellent Order of the British Empire in recognition of gallant and distinguished services in North West Europe. To be additional Members of the Military Division of the said Most Excellent Order. Captain (temporary) Ernest Stanley Pont (6621) Royal Regiment of Artillery (Swindon)."
LG: 21 Jun 1945, page 3221.

RICHARDSON, Edward, 268693 Lt, 5 DWR (600 Regt RA), r. Leeds.
Mentioned in Despatches, NW Europe, WW2.
Citation not currently available.
LG: 13 Jan 1944, page 260.

ROBINSON, Charles Portland, 56501 Capt (later Col), 5 DWR (RE Bn)
(from RE to 43 S/L Bn RE (5 DWR) Oct 1940, later 600 Regt RA)**,** r. Ilkley.
Military Cross, for Dunkirk, Normandy Campaign, 1945, WW2.
Announcement: "The King has been graciously pleased to approve the following awards in recognition of gallant and distinguished services in North West Europe."
LG: 24 May 1945, page 2648.
Citation: "For leadership and bravery in an action on the outskirts of Dunkirk."
Iron Duke: 230-1996, page 38.
Efficiency Decoration (Territorial), WW2.
"The King has been graciously pleased to confer the award of the Efficiency Decoration upon the following Officers of the Territorial Army - R Art, Major C P Robinson MC (56501)."
LG: 14 Nov 1947, page, 5356.
Efficiency Decoration (Territorial), WW2.
"The King has been graciously pleased to confer the award of two clasps to the Efficiency Decoration upon the following Officers - R Art, Major C P Robinson MC TD (56501)."
LG: 15 Jun 1951, page 3284.
Officer, the Most Excellent Order of the British Empire.
"The King has been graciously pleased to give orders for the following promotions in, and appointments to, the Most Excellent Order of the British Empire. To be ordinary Officers of the Military Division of the said Most Excellent Order."
LG: 31 May 1956, page 3105.
Territorial Efficiency Decoration.
"The Queen has been graciously pleased to confer the award of the 3rd Clasp to the Territorial Efficiency Decoration upon the following Officers - Comds & Staff, Col C P Robinson OBE MC TD (56501)."
LG: 14 Nov 1957, page, 5356.

SHAW, James Cameron, 69612 Maj, 5 DWR (43 SL Bn RE, 600 Regt RA), r. Huddersfield.
Member, the Most Excellent Order of the British Empire, NW Europe, WW2.
"The King has been graciously pleased to give orders for the following promotions in, and appointments to, the Most Excellent Order of the British Empire in recognition of gallant and distinguished services in North West Europe. To be additional Members of the Military Division of the said Most Excellent Order."
LG: 24 Jan 1946, page 624.

Czechoslovakian Military Cross.
Citation not currently available.
LG: Not Known. Iron Duke: 239-1999, page 46.

TAYLOR, John William, 240514 Pte, 1/5th DWR
(later CSM, also served throughout WW2, seeing action at Dunkirk with 600 Regt RA, 1945).
Military Medal, for Ypres, 9 Oct 1917, France & Flanders, WW1.
"For Zonnebeke, Abraham Heights, October, 1917."
LG: 28 Jan 1918, page 1399. Unit WD: MM award, 30 Nov 1917.
"This soldier showed great gallantry during an attack on the 9th October, 1917. He constantly carried messages and volunteered for every duty. He acted as guide to his Company to the firing line on the 9th October, 1917, and went back for others, lost, under shell fire."
Boston Guardian: MM award, 24 Nov 1917. Carline F A, Iron Duke: 1946, page 74.

On 26th October, 1969, members of the 5th Battalion, including the Commanding Officer, were invited to attend the unveiling of the Czech Armoured Brigade War Memorial in Leamington, where the Brigade group had been formed after the Fall of France, The Battalion was given a very warm and enthusiastic welcome by the Czech veterans and the inhabitants of Leamington.

5th Bn. Searching for German snipers near Dunkirk, March 1945

DWR Crew of captured German midget submarine, Dunkirk, 1945.

Part 3
SECOND WORLD WAR

1/7th Battalion The Duke of Wellington's Regiment
1944-45
2/7th Battalion (115 Regiment RAC)
1939-1940 & 1944-45

THE MEMORIALS

THE FALLEN
1/7th, 2/7th Battalions and 115 Regiment (RAC)

ADAMS, Herbert, 4977000 LSgt, 1/7th DWR (also Sherwood Foresters).
Son of William Albert George and Alice Kate Adams, St Leonards on Sea, Sussex.
    Killed in Action: 16 Jul 1944, Normandy Campaign, aged 33.
    Buried: Hottot les Bagues War Cemetery, 8, G, 3.
    Commemorated: **7 DWR WW2 War Memorial, Col 1.**
    Barclay History RoH, page 368.
    DWR Enlistment Books: Over Numbers, page 152.
"IN PROUD MEMORY OF HERBERT ALWAYS IN OUR THOUGHTS. MUM, DAD AND FAMILY"

ALLEN, John William, 4617804 Pte, 2/7th DWR.
    Reported missing: Died 11 Jun 1940, France & Belgium Campaign, 1939/40.
    Buried: Sainte Marie Cemetery, Le Havre, 67, T, 16.
    Previously Interred: Sotteville sur Mer Temp Burial Ground, 6, 9 (until Oct 1947).
    Commemorated: **7 DWR WW2 War Memorial, Col 1.**
    Barclay History RoH, page 371.
    DWR Enlistment Books: TED 17, page 81.

APPLEYARD, Bernard, 4618813 Pte, 2/7th DWR.
Son of John William and Alice Appleyard, Wadlsey, Sheffield, Yorks.
    Killed in Action: 11/12 Jun 1940, France & Belgium Campaign, 1939/40.
    Buried: Sainte Marie Cemetery, Le Havre, 67, T, 1.
    Previously Interred: Sotteville sur Mer Temp Burial Ground, 5, 6 (until Oct 1947).
    Commemorated: **7 DWR WW2 War Memorial, Col 1.**
    Barclay History RoH, page 371.
    DWR Enlistment Book: TED 18, page 82.
"HIS SMILING FACE, HIS HEART OF GOLD, HIS WORTH TO US, WAS WEALTH UNTOLD"

BARROW, George Geoffrey, 4398009 Pte, 1/7th DWR (also Green Howards).
Son of Charles Henry and Helena Georgina Barrow, husband of Lily Dorothy Barrow, Clapton, London.
    Killed in Action: 10 Aug 1944, Normandy Campaign, aged 35.
    Buried: Ranville War Cemetery, 8, B, 20.
    Commemorated: **7 DWR WW2 War Memorial, Col 1; D Coy Memorial, Col 1.**
    Barclay History RoH, page 368.
    DWR Enlistment Book: Under 30, page 90, & Over 30, page 90.
"THAT WE MIGHT FREEDOM'S SONG RENEW; THERE IS NO GREATER DEED MORTAL MAN CAN DO" LILLIAN

BATES, Leonard Isaac, 14719002 Pte, 1/7th DWR.
Son of Samuel and Matilda Bates, Milnsbridge, Huddersfield, Yorks.
    Killed in Action: 28 Oct 1944, Normandy Campaign, Netherlands, aged 20.
    Buried: Bergen Op Zoom War Cemetery, 9, A, 14.
    Commemorated: **7 DWR WW2 War Memorial, Col 1.**
    Barclay History RoH, page 368.
    DWR Enlistment Book: Over 33, page 79.
"SOME CORNER OF A FOREIGN FIELD THAT IS FOREVER ENGLAND. REST IN PEACE"

BAXTER, Frank, 4547028 Pte, 1/7th DWR.
Son of Albert Edward and Gertrude F Baxter, West Bowling, Bradford, Yorks.
  Died of Wounds: 26 Jun 1944, Normandy Campaign.
  Buried: Killowen Churchyard, 282.
  Commemorated: **7 DWR WW2 War Memorial, Col 1.**
    Barclay History RoH, page 375.
  DWR Enlistment Book: Under 30, page 77, & Over 30, page 77.

BAXTER, Robert, 3782559 Pte, 1/7th DWR.
Son of James and Eileen Baxter, Coleraine, Ireland.
  Died: 3 Feb 1944, aged 20.
  Buried: Killowen (St John) Church of Ireland Churchyard, grave 282.
  Commemorated: **7 DWR WW2 War Memorial, Col 1.**
    Barclay History RoH, page 368.
  DWR Enlistment Book: Under 30, page 71, & Over 30, page 71.
"THE LORD GAVE AND THE LORD HATH TAKEN AWAY"

BEGLEY, John, 5053570 Pte, B Company, 1/7th DWR.
Son of Mark and Annie Begley, Burslem, Stoke on Trent, Staffs.
  Killed in Action: 29 Oct 1944, Normandy Campaign, Netherlands, aged 31.
  Buried: Bergen Op Zoom War Cemetery, 7, C, 12.
  Commemorated: **7 DWR WW2 War Memorial, Col 1.**
    Barclay History RoH, page 368.
  DWR Enlistment Book: Over 35, page 139.
"ETERNAL REST GIVE TO HIM, OH LORD; AND LET PERPETUAL LIGHT SHINE UPON HIM R.I.P."

BELLAMY, John Minard, 4612801 LSgt, 1/7th DWR.
Son of Sidney and Ada Bellamy, Southport, Lancs. Resided Huddersfield, Yorks.
  Killed in Action: 29 Jul 1944, Normandy Campaign, aged 29.
  Buried: Ranville War Cemetery, 1, D, 35.
  Commemorated: **7 DWR WW2 War Memorial, Col 1.**
    Barclay History RoH, page 368.
  DWR Enlistment Book: EB 12, page 134, enlisted 11 Oct 1933.
"IN EVERLOVING MEMORY OF A DEAR SON AND BROTHER, RESTING WHERE NO SHADOWS FALL"

BENTLEY, Cecil Farnsworth Burley, 4618951 Pte, 2/7th DWR.
Son of Harry and Ellen Bentley, Hull, husband of Clarice Irene Bentley, Hull, Yorks.
  Died: 11 Oct 1941, aged 21.
  Buried: Hull Western Cemetery, 173, 16891.
  Commemorated: Commonwealth War Graves Commission, Vol 5, page 67.
    Not listed on 7 DWR WW2 Memorial.
  DWR Enlistment Book: TED 18, page 96, discharged 27 Dec 1940.
"PEACEFULLY SLEEPING"

BETTSWORTH, William, 4613755 LCpl, 2/7th DWR.
  Killed in Action: 11/12 Jun 1940, France & Belgium Campaign, 1939/40, aged 22.
  Buried: Sainte Marie Cemetery, Le Havre, 67, S, 17.
  Commemorated: **7 DWR WW2 War Memorial, Col 1.**
    Barclay History RoH, page 371.

DWR Enlistment Book: TED 13, page 76.

BIRD, John, 4616407 Pte, S Coy Carrier Platoon, 1/7th DWR.
Son of George and Annie Bird, husband of Vera Bird, Oldham, Lancs.
Killed in Action: 2 Oct 1944, Normandy Campaign, Belgium, aged 25.
Buried: Leopoldsburg War Cemetery, 5, C, 20.
Commemorated: **7 DWR WW2 War Memorial, Col 1.**
Barclay History RoH, page 368.
DWR Enlistment Book: TED 16, page 41.
"A CORNER OF A FOREIGN FIELD FOR EVER ENGLAND"

BIRKHEAD, Tom, 86438 2Lt, 2/7th DWR.
Son of Percy and Annie Katherine Mary Birkhead, Holmfirth, Yorks.
Killed in Action: 7 Jun 1940, France & Belgium Campaign, 1939/40, aged 19..
Buried: Eu Communal Cemetery, 16.
Commemorated: **7 DWR WW2 War Memorial, Col 1.**
Barclay History RoH, page 371.
Commissioned: 28 Mar 1939; War Diary, Offrs' Roll, 5 May 1940.

BLACKMORE, Edgell Albert, 4626174 Pte, 1/7th DWR.
Resided Exeter, Devon.
Killed in Action: 2 Jul 1944, Normandy Campaign, France, aged 31.
Buried: St Manvieu War Cemetery, 5, J, 15.
Commemorated: **7 DWR WW2 War Memorial, Col 1.**
Barclay History RoH, page 368.
DWR Enlistment Book: TED 26.

BLACKWELL, John Francis, 14555541 Pte, D Coy 1/7th DWR.
Resided Hull, Yorks.
Killed in Action: 10 Aug 1944, Normandy Campaign.
Buried: No known grave.
Commemorated: Bayeux War Memorial, p15, Col 1;
7 DWR WW2 War Memorial, Col 1; D Coy Memorial, Col 3.
Barclay History RoH, page 368.
DWR Enlistment Book: Over 31, page 101.

BLACKWELL, Roy, 14624413 Pte, 1/7th DWR.
Son of William Henry and Ethel Blackwell, Sheffield, Yorks.
Killed in Action: 26 Jun 1944, Normandy Campaign, France, aged 26.
Buried: Jerusalem War Cemetery, Chouain, A, 9.
Commemorated: **7 DWR WW2 War Memorial, Col 1.**
Barclay History RoH, page 375.
DWR Enlistment Book: Over 33, page 50.
"HOLD HIM, DEAR LORD NOW HE IS THINE, LOVE HIM AS WE LOVED HIM WITH THY LOVE DIVINE"

BLAKE, Leslie Francis, 5337474 (5337174?) Pte, 1/7th DWR (also Royal Berkshire Regt).
Son of William F and Mabel F Blake, husband of Doris M Blake, Plumstead, London.
Died of Wounds: 22 Oct 1944, Normandy Campaign, Belgium, aged 24.
Buried: Lier Belgian Military Cemetery, 5, A, 16.
Commemorated: **7 DWR WW2 War Memorial, Col 1.**
Barclay History RoH, page 368.

DWR Enlistment Book: Over 35, page 112.
"ONLY GOOD-NIGHT, BELOVED, NOT FAREWELL"

BOYLE, Selwyn Hopkinson, 4618807 Pte, 2/7th DWR.
Son of Thomas and Annie Mary Boyle, nephew of Fred Sykes, Sowerby Bridge, Yorks. His brother John Leslie also died in service.
> **Killed in Action:** 11 Jun 1940, France & Belgium Campaign, 1939/40, aged 23.
> **Buried:** Sainte Marie Cemetery, Le Havre, 67, T, 3.
> **Previously Interred:** Sotteville sur Mer Temp Burial Ground, 5, 8 (until Oct 1947.
> **Commemorated:** **7 DWR WW2 War Memorial, Col 1.**
> Barclay History RoH, page 371.
> **DWR Enlistment Book:** TED 18, page 81.

"CHRIST WILL LINK THE BROKEN CHAIN CLOSER WHEN WE MEET AGAIN"

BREWER, Barrie Morton, 258672 2Lt, 1/7th DWR.
Son of Thomas Dobson and Lilian Morton Brewer, Paddington, London.
> **Killed in Action:** 11 Jun 1944, Normandy Campaign, aged 23.
> **Buried:** Ranville War Cemetery, 4A, B, 1.
> **Commemorated:** **7 DWR WW2 War Memorial, Col 1.**
> Barclay History RoH, page 368.
> **Commissioned:** Jan 1943; Army List 1944, page 1048h.

BRIDGE. Harold, 33963 Lt Col, 1/7th DWR. Territorial Decoration, *LG: 25 Mar 1943, page 1406.*
Son of William and Elizabeth Bridge, husband of Helen Burd Bridge, Handforth, Cheshire.
> **Died:** 30 Jun 1943, aged 38.
> **Buried:** Wilmslow Cemetery, A, 51.
> **Commemorated:** **7 DWR WW2 War Memorial, Col 1.**
> Barclay History RoH, page 368.
> Iron Duke 057-1944, page 121.
> **Commissioned:** 1926; embodied, 1 Sep 1939 as Major.

BRIGGS, Geoffrey, 14551231 Pte, 1/7th DWR.
Son of James and Annie Briggs, Whitefield, Lancs.
> **Died of Wounds:** 18 Jun 1944, Normandy Campaign, aged 19.
> **Buried:** Bayeux War Cemetery, 15, D, 13.
> **Commemorated:** **7 DWR WW2 War Memorial, Col 1; D Coy Memorial, Col 2.**
> Barclay History RoH, page 368.
> **DWR Enlistment Book:** Over 32, page 52.

BRINDLEY, David, 3771448 Pte, 1/7th DWR.
Son of Benjamin and Florence Brindley, Willenhall, Staffs.
> **Killed in Action:** 29 Oct 1944, Normandy Campaign, Netherlands, aged 24.
> **Buried:** Bergen Op Zoom War Cemetery, 9, A, 16.
> **Commemorated:** **7 DWR WW2 War Memorial, Col 1.**
> Barclay History RoH, page 368.
> **DWR Enlistment Book:** Under 34, page 41.

"HE IS SHELTERED FROM THE STORMY BLAST AND GONE TO HIS ETERNAL REST. R.I.P"

BROADBENT, Gordon, 144997470 Pte, 1/7th DWR.
Son of Stanley and Dorothea C Broadbent, Bradford, Yorks.
> **Killed in Action:** 2 Apr 1945, Normandy Campaign, Netherlands, aged 19.
> **Buried:** Jonkerbos War Cemetery, 2, F, 4.

Commemorated:	**7 DWR WW2 War Memorial, Col 1; D Coy Memorial, Col 2.**
	Barclay History RoH, page 368.
DWR Enlistment Book:	Over 33, page 94.

"LOVED SON OF DOROTHEA AND THE LATE STANLEY BROADBENT, BRADFORD, ENGLAND"

BROADBENT, Jack, 4619025 Pte, 2/7th DWR.
Son of Edith Broadbent, husband of Ivy Broadbent, Blackpool, Lancs.
Killed in Action:	11 Jun 1940, France & Belgium Campaign, 1939/40, aged 19.
Buried:	Sainte Marie Cemetery, Le Havre, 67, T, 2.
Previously Interred:	Sotteville sur Mer Temp Burial Ground, 5, 7 (until Oct 1947).
Commemorated:	**7 DWR WW2 War Memorial, Col 1.**
	Barclay History RoH, page 371.
DWR Enlistment Book:	TED 19, page 3.

"HEAVENLY WINDS BLOW SOFTLY O'ER THIS HALLOWED SPOT. THE ONE WE LOVED LIES ASLEEP"

BRODERICK, George, 14686689 Pte, 1/7th DWR.
Son of Matthew and Isabella Broderick, Hull, Yorks.
Killed in Action:	4 Dec 1944, Normandy Campaign, Netherlands, aged 19.
Buried:	Jonkerbos War Cemetery, 15, D, 2.
Commemorated:	**7 DWR WW2 War Memorial, Col 1; D Coy Memorial, Col 2.**
	Barclay History RoH, page 368.
DWR Enlistment Book:	Over 35, page 99.

"MAY HIS SACRIFICE NOT BE IN VAIN. MAM AND DAD"

BROOK, Gordon, 14677008 Pte, 1/7th DWR.
Killed in Action:	29 Oct 1944, Normandy Campaign, Netherlands, aged 19.
Buried:	Bergen Op Zoom War Cemetery, 9, A, 19.
Commemorated:	**7 DWR WW2 War Memorial, Col 1; D Coy Memorial, Col 1.**
	Barclay History RoH, page 368.
DWR Enlistment Book:	Over 33, page 79.

BUCKLEY, Ernest Gordon, 4616060 Pte, 2/7th DWR.
Son of Herbert and Martha Ann Buckley, Delph, Oldham, Lancs.
Killed in Action:	11 Jun 1940, France & Belgium Campaign, 1939/40, aged 20.
Buried:	Sainte Marie Cemetery, Le Havre, 76, T, 6.
Previously Interred:	Sotteville sur Mer Temp Burial Ground, 5, 11 (until Oct 1947).
Commemorated:	**7 DWR WW2 War Memorial, Col 1.**
	Barclay History RoH, page 371.
DWR Enlistment Book:	TED 16, page 7.

"HIS MEMORY WE TREASURE HIS PRESENCE WE MISS"

BURGESS, John, 4619035 Pte, 2/7th DWR.
Son of Francis George and Hannah Maria Burgess, Dewsbury, Yorks.
Killed in Action:	11 Jun 1940, France & Belgium Campaign, 1939/40.
Buried:	Sainte Marie Cemetery, Le Havre, 76, T, 11.
Previously Interred:	Sotteville sur Mer Temp Burial Ground, 6, 4 (until Oct 1947).
Commemorated:	**7 DWR WW2 War Memorial, Col 1.**
	Barclay History RoH, page 371.
DWR Enlistment Book:	TED 19, page 4.

"IN GOD'S BEAUTIFUL GARDEN OF REST IS SOMEONE WE LOVE AND NEVER FORGET"

BUTTERWORTH, Brian, 4616283 Pte, 2/6th DWR [the only B Butterworth listed in CWGC records].
Son of James and Florence Butterworth, Milnsbridge, Huddersfield, Yorks.
    Killed in Action: 19 Oct 1940, France & Belgium Campaign, 1939/40, aged 19.
    Buried: Huddersfield, Lockwood, Cemetery, B, 29.
    Commemorated: **7 DWR WW2 War Memorial, Col 3.**
    Barclay History RoH, page 367.
    DWR Enlistment Book: TED 16, page 29.

CADDY, Joseph Donald, 14708384 Pte, 1/7th DWR.
Son of John Niles and Phillis Annie Caddy, Summercourt, Cornwall.
    Killed in Action: 30 Sep 1944, Normandy Campaign, Belgium, aged 19..
    Buried: Leopoldsburg War Cemetery, 5, C, 16.
    Commemorated: **7 DWR WW2 War Memorial, Col 1.**
    Barclay History RoH, page 368.
    DWR Enlistment Book: OVER 33, page 68.
"IN TREASURED MEMORY OF DONALD ALWAYS IN THE THOUGHTS OF MUM, DAD AND BERYL"

CAMBELL, Herbert Alexander, 326885 Lt, 1/7th DWR, also 11 R Scots Fus.
Son of Edgar and Alice Eva Campbell, husband of Violet Campbell, West Hartlepool, Co Durham.
    Killed in Action: 17 Apr 1945, Normandy Campaign, Netherlands, aged 28.
    Buried: Arnhem Oosterbeek War Cemetery, 7, A, 1.
    Commemorated: **Not listed on 7 DWR WW2 Memorial.**
    Barclay History RoH, page 375.
    Commissioned: Aug 1944.
"TREASURED MEMORIES OF MY LOVING HUSBAND. HE DIED THAT WE MIGHT LIVE"

CAREY, Peter Vivian, 112899 Lt, 1/7th DWR.
Son of Major Peter and Dorothy Madeline Carey, St Peter Port, Guernsey, Channel Islands.
    Died: Drowned off the Azores, 7 Dec 1942, aged 22.
    Buried: No known grave.
    Commemorated: Brookwood 1939-1945 Memorial, 11, 3.
    7 DWR WW2 War Memorial, Col 1.
    Barclay History RoH, page 368.
    Commissioned: Dec 1939.

CARNELL, Percy, D/34915 Pte, 1/7th DWR.
Son of Percy and Mary Alice Carnell, husband of L Carnell, Netherfield, Notts.
    Died of Wounds: 29 Jun 1944, Home Duties.
    Buried: Carlton (Notts) Cemetery, C, D7, 27.
    Commemorated: **7 DWR WW2 War Memorial, Col 1.**
    Barclay History RoH, page 368.
    DWR Enlistment Book: UNDER 30, page 90, OVER 30, page 90.

CAVAN, John Baptist, 4618838 Pte, 2/7th DWR.
Son of John B and Robina Cavan.
    Killed in Action: 12 Jun 1940, France & Belgium Campaign, 1939/40.
    Buried: Sainte Marie Cemetry, Le Havre, 67, S, 14.
    Commemorated: **7 DWR WW2 War Memorial, Col 1.**
    Barclay History RoH, page 371.
    DWR Enlistment Book: TED 18, page 84.

CHAPMAN, Arthur, 4622104 Cpl, 1/7th DWR, att HQ 1st Abn Div.
    Killed in Action: 24 Sep 1944, Normandy Campaign, Netherlands.
    Buried: Arnhem Oosterbeek War Cemetery, 20, C, 17.
    Commemorated: **Not listed on 7 DWR WW2 Memorial.**
        Barclay History RoH, page 375.
    DWR Enlistment Book: TED 22, page 11.

CLENNETT, John, 4619020 Pte, 1/7th DWR.
    Reported Missing: Presumed killed 11 Jun 1940, aged 20.
    Buried: Sainte Marie Cemetry, Le Havre, 67, S, 16.
    Commemorated: **7 DWR WW2 War Memorial, Col 1.**
        Barclay History RoH, page 371.
    DWR Enlistment Book: TED 19, page 3.

CLUMPUS, Samuel, 4546248 Pte, 1/7th DWR.
    Killed in Action: 23 Mar 1944, Normandy Campaign, Netherlands, aged 22.
    Buried: Groesbeek Canadian War Cemetery, 6, A, 11.
    Commemorated: **7 DWR WW2 War Memorial, Col 2.**
        Barclay History RoH, page 368.
    DWR Enlistment Book: UNDER 30, page 76, OVER 30, page 76.

COBB, George, 258676 Lt, 1/7th DWR att 1 Bn Gold Coast Regt.
Son of Richard John and Honoria Winifred Cobb, Market Weighton, Yorks.
    Died of Wounds: 6 Dec 1945, Burma Campaign, aged 22.
    Buried: No known grave.
    Commemorated: Rangoon Memorial, Face 13.
        7 DWR WW2 War Memorial, Col 1.
        Barclay History RoH, page 368.
    Commissioned: Jan 1943, posted to Royal West African Frontier Force, 1945.

COHEN, Harry, 4622606 Pte, 2/7th DWR.
Son of Samuel and Ada Cohen, husband of Mary H Cohen, Marylebone, London.
    Killed in Action: 6 Oct 194, Home Duties, aged 28.
    Buried: Brookwood Military Cemetery, 11, BB, 10.
    Commemorated: **7 DWR WW2 War Memorial, Col 2.**
        Barclay History RoH, page 371.
    DWR Enlistment Book: TED 22, page 61.
"HOW LITTLE, BUT HOW MUCH"

COOKSON, Edmund, 1691273 Pte, 1/7th DWR.
Son of Sethur Edmund and Laura Mabel Cookson, Fallowfield, Manchester, Lancs.
    Killed in Action: 1 Dec 1944, Normandy Campaign, Netherlands, aged 29.
    Buried: Jonkerbos War Cemetery, 7, E, 4.
    Commemorated: **7 DWR WW2 War Memorial, Col 2. D Coy Memorial, Col 3.**
        Barclay History RoH, page 368.
    DWR Enlistment Book: UNDER 34, page 34.

COOMBS, Alexander Douglas, 3773440 Pte, 1/7th DWR.
Son of Samuel and Julia Coombs, Liverpool, Lancs.
    Died: 12 Jul 945, aged 23.
    Buried: Liverpool (Anfield) Cemetery, 22, 1424.

Commemorated:	**7 DWR WW2 War Memorial, Col 2.**
	Barclay History RoH, page 368.
DWR Enlistment Book:	UNDER 34, page 43.

COWBURN, Edward, 14623087 Pte, 1/7th DWR. [Memorial shows initial F].
Son of Edward and Ivy Cowburn, Rotherham, Yorks.

Killed in Action:	18 Jun 1944, Normandy Campaign, France, aged 19.
Buried:	Bayeux War Cemetery, 12, J, 22.
Commemorated:	Rotherham War Memorial.
	7 DWR WW2 War Memorial, Col 2; D Coy Memorial, Col 1.
	Barclay History RoH, page 368.
DWR Enlistment Book:	OVER 32, page 58.

"GOD HAS GAINED WHAT WE HAVE LOST. WE SHALL MEET AGAIN SOME DAY. MOTHER AND BROTHERS"

COX, Ernest, 4618296 Pte, 1/7th DWR.
Son of Dennis and Gertrude Cox, Grimethorpe, Yorks.

Killed in Action:	18 Jun 1944, Normandy Campaign, France, aged 26.
Buried:	Bayeux War Cemetery, 12, J, 17.
Commemorated:	**7 DWR WW2 War Memorial, Col 2.**
	Barclay History RoH, page 368.
DWR Enlistment Book:	TED 18, page 30.

CROSSLAND, John, 96765 Capt, 1/7th DWR att 147 Bde HQ, GSO3.
Son of Dan and Annie Crossland, Oakes, Huddersfield, Yorks.

Killed in Action:	6 Aug 1944, Normandy Campaign, France, aged 34.
Buried:	Ranville War Cemetery, 1, D, 15.
Commemorated:	**7 DWR WW2 War Memorial, Col 1.**
	Barclay History RoH, page 368.
Commissioned:	6 Sep 1939, from Leeds University OTC, embodied 1 Sep 1939.

"AT THE GOING DOWN OF THE SUN AND IN THE MORNING WE WILL REMEMBER HIM"

CROSSLEY, Alfred, 4537947 Sgt, 1/7th DWR.
Husband of Sylvia E Crossley, Barnetby, Lincs.

Killed in Action:	12 Jul 1944, Normandy Campaign.
Buried:	St Manvieu War Cemetery, Cheux, 3, C, 2.
Commemorated:	**7 DWR WW2 War Memorial, Col 2.**
	Barclay History RoH, page 368.
DWR Enlistment Book:	UNDER 34, page 35.

CROSSLEY, John, 14661157 Pte, 1/7th DWR.
Son of James Whiteley and Florence Crossley, Sowerby Bridge, Yorks.

Killed in Action:	17 Jun 1944, Normandy Campaign, France, aged 19.
Buried:	Hottot les Bagues War Cemetery, 8, G, 13.
Commemorated:	**7 DWR WW2 War Memorial, Col 2; D Coy Memorial, Col 1.**
	Barclay History RoH, page 368.
DWR Enlistment Book:	OVER 33, page 36.

"UNTIL THE DAY BREAK"

DAVIES, Gwyn Wood, 4615594 Sgt, 2/7th DWR.

Killed in Action:	11 Jun 1940, France & Belgium Campaign, 1939/40, aged 25.
Buried:	No known grave.

Commemorated:	Dunkirk Memorial, Col 61.
	Not listed on 7 DWR WW2 Memorial.
	Barclay History RoH, page 371.
DWR Enlistment Book:	TED 15, page 60.

DAVIS, Henry, 4692211 Pte, 1/7th DWR, also KOYLI.
Son of John and Eliza Davis, Leeds, husband of Mabel Davis, Leeds, Yorks.

Died:	10 Mar 1943.
Buried:	No known grave.
Commemorated:	Leeds (Lawnswood) Crematorium, Panel 1.
	7 DWR WW2 War Memorial, Col 2.
DWR Enlistment Book:	OVER 36, page 128.

DAY, William Durrans, 7617832, 2/7th DWR.
Son of Norman Brook and Martha Ann Day, Crosland Moor, Huddersfield, Yorks.

Died:	30 Aug 1941, Home Duties, aged 23.
Buried:	Huddersfield (Lockwood) Cemetery, D, 355.
Commemorated:	**7 DWR WW2 War Memorial, Col 2.**
	Barclay History RoH, page 371.
DWR Enlistment Book:	Over Numbers, page 126 (initials shown as W P).

DEARING, Roy, 14579246 Pte, C Coy, 1/7th DWR.
Son of Thomas Richard and Easter Ann Dearing, Elland, Yorks.

Killed in Action:	4 Dec 1944, Normandy Campaign (Netherlands), aged 19.
Buried:	Jonkerbos War Cemetery, 19, D, 8.
Commemorated:	**7 DWR WW2 War Memorial, Col 2.**
	Barclay History RoH, page 368.
DWR Enlistment Book:	OVER 32, page 12.

"WITH COMRADES HE LIES FAR FROM THOSE HE LOVED. HE GAVE HIS LIFE FOR FREEDOM"

DERMODY, John, 14454064 Pte, 1/7th DWR.
Son of Donald and Mary Dermody, Waun-wen, Swansea, Wales.

Died:	28 Aug 1946, Normandy Campaign, Germany, aged 20.
Buried:	Reichswald Forest War Cemetery, 59, J, 7.
Commemorated:	**Not listed on 7 DWR WW2 Memorial.**
DWR Enlistment Book:	OVER 36, page 205.

"ETERNAL REST GIVE UNTO HIM, O LORD; AND LET PERPETUAL LIGHT SHINE UPON HIM"

DEWE, Walter Britford, 4616993 Cpl, Carrier Pl, 1/7th DWR.
Son of Leonard and Pamela Dewe, husband of Dorren Dewe, Rawmarsh, Rotherham, Yorks.

Killed in Action:	17 Apr 1945, Normandy Campaign, Netherlands, aged 26.
Buried:	Arnhem Oosterbeek War Cemetery, 7, A, 3.
Commemorated:	Rotherham War Memorial.
	7 DWR WW2 War Memorial, Col 2.
	Barclay History RoH, page 368.
DWR Enlistment Book:	TED 16, page 100.

"IN LOVING MEMORY. MY DARLING HUSBAND WALTER. TILL WE MEET AGAIN. MUD, DAD, SIS & TWINS"

DILWORTH, Arthur, 14409161 LCpl, 1/7th DWR.
Son of Edgar and Kezia Caroline Dilworth, Halifax, Yorks.

Reported missing:	presumed dead, 27 Aug 1944, Normandy Campaign, France, aged 19.
Buried:	No known grave.
Commemorated:	Bayeux Memorial, panel 15, Col 1.
	7 DWR WW2 War Memorial, Col 2; D Coy Memorial, Col 2.
	Barclay History RoH, page 368.
DWR Enlistment Book:	OVER 32, page 36.

DOWNES, John Henry, 4626078 Pte, 1/7th DWR [7 DWR Memorial shows initials J B].
Killed in Action:	25 Jun 1944, Normandy Campaign.
Buried:	Hottot les Bagues War Cemetery, 8, G, 8.
Commemorated:	Rotherham War Memorial.
	7 DWR WW2 War Memorial, Col 2.
	Barclay History RoH, page 368.
DWR Enlistment Book:	TED 26.

DRACUP, Alfred, 4619016 Pte, 2/7th DWR.
Son of John William and Mary Dracup, Turnbridge, Huddersfield, Yorks.
Killed in Action:	11 Jun 1940, France & Belgium Campaign, 1939/40, aged 20.
Buried:	Sainte Marie Cemetery, Le Havre, 67, S, 20.
Previously Interred:	Sotteville sur Mer Temp Burial Ground, 5, 5 (until Oct 1947).
Commemorated:	**7 DWR WW2 War Memorial, Col 2.**
	Barclay History RoH, page 371.
DWR Enlistment Book:	TED 19, page 2.

"LOVING SHEPHERD OF THY SHEEP KEEP THY LAMB, IN SAFETY KEEP"

DUNN, Bernard, 2365534 Pte, 1/7th DWR [D Coy Memorial shows initial W].
Son of Sydney Edward and Eleanor Sarah Dunn, Forest Hill, London.
Killed in Action:	4 Dec 1944, Normandy Campaign, Netherlands, aged 35.
Buried:	Jonkerbos War Cemetery, 15, D, 4.
Commemorated:	**7 DWR WW2 War Memorial, Col 2, D Coy Memorial, Col 2.**
	Barclay History RoH, page 368.
DWR Enlistment Book:	UNDER 34, pages 43 & 53.

"A LOVING SON AND BROTHER TRUE AND KIND A BEAUTIFUL MEMORY LEFT BEHIND"

DYSON, J, 7th DWR. Unable to identify.
Killed in Action:	4 x J Dyson in CWGC records.
Buried:	No known grave.
Commemorated:	**7 DWR WW2 War Memorial, Col 2.**
	4616443 J E Dyson, 1/7th DWR, Barclay History RoH, page 368.
DWR Enlistment Book:	[4616443 Joe Edwin Dyson, 2/7th DWR, discharged 22 Sep 1940].
	[4618623 John Dyson, transferred to Royal Signals 13 Apr 1940].

ELLIS, Graham Ellis, 189384 Capt, 1/7th DWR, from South Staffs Regt, awarded MC, *LG 21 Dec 1944, p 5856 & Unit WD, 31 Mar 1945.*
Killed in Action:	15 Mar 1945, France & Belgium Campaign, 1939/40, Netherlands,
Buried:	Jonkerbos War Cemetery, 19, D, 8.
Commemorated:	**7 DWR WW2 War Memorial, Col 1; D Coy Memorial, Col 3.**
Commissioned:	May 1941.

ELLWOOD, John, 14409409 Pte, 1/7th DWR.
Died of Wounds:	18 Jun 1944, Normandy Campaign, France, aged 19.
Buried:	Bayeux War Cemetery, 12, J, 12.

    Commemorated: **7 DWR WW2 War Memorial, Col 2.**
                                             Barclay History RoH, page 369.
    DWR Enlistment Book: OVER 32, page 65.

ENION, Joel, 4615837 Pte, 2 DWR, from 5 Dragoon Gds RAC to DWR 8 Apr 1941.
    Killed in Action: 10 Mar 1942, Burma Campaign, aged 23.
    Buried: No known grave.
    Commemorated: Rangoon Memorial, Face 13.
                                          7 DWR WW2 War Memorial, Col 2.
                                           Barclay History RoH, page 359.
    DWR Enlistment Book: TED 15, page 84.

EVANS, Clifford, 4616999 Sgt, 1/7th DWR.
Son of Enoch and Florence Evans, Dunsford, Yorks, husband of Iris Evans.
    Killed in Action: 24 Sep 1944, Normandy Campaign, Belgium, aged 26.
    Buried: Leopoldsburg War Cemetery, 5 C, 18.
    Commemorated: **7 DWR WW2 War Memorial, Col 2.**
                                           Barclay History RoH, page 369.
    DWR Enlistment Book: TED 16, page 100.
"WITHOUT FAREWELL YOU FELL ASLEEP ONLY A MEMORY FOR US TO KEEP"

EVEMY, Reginald James, 14204889 Pte, 1/7th DWR.
Son of Ernest Frank and Maude Mabel Evemy, Pitt, Hants.
    Died of Wounds as POW: 2 Dec 1944, Normandy Campaign, Netherlands, aged 21.
    Buried: Arnhem Oosterbeek War Cemetery, 14, B, 12.
    Commemorated: **7 DWR WW2 War Memorial, Col 2.**
                                           Barclay History RoH, page 369.
    DWR Enlistment Book: OVER 31, page 16.
"FOREVER IN OUR HEARTS"

FELLOWS, Thomas, 4911353 WO2, CSM A Coy, 1/7th DWR [one source shows Fellowes].
SON OF Mr and Mrs C R Fellows, Harden, Bloxwich, Staffs, husband of Hilda Fellows, Llangollen, Denbighshire, Wales.
    Died of Wounds: 15 Apr 1945, Normandy Campaign, Netherlands, aged 36
    Buried: Milsbeek War Cemetery, 2, F, 12.
    Commemorated: **7 DWR WW2 War Memorial, Col 2.**
                                           Barclay History RoH, page 369.
    DWR Enlistment Book: OVER 35, page 131.
"PEACEFULLY SLEEPING FREE FROM PAIN IN GOD'S OWN TIME WE'LL MEET AGAIN"

FINN, Thomas, 14623110 Pte, 1/7th DWR.
Son of James and Mary Finn, Whitwood Mere, Castleford, Yorks.
    Died of Wounds: 19 Jun 1944, Normandy Campaign, France, aged 19.
    Buried: Bayeux War Cemetery, 14, H, 7.
    Commemorated: **7 DWR WW2 War Memorial, Col 2.**
                                           Barclay History RoH, page 369.
    DWR Enlistment Book: OVER 32, page 59.
"GIVE HIM, O LORD, ETERNAL REST; LET PERPETUAL LIGHT SHINE UPON HIM R.I.P.

FISHER, John Edward, 831285 Pte, 1/7th DWR.
SON OF Samual Sidney and Catherine Fisher, Willington Quay, Northumberland.

Killed in Action:	15 Aug 1945, Normandy Campaign, Germany (BLA Duties).
Buried:	Munster Heath War Cemetery, 2, C, 13.
Commemorated:	**7 DWR WW2 War Memorial, Col 2.**
	Barclay History RoH, page 369.
DWR Enlistment Book:	UNDER 34, page 93.

"ON HIS SOUL, SWEET JESUS, HAVE MERCY R.I.P.

FITZJOHN, Norman,   4622643 Pte, 2/7th DWR.
Son of Mr and Mrs Bertie Alfred Fitzjohn, Stoke Newington, London.

Killed in Action:	20 Apr 1942, Home Duties, aged 26.
Buried:	Shorncliffe Military Cemetery, Q, 1118.
Commemorated:	**7 DWR WW2 War Memorial, Col 2.**
	Barclay History RoH, page 369.
DWR Enlistment Book:	TED 22, page 65.

"LOST BUT NOT FORGOTTEN. DAD, ALBERT AND BERTIE"

FLANNERY, John, 14287088 Pte, 1/7th DWR.
Son of Patrick and Julia Flannery, Kilbride, Co Mayo, Irish Republic.

Killed in Action:	4 Dec 1944, Normandy Campaign, Netherlands, aged 29.
Buried:	Jonkerbos War Cemetery, 1, C, 1.
Commemorated:	**7 DWR WW2 War Memorial, Col 2; D Coy Memorial, Col 2.**
	Barclay History RoH, page 369.
DWR Enlistment Book:	OVER 31, page 38.

FROST, Eric, 14551255 Pte, 1/7th DWR.
Son of John Edward and May Frost, Wilmslow, Cheshire.

Killed in Action:	26 Jul 1944, Normandy Campaign, France, aged 20.
Buried:	Ranville War Cemetery, 4, E, 19.
Commemorated:	**7 DWR WW2 War Memorial, Col 2.**
	Barclay History RoH, page 369.
DWR Enlistment Book:	OVER 32, page 52.

"BLESSED ARE THE PURE IN HEART; FOR THEY SHALL SEE GOD" MOTHER, DAD AND FAMILY

GARDNER, Stanley Edward Samuel, 4613789 Pte, 2/7th DWR.
Son of John William and Emily Maud Gardner, husband of Maria Annugaita Gardner, Halifax, Yorks.

Died:	21 Feb 1941, Home Duties, aged 21.
Buried:	Halifax (Stoney Royd) Cemetery, H, 144.
Commemorated:	**7 DWR WW2 War Memorial, Col 2.**
	Barclay History RoH, page 371.
DWR Enlistment Books:	EB 1938 & TED 13, page 79 [EB 1938 shows initials E S].

"TREASURED MEMORIES. ALSO HIS SISTER-IN-LAW CELESTA FUSCO DIED 4TH NOVEMBER 1936"

GARMORY, John Bird, 1836920 Pte, 1/7th DWR.
Son of Robert and Elizabeth Garmoy, Lochgelly, Scotland.

Died of Wounds:	21 Oct 1944, Normandy Campaign, Belgium, aged 22.
Buried:	Wuustwezel Churchyard, 6.
Commemorated:	**7 DWR WW2 War Memorial, Col 2.**
	Barclay History RoH, page 369.
DWR Enlistment Book:	UNDER 34, page 44.

"OUR LOVE GOES WITH YOU. BORN AT LOCHGELLY, SCOTLAND"

GARVEY, Christopher William, 4617095 LCpl, Sigs Platoon, 1/7th DWR.
Son of James and Mary Garvey, Halifax, Yorks.
Killed in Action:	12 Oct 1944, Normandy Campaign, Belgium, aged 26.
Buried:	Leopoldsburg War Cemetery, 5, E, 11.
Commemorated:	**7 DWR WW2 War Memorial, Col 2.**
	Unit War Diary, 12 Oct 1944.
	Barclay History RoH, page 369.
DWR Enlistment Book:	TED 17, page 10.

"MY CHRISTY WHOM I SHALL NOT SEE AGAIN TILL MY EARTHLY RACE BE RUN R.I.P. MOTHER"

GAWTHORPE, Herbert Edward, 4616271 Sgt, 2/7th DWR.
Son of George Henry and Annie Gawthorpe, Halifax, Yorks.
Killed in Action:	11 Jun 1940, France & Belgium Campaign, 1939/40, aged 20.
Buried:	Blosseville sur Mer Churchyard Military Cemetery, 1, 3.
Commemorated:	**7 DWR WW2 War Memorial, Col 2.**
	Barclay History RoH, page 371.
DWR Enlistment Book:	TED 16, page 28.

"GREATER LOVE HATH NO MAN THAN THIS, THAT A MAN LAY DOWN HIS LIFE FOR HIS FRIENDS"

GERRARD, Robert Anthony Herbert, 42195 Maj, OC W Coy, 2/7th DWR, also 1 & 2 DWR pre war. Mentioned in Despatches, *LG 11 Oct 1945, page 23*.
Son of Major General J J Gerrard CB CMG and Mrs Gerrard, husband of Muriel Gerrard, Woking, Surrey.
Killed in Action:	13 Jun 1940, France & Belgium Campaign, 1939/40.
Buried:	Veules les Roses, 1, 10.
Commemorated:	**7 DWR WW2 War Memorial, Col 1.**
	Barclay History RoH, page 372.
Commissioned:	c1931, 2 DWR. MID awarded, LG 11 Oct 1945, page 5009.

GIBSON, Ernest, 14409160 Pte, 1/7th DWR.
Son of J C and Rebecca Gibson, Sowerby Bridge, Yorks.
Killed in Action:	6 Jul 1944, Normandy Campaign, France, aged 19.
Buried:	Hottot les Bagues War Cemetery, 10, G, 7.
Commemorated:	**7 DWR WW2 War Memorial, Col 2, D Coy Memorial, Col 2.**
	Barclay History RoH, page 369.
DWR Enlistment Book:	OVER 32, page 36.

"WHEN HIS YEARS WERE BEST GOD TOOK HIM FROM AMONG US TO ETERNAL REST"

GLANISTER, Herbert, 4615991 LSgt, S Coy 1/7th DWR.
Son of Mr and Mrs George Henry Glanister, Mossley, Lancs.
Killed in Action:	1 Dec 1944, Normandy Campaign, Netherlands, aged 25.
Buried:	Jonkerbos War Cemetery, 19, D, 4.
Commemorated:	**7 DWR WW2 War Memorial, Col 2.**
	Barclay History RoH, page 369.
DWR Enlistment Book:	TED 15, page 100.

"NEVER SHALL YOUR MEMORY FADE SWEET THOUGHTS EVER LINGER WHERE YOU ARE LAID"

GLEDHILL, Norman, 4616503 Pte, 2/7th DWR.
Son of John Edwin and Agnes Gledhill, Golcar, Yorks.

Died of Wounds as POW:	13 Apr 1945, France & Belgium Campaign, 1939/40, died Marienburg Camp, aged 23.
Buried:	No known grave.
Commemorated:	Dunkirk Memorial, Col 62.
	7 DWR WW2 War Memorial, Col 2.
	Barclay History RoH, page 372.
DWR Enlistment Book:	TED 16, page 51.

GREENWOOD, Clifford, 4617399 Pte, 2/7th DWR.
Son of Thomas and Nellie Beardsell Greenwood, Halifax, Yorks.

Killed in Action:	11 Jun 1940, France & Belgium Campaign, 1939/40, aged 21.
Buried:	Sainte Marie Cemetery, Le Havre, 67, T, 14.
Previously Interred:	Sotteville sur Mer Temp Burial Ground, 6, 7 (until Oct 1947).
Commemorated:	**7 DWR WW2 War Memorial, Col 2.**
	Barclay History RoH, page 372.
DWR Enlistment Book:	TED 17, page 40.

"WE WILL ALWAYS REMEMBER AND WONDER WHY HE HAD TO DIE. MOTHER, BROTHERS AND SISTERS"

GREENWOOD, James, 4616713 Pte, 1/7th DWR.
Son of Percy and Agnes Greenwood, husband of Marjorie Greenwood, Halifax, Yorks.

Died:	30 Aug 1941, Home Duties, aged 21.
Buried:	Halifax (Stoney Royd) Cemetery, Spec Mem.
Commemorated:	**7 DWR WW2 War Memorial, Col 2.**
	Barclay History RoH, page 372.
DWR Enlistment Book:	TED 16, page 72.

"AT THE GOING DOWN OF THE SUN AND IN THE MORNING WE WILL REMEMBER HIM"

GREENWOOD, Kevin Barrett, 14693520 Pte, 1/7th DWR.
Son of Fred and Emily Greenwood, Hebden Bridge, Yorks.

Killed in Action:	16 Jul 1944, Normandy Campaign, France, aged 18.
Buried:	Hottot les Bagues War Cemetery, 10, E, 1.
Commemorated:	**7 DWR WW2 War Memorial, Col 2, D Coy Memorial, Col 2.**
DWR Enlistment Book:	OVER 35, page 112.

"ETERNAL HONOUR GIVE TO THOSE WHO DIED THAT WE MIGHT LIVE"

GREENWOOD, William Kenneth, HQ Coy Sigs 4545999 Pte, 1/7th DWR.
Son of William Henry and Kathleen Greenwood, Leeds, Yorks.

Killed in Action:	25 Jun 1944, Normandy Campaign, France, aged 20.
Buried:	Hottot les Bagues War Cemetery, 10, G, 8.
Commemorated:	**7 DWR WW2 War Memorial, Col 2.**
	Barclay History RoH, page 369.
DWR Enlistment Book:	UNDER 30, page 75 & OVER 30, page 75.

"TREASURED MEMORIES OF OUR ONLY SON KENNETH WHO GAVE HIS LIFE IN BATTLE"

GROOM, William John Athur, 14424494 Pte, 1/7th DWR.
Son of James Arthur and Elizabeth Groom (nee Barnett).

Killed in Action:	16 Oct 1944, Normandy Campaign, Belgium.
Buried:	Leopoldsburg War Cemetery, 2, D, 7.
Commemorated:	**7 DWR WW2 War Memorial, Col 2.**
	Barclay History RoH, page 369.
DWR Enlistment Book:	OVER 35, page 131.

"I HAVE FOUGHT A GOOD FIGHT, I HAVE FINISHED MY COURSE, I HAVE KEPT THE FAITH"

HAINSWORTH, Harold, 4617702 Pte, 2/7th DWR.
Son of Harry and Loui Hainsworth, Lee Mount, Halifax, Yorks, husband of Annie Hainsworth.
> **Killed in Action:** 11 Jun 1940, France & Belgium Campaign, 1939/40, aged 20.
> **Buried:** Sainte Marie Cemetery, Le Havre, 67, T, 15.
> **Previously Interred:** Sotteville sur Mer Temp Burial Ground, 6, 8 (until Oct 1947).
> **Commemorated:** **7 DWR WW2 War Memorial, Col 2.**
> Barclay History RoH, page 372.
> **DWR Enlistment Book:** TED 17, page 71.

"ALWAYS REMEMBERED BY HIS WIFE ANN, MOTHER, FATHER AND SISTERS."

HALL, Donald, 268898 Lt, 1/7th DWR.
Son of Percy Foster and Edith Hall, Brough, Hull, Yorks.
> **Died Accidentally:** 16 Jan 1944, Home Duties, aged 20.
> **Buried:** Hull Northern Cemetery, 298, 35.
> **Commemorated:** **7 DWR WW2 War Memorial, Col 2.**
> **Commissioned:** Mar 1943.

"PROUD AND HAPPY MEMORIES OF OUR LOVING AND DEVOTED YOUNGEST SON DONALD"

HALL, H, 7 DWR.   Unable to identify [14660700 Pte Hall H, 1 DWR, in Barclay RoH].
> **Killed in Action:** No trace - 18 x Hall H listed in CWGC.
> **Buried:** No known grave.
> **Commemorated:** **7 DWR WW2 War Memorial, Col 2.**
> **DWR Enlistment Book:** No trace.

HALLIDAY, Reginald, 4615921, 2/7th DWR.
> **Killed in Action:** 10 Jun 1940, France & Belgium Campaign, 1939/40, aged 26.
> **Buried:** No known grave.
> **Commemorated:** Dunkirk Memorial, Col 62.
> **Not listed on 7 DWR WW2 Memorial.**
> Barclay History RoH, page 367.
> **DWR Enlistment Book:** TED 15, page 93.

HALSE, William James, 153949 Lt, C Coy, 1/7th DWR, from Royal Armoured Corps.
Son of E Stanley and Ethel W Halse, South Littleton. Worcs.
> **Died of Wounds:** 28 Jun 1944, Normandy Campaign, France, aged 26.
> **Buried:** Bayeux War Cemetery, 13, J, 25.
> **Commemorated:** **7 DWR WW2 War Memorial, Col 1.**
> Barclay History RoH, page 369.
> **Commissioned:** Oct 1940.

"ALL THAT IS BROKEN SHALL BE MENDED; ALL THAT IS LOST SHALL BE FOUND"

HAMPSON, Cyril, 4618811 Pte, 2/7th DWR.
SON OF John Arthur and Mahalah Hampson, Sheffield, Yorks.
> **Killed in Action:** 11 Jun 1940, France & Belgium Campaign, 1939/40, aged 22.
> **Buried:** Sainte Marie Cemetery, Le Havre, 67, T, 13.
> **Previously Interred:** Sotteville sur Mer Temp Burial Ground, 6, 6 (until Oct 1947).
> **Commemorated:** **7 DWR WW2 War Memorial, Col 2.**
> Barclay History RoH, page 372.

> DWR Enlistment Book: TED 18, page 82.

"HIS DUTY NOBLY DONE. HE DIED THAT WE MIGHT LIVE"

HARESIGN, Harold, 14546078 Pte, 1/7th DWR (CWGC shows 6 DWR).
Son of Albert and Edith Haresign, Balby, Doncaster, Yorks.
> **Killed in Action:** 18 Aug 1944, Normandy Campaign, France, aged 19.
> **Buried:** No known grave.
> **Commemorated:** Bayeux Memorial, Panel 15, Col 1.
> **Not listed on 7 DWR WW2 Memorial.**
> Barclay History RoH, page 366.
> **DWR Enlistment Book:** OVER 31, page 98.

HARKER, Raymond, 4617199 Cpl, 1/7th DWR.
Son of Elizabeth Harker, husband of Doris Harker, Todmorden, Lancs.
> **Killed in Action:** 28 Oct 1944, Normandy Campaign, Netherlands, aged 26.
> **Buried:** Bergen Op Zoom War Cemetery, 9, A, 20.
> **Commemorated:** Todmorden War Memorial.
> St Andrew's Church, Finghall
> **7 DWR WW2 War Memorial, Col 2.**
> Barclay History RoH, page 369.
> **DWR Enlistment Book:** TED 17, page 20.

"HE THAT DWELLETH IN THE SECRET PLACE OF THE MOST HIGH SHALL ABIDE…"

HEAD, Stanley Ernest, 14708390 Pte, 1/7th DWR.
Son of Ernest and Mary Head, Highworth, Wilts.
> **Killed in Action:** 31 Oct 1943, Normandy Campaign, Netherlands, aged 18.
> **Buried:** Dordrecht General Cemetery, A, 5.
> **Commemorated:** **7 DWR WW2 War Memorial, Col 2.**
> Barclay History RoH, page 369.
> **DWR Enlistment Book:** OVER 33, page 69.

"GREATER LOVE HATH NO MAN THAN THIS, THAT A MAN LAY DOWN HIS LIFE FOR HIS FRIENDS"

HEARSON, Eric, 5049825 Cpl, 1/7th DWR, from N Staffs Regt.
Son of George and Margaret Hearson, husband of Alice Hearson, Sandyford, Staffs.
> **Killed in Action:** 17 Jun 1944, Normandy Campaign, France, aged 26, first casualty.
> **Buried:** Bayeux War Cemetery, 14, F, 3 [shows date of death as 21 Jun].
> **Commemorated:** **7 DWR WW2 War Memorial, Col 2.**
> Barclay History RoH, page 369.
> **DWR Enlistment Book:** OVER Numbers, page 84.

"PEACEFULLY SLEEPING NOW AT REST IN GOD'S OWN GARDEN LIES ONE OF THE BEST"

HEELEY, Albert, 4611484 LCpl, 1/7th DWR, previously served 19 May 1931 - 31 Aug 1935.
Son of Albert and Winifred Heeley, Staybridge, Cheshire.
> **Killed in Action:** 19 Jun 1944, Normandy Campaign, France, aged 32.
> **Buried:** Hottot les Bagues War Cemetery, 10, E, 9.
> **Commemorated:** **7 DWR WW2 War Memorial, Col 2.**
> Barclay History RoH, page 369.
> **DWR Enlistment Book:** EB 11, page 97 & EB 1935. [some sources show HEALEY].

"LORD HAVE MERCY ON HIS SOUL R.I.P"

HEMINSLEY, Raymond, 4389129 LCpl, 1/7ᵗʰ DWR, from Green Howards.
Son of Robert and Florence Heminsley, husband of Lucy Heminsley, Normandby, Middlesbrough, Yorks.
    Killed in Action: 2 Apr 1944, Normandy Campaign, Netherlands, aged 29.
    Buried: Jonkerbos War Cemetery, 10, A, 2.
    Commemorated: **7 DWR WW2 War Memorial, Col 2.**
    DWR Enlistment Book: UNDER 34, page 28.

HEWITT, Alfred, 4749025 Pte, 1/7ᵗʰ DWR.
Son of Charles and May Hewitt, Kinsley, Yorks.
    Killed in Action: 7 Aug 1944, Normandy Campaign, France, aged 29.
    Buried: Banneville la Campagne War Cemetery, 14, C, 4.
    Commemorated: Hemsworth War Memorial.
        7 DWR WW2 War Memorial, Col 2.
        Barclay History RoH, page 369.
    DWR Enlistment Book: EB 7, page 186.
"HE DIED AND LEFT SO SWEET A MEMORY THAT STILL HE SEEMS TO LIVE"

HIGGINBOTTOM, Henry, 4616295 Sgt, 1/7ᵗʰ DWR, awarded MID, LG 22 Mar 1945, page 1559.
    Killed in Action: 25 Jun 944, Normandy Campaign, France, aged 24.
    Buried: Hottot les Bagues War Cemetery, 8, G, 25.
    Commemorated: **7 DWR WW2 War Memorial, Col 2.**
        Barclay History RoH, page 369.
    DWR Enlistment Book: TED 16, page 30.

HIGHAM, James, 4618948 Pte, 2/7ᵗʰ DWR att DEMS.
Son of William and Susan Higham, Hull, Yorks.
    Died: 19 Feb 1941, Home Convoy Duties, aged 21.
    Buried: At sea.
    Commemorated: Plymouth Naval Memorial, Panel 62, Col 2.
        7 DWR WW2 War Memorial, Col 3.
        Barclay History RoH, page 372.
    DWR Enlistment Book: TED 18, page 95.

HILDRETH, Frank, 4979963 LCpl, C Coy, 1/7ᵗʰ DWR.
Son of John Atkinson and Mary Emma Hildreth, Ferriby Sluice, Lincs.
    Killed in Action: 18 Jun 1944, Normandy Campaign, France, aged 25.
    Buried: Hottot les Bagues War Cemetery, 10, E, 11.
    Commemorated: **7 DWR WW2 War Memorial, Col 3.**
        Barclay History RoH, page 369.
    DWR Enlistment Book: OVER Numbers, page 157.
"HIS FACE WE NEVER FORGET FOR IN OUR HEARTS HE IS WITH US YET. FAMILY"

HILL, Charles Herbert, 117116 Maj, D Coy 1/7ᵗʰ DWR, Gallantry Certificate awarded Dec 1944.
Son of Charles J and Eleanor E Hill, Battersea, London.
    Killed in Action: 10 Aug 1944, Normandy Campaign, France, aged 28.
    Buried: Ranville War Cemetery, 8, B, 16.
    Commemorated: **7 DWR WW2 War Memorial, Col 3.**
        Barclay History RoH, page 366.
        Iron Duke Journal, 061-1945, page 107.
    Commissioned: Jan 1940.
"RATHER DEATH THAN FALSE OF FAYTHE"

HILTON, Eric, 14687366 LCpl, 1/7th DWR.
Son of Rupert and Ethel Hilton, Middleton, Manchester, Lancs.
Died:	2 Jun 1946, BLA, Germany, aged 21.
Buried:	Reichswald Forest War Cemetery, 59, J, 8.
Commemorated:	**Not listed on 7 DWR WW2 Memorial.**
DWR Enlistment Book:	OVER 33, page 53.

"THOUGH ABSENT YOU ARE ALWAYS NEAR, STILL LOVED, STILL MISSED, AND VERY DEAR"

HIRST, Fred, 3300461 CSgt (CQMS), 2/7th DWR.
Died of Wounds:	14 Jun 1940, France & Belgium Campaign, 1939/40, aged 39.
Buried:	Auppegard Churchyard, 1.
Commemorated:	**7 DWR WW2 War Memorial, Col 3.**
	Barclay History RoH, page 372.
DWR Enlistment Book:	No trace.

HOCKING, John Hepton, 4691312 Sgt, 1/7th DWR.
Son of Alfred Charles and Mary Elizabeth Hocking, Langcliffe, Yorks
Killed in Action:	4 Dec 1944, Normandy Campaign, Netherlands.
Buried:	Jonkerbos War Cemetery, 11, D, 7.
Commemorated:	Langcliffe (Settle) War Memorial.
	7 DWR WW2 War Memorial, Col 3; D Coy Memorial, Col 2.
	Barclay History RoH, page 369.
DWR Enlistment Book:	OVER 32, page 10.

"AT THE GOING DOWN OF THE SUN AND IN THE MORNING WE WILL REMEMBER HIM"

HOPE, Bragan Joseph, 14410818 Pte, 1/7th DWR [memorial shows initials J B].
Son of Thomas F and Mary Hope, Morley, Yorks.
Killed in Action:	25 Jun 1944, Normandy Campaign, France, aged 18.
Buried:	Hottot les Bagues War Cemetery, 8, G, 5.
Commemorated:	**7 DWR WW2 War Memorial, Col 3.**
	Barclay History RoH, page 369.
DWR Enlistment Book:	OVER 32, page 37.

"IN THE SUNSET WHERE LOVELINESS NEVER DIES HE LIVES IN GLORY NEATH THE GOLDEN SKIES"

HOUGH, Herbert, 4610272 WO2 (CSM), 7 DWR (posted to 2 DWR?).
Son of Benjamin and Elizabeth Hough, husband of Elizabeth Hough, Stalybridge, Cheshire.
Died:	13 Apr 1942, en route for Far East, aged 44.
Buried:	Pietermaritzburg (Fort Napier), D, 9.
Commemorated:	**7 DWR WW2 War Memorial, Col 3.**
	Barclay History RoH, page 372.
DWR Enlistment Book:	EB 10, page 55.

"ONLY THOSE WHO HAVE LOST CAN TELL THE PAIN OF PARTING WITHOUT FAREWELL"

HOUNDSFIELD, Kenneth Denholm, 258669 Lt, 1/7th DWR, MID awarded, *LG 22 Mar 1945, page 1559.* Son of the Reverend Norman Geary and Edith Margaret Houndsfield, Thurstonland Vicarage, Yorks.
Killed in Action:	11 Sep 1944, Normandy Campaign, France, aged 23.
Buried:	Sainte Marie Cemetery, Le Havre, 67, H, 14.
Commemorated:	**7 DWR WW2 War Memorial, Col 1.**
	Barclay History RoH, page 369.

Commissioned: Jan 1943.
"IN PROUD AND HAPPY MEMORY OF A BELOVED SON AND BROTHER"

HUDSON, Frank, 4394857 Cpl, 1/7th DWR.
Son of Thomas Holder and Sarah Jane Hudson, husband of Evelyn Watts Hudson, Eston, Yorks.
- **Killed in Action:** 4 Dec 1944, Netherlands, aged 31.
- **Buried:** Jonkerbos War Cemetery, 19, D, 3.
- **Commemorated:** **7 DWR WW2 War Memorial, Col 3, D Coy Memorial, Col 3.**
  Barclay History RoH, page 369.
- **DWR Enlistment Book:** UNDER 30, page 91 & OVER 30, page 91.

"LIFE'S SWEETEST GIFT, REMEMBRANCE. HIS LOVING WIFE, JEAN, BRIAN, MAM AND DAD"

HUGHES, Edwin James, 4620609 LSgt, 1/7th DWR.
- **Killed in Action:** 25 Jun 1944, Normandy Campaign, France.
- **Buried:** Ryes War Cemetery 8, H, 2.
- **Commemorated:** **7 DWR WW2 War Memorial, Col 3.**
  Barclay History RoH, page 369.
- **DWR Enlistment Book:** TED 20, page 61.

HUGHES, Robert, 4618829 Pte, 2/7th DWR.
Son of William Henry and Nellie Hughes, Sheffield' Yorks.
- **Reported missing:** presumed killed 10-11 Jun 1940, France & Belgium Campaign, 1939/40, aged 22.
- **Buried:** Sainte Marie Cemetery, Le Havre, 67, T, 12.
- **Previously Interred:** Sotteville sur Mer Temp Burial Ground, 6, 5 (until Oct 1947).
- **Commemorated:** **Not listed on 7 DWR WW2 Memorial.**
  Barclay History RoH, page 372.
- **DWR Enlistment Book:** TED 18, page 83.

"WORTHY OF EVERLASTING REMEMBRANCE. GOODNIGHT BOB, GOD BLESS"

ILLINGWORTH, Jack, 4623702 Pte, 1/7th DWR.
Son of J H and Edith Illingworth, Farsley, Yorks.
- **Killed in Action:** 27 Jun 1944, Normandy Campaign, France.
- **Buried:** Bayeux War Cemetery, 3, J, 19.
- **Commemorated:** **7 DWR WW2 War Memorial, Col 3.**
  Barclay History RoH, page 369.
- **DWR Enlistment Book:** TED 23.

"MAY HIS REWARD BE AS GREAT AS HIS SACRIFICE, SAFE IN GOD'S KEEPING"

JONES, John Thomas, 4201131 LCpl, 1/7th DWR.
Son of Edward and Dorothy Jones, Altrincham, Cheshire.
- **Killed in Action:** 4 Dec 1944, Normandy Campaign, Netherlands.
- **Buried:** Jonkerbos War Cemetery, 15, D 3.
- **Commemorated:** **7 DWR WW2 War Memorial, Col 3.**
  Barclay History RoH, page 369.
- **DWR Enlistment Book:** UNDER 30, page 71, OVER 30, page 71 (number D/16688).

"BRAVE AND TRUE, FOR ALL HE DID HIS BEST, GOD GRANT HIM ETERNAL REST, MOTHER, DAD AND FAMILY"

JORDAN, Francis, 4618318 Pte, 2/7th DWR.
Son of John T and Margaret Jordan, Sheffield, husband of Vera Jordan, Sheffield, Yorks.

       Died of Wounds: 31 Jun 1940, France & Belgium Campaign, 1939/40.
       Buried: Sheffield (City Road) Cemetery, E6, 22530 [shows JORDON].
       Commemorated: **7 DWR WW2 War Memorial, Col 3.**
                       Barclay History RoH, page 372.
       DWR Enlistment Book: TED 18, page 32.
"HOLD HIM, DEAR LORD NOW HE IS THINE LOVE HIM, AS WE LOVED HIM WITH THY LOVE DIVINE"

KAYE, Sam, 4621929 Pte, 2/7th DWR.
Son of Joe Edward and Ethel Kaye, Shelley, husband of Edith Kaye, Shelley, Huddersfield, Yorks.
       Died: 19 Jan 1942, Home Duties.
       Buried: Shelley (Emmanuel) Churchyard, K, 452.
       Commemorated: **7 DWR WW2 War Memorial, Col 3.**
                       Barclay History RoH, page 372.
       DWR Enlistment Book: TED 21, page 93.
"YEARS ROLL BY BUT MEMORIES LINGER ON"

KELWICK, James Frederick, 4749088 LCpl, C Coy, 1/7th DWR.
       Killed in Action: 28 Sep 1944, Normandy Campaign, Belgium, aged 25.
       Buried: Leopoldsburg War Cemetery, 5, C, 13.
       Commemorated: **7 DWR WW2 War Memorial, Col 3.**
                       Barclay History RoH, page 369.
       DWR Enlistment Book: OVER Numbers, page 116.

KEMBERY, Donald Arthur, 14708700 Pte, 1/7th DWR.
       Killed in Action: 30 Sep 1944, Normandy Campaign, Belgium, aged 18.
       Buried: Leopoldsburg War Cemetery, 5, C, 14.
       Commemorated: **7 DWR WW2 War Memorial, Col 3.**
                       Barclay History RoH, page 369.
       DWR Enlistment Book: OVER 33, page 83.

KERSHAW, Joseph, 4616583 Pte, B Coy, 1/7th DWR.
       Killed in Action: 24 Sep 1944, Normandy Campaign, Belgium, aged 24.
       Buried: Geel War Cemetery, 5, C, 14.
       Commemorated: **7 DWR WW2 War Memorial, Col 3.**
                       Barclay History RoH, page 369.
       DWR Enlistment Book: TED 16, page 59.

KNIGHT, Clifford Aubrey, 262161 Lt, 1/7th DWR, att 4 Welch Regt.
Son of Edward Ernest and Charlotte Eleanor Knight, husband of Florence Mary Knight, Leyburn, Yorks.
       Killed in Action: 18 Sep 1944, Normandy Campaign, Belgium, aged 29.
       Buried: Bergen op Zoom War Cemetery, 11, B, 4.
       Commemorated: **Not listed on 7 DWR WW2 Memorial.**
                       Barclay History RoH, page 376.
       Commissioned: Feb 1943.

LAMBERT, D N, 82 Lt, B Coy 1/7th DWR, Canadian Officer (canloan).
       Killed in Action: No record of death, wounded by looters, 12 Sep 1944.
       Buried: No known grave.
       Commemorated: **7 DWR WW2 War Memorial, Col 1.**
       Commissioned: Canada.

LANDY, John William Retford, 1554399 Pte, 1/7th DWR (D Coy Memorial shows initisls J K R).
Son of John James Edwin and Ruby Landy, Ilford, Essex.
    Killed in Action: 4 Dec 1944, Normandy Campaign, Netherlands, aged 27.
    Buried: Jonkerbos War Cemetery, 15, D, 1.
    Commemorated: **7 DWR WW2 War Memorial, Col 3; D Coy Memorial, Col 3.**
    Barclay History RoH, page 369.
    DWR Enlistment Book: UNDER 34, page 38.
"EVER IN OUR THOUGHTS"

LANGLEY, Henry, 13033867 Pte, 1/7th DWR.
Son of Mr and Mrs Henry Langley, husband of Martha Velma Rose Langley, Braintree, Essex.
    Killed in Action: 13 Oct 1944, Normandy Campaign, Belgium, aged 31.
    Buried: Leopoldsburg War Cemetery, 5, E, 10.
    Commemorated: **7 DWR WW2 War Memorial, Col 3.**
    Barclay History RoH, page 369.
    DWR Enlistment Book: OVER 33, page 54.
"YOU ARE ALWAYS IN OUR THOUGHTS DEAR, YOUR WIFE ROSE AND CHILDREN HENRY, HAZEL AND SHIRLEY"

LAWTON, James William, 4617712 Pte, 2/7th DWR.
    Killed in Action: 11 Jun 1940, France & Belgium Campaign, 1939/40, aged 20.
    Buried: Veules les Roses, 1, 1.
    Commemorated: **7 DWR WW2 War Memorial, Col 3.**
    Barclay History RoH, page 372.
    DWR Enlistment Book: TED 17, page 72.

LEE, Frederick Dennis, 4748803 Pte, 1/7th DWR.
Son of Joseph Frederick and Ellen Lee, Woodseats, Sheffield, Yorks.
    Died of Wounds: 19 Jun 1944, Normandy Campaign, France, aged 25.
    Buried: Bayeux War Cemetery, 15, J, 15.
    Commemorated: **7 DWR WW2 War Memorial, Col 3.**
    Barclay History RoH, page 369.
    DWR Enlistment Book: OVER Numbers, page 122.
"I HAVE ENDEAVOURED TO FOLLOW WITH UNSWERVING FIDELITY THE LINE OF DUTY"

LEE, Thomas, 4617114 Pte, 2/7th DWR.
Son of Thomas and Betsy Lee, Siddal, Halifax, Yorks.
    Reported Missing: presumed killed 11 Jun 1940, France & Belgium Campaign, 1939/40, aged 21.
    Buried: No known grave.
    Commemorated: Dunkirk Memorial, Col 62.
    Not listed on 7 DWR WW2 Memorial.
    Barclay History RoH, page 372.
    DWR Enlistment Book: TED 17, page 12.

LEFEVRE, Thomas William, 4616400 Pte, 1/7th DWR.
Husband of Ellen Lefavre Blakenall, Bloxwich, Staffs.
    Killed in Action: 29 Oct 1944, Normandy Campaign, Netherlands, aged 24.
    Buried: Bergen op Zoom War Cemetery, 9, A, 13.
    Commemorated: **7 DWR WW2 War Memorial, Col 3.**
    Barclay History RoH, page 369.
    DWR Enlistment Book: OVER 35, page 133.

"A SMILING FACE, HEAR OF GOLD MEMORIES OF YOU WILL NEVER GROW OLD. WIFE AND SON"

LEWIS, William John, 4620635 Pte, 1/7th DWR [memorial shows initial W].
Son of Joshua John and Anna Catherine Lewis, husband of Evelyn Phillis Lewis, Walthamstow, Essex.
    Died: 8 Mar 1943, Home Duties, aged 22.
    Buried: Manor Park Cemetery (Essex), 146, 431.
    Commemorated: **7 DWR WW2 War Memorial, Col 3.**
        Barclay History RoH, page 372.
    DWR Enlistment Book: TED 20, page 64.

LOFTHOUSE, Kenneth Edward, 14663793 Pte, 1/7th DWR.
    Killed in Action: 7 Aug 1944, Normandy Campaign, France, aged 19.
    Buried: Banneville la Campagne War Cemetery, 14, A, 14.
    Commemorated: **7 DWR WW2 War Memorial, Col 3.**
        Barclay History RoH, page 369.
    DWR Enlistment Book: OVER 33, page 22.
"THO' NO ONE KNOWS THE COST OF PARTING GOD HAS, IN HIS MERCY GAINED WHAT WE LOST. MAM"

LONG, Harry, 4617497 Pte, 2/7th DWR.
Son of Frank and Lucy Long, Dewsbury, Yorks.
    Died as POW: 26 Jun 1940, France & Belgium Campaign, 1939/40, aged 21.
    Buried: Rouen (St Sever) Cemetery Extension, S, 4, Q, 19.
    Commemorated: **7 DWR WW2 War Memorial, Col 3.**
        Barclay History RoH, page 372.
    DWR Enlistment Book: TED 17, page 50.
"HE GAVE HIS LIFE THAT WE MAY LIVE. R.I.P"

LONGMAN, Reginald Leslie, 5729651 Cpl, 1/7th DWR.
Husband of Rosina Longman, Stoke Newington, London.
    Killed in Action: 29 Sep 1944, Normandy Campaign, Belgium, aged 24.
    Buried: Lier Belgian Military Cemetery, 3, B, 1.
    Commemorated: **7 DWR WW2 War Memorial, Col 3.**
        Barclay History RoH, page 369.
    DWR Enlistment Book: OVER 35, page 138 & 167 (shows number as 5727651).
"HE BRAVELY FOUGHT FOR THOSE HE LOVED AND LEFT US TO REMEMBER"

LOWE, Ernest, 4616387 Pte, 2/7th DWR.
    Died: 12 Jun 1940, France & Belgium Campaign, 1939/40, aged 29.
    Buried: Sainte Marie Cemetery, Le Havre, 67, T, 10:
    Previously interred: Sotteville sur Mer Temp Burial Ground, 6, 3 (until Oct 1947).
    Commemorated: **7 DWR WW2 War Memorial, Col 3.**
        Barclay History RoH, page 372.
    DWR Enlistment Book: TED 16, page 39.

LUNN, Ronald Fitzroy, 4621941 Pte, 1/7th DWR.
Son of Thomas and Fanny Lunn, Newsome, Huddersfield, Yorks.
    Killed in Action: 19 Jun 1944, Normandy Campaign, France, aged 30.
    Buried: Bayeux War Cemetery, 15, H, 6.
    Commemorated: **7 DWR WW2 War Memorial, Col 3.**
        Barclay History RoH, page 369.

DWR Enlistment Book: TED 21, page 95.
"DEARLY LOVED SON OF FANNY AND THE LATE THOMAS LUNN. WORTHY OF REMEMBRANCE"

MARKS, Albert, 14660114 Pte, 1/7th DWR.
    Killed in Action: 26 Jun 1944, Normandy Campaign, France, aged 19.
    Buried: Banneville la Campagne War Cemetery, 14, C, 11.
    Commemorated: **7 DWR WW2 War Memorial, Col 3.**
    Barclay History RoH, page 369.
    DWR Enlistment Book: OVER 33, page 38.
"HIS DUTY NOBLY DONE"

MARSHALL, Joffre, 4613457 LCpl, 2/7th DWR.
    Killed in Action: 11 Jun 1940, France & Belgium Campaign, 1939/40, aged 23.
    Buried: Sainte Marie Cemetery, Le Havre, 67, S, 19 (2 Oct 1947).
    Previously Interred: Sotteville sur Mer Temp Burial Ground, 5, 2 (until Oct 1947).
    Commemorated: **7 DWR WW2 War Memorial, Col 3.**
    Barclay History RoH, page 372.
    DWR Enlistment Book: TED 13, page 46.

MARSHALL, William Robert, 4616407 Pte, 1/7th DWR.
Son of Thomas and Sarah Marshall, Lees, Lancs.
    Died of Wounds: 21 Jun 1944, Normandy Campaign, France, aged 24.
    Buried: Lees (Lancashire) Cemetery, 2J, 57.
    Commemorated: **7 DWR WW2 War Memorial, Col 4.**
    Barclay History RoH, page 369.
    DWR Enlistment Book: TED 16, page 5.
"THEY SHALL NOT GROW OLD AS WE THAT ARE LEFT GROW OLD"

McCREESH, John William, 4619980 Pte, 1/7th DWR.
    Died: 24 Dec 1944, Normandy Campaign, Belgium, aged 28.
    Buried: Gent City Cemetery, 18, A, 40.
    Commemorated: **7 DWR WW2 War Memorial, Col 4** [shows initials J F].
    Barclay History RoH, page 369.
    DWR Enlistment Book: TED 19, page 99.

McMANUS, Benjamin, 4615607 Pte, 1/7th DWR.
Son of Thomas and Elizabeth Ann McManus, husband of Lily McManus, Stalybridge.
    Killed in Action: 14 Sep 1939, Home Duties, aged 37.
    Buried: Stalybridge (St Paul's) Churchyard, New yard, Range 32, Grave 43.
    Commemorated: Stalybridge Churchyard memorial.
    7 DWR WW2 War Memorial, Col 4.
    Barclay History RoH, page 370.
    DWR Enlistment Book: TED 15, page 61.
"MEMORIES OF A DEAR FATHER TREASURED STILL WITH LOVE SINCERE BY SONS AND DAUGHTERS"

MEE, Harry Alexander 13096137 Pte, S Coy, 1/7th DWR.
Son of Mr and Mrs Henry Mee, husband of Ivy Mee, Marsden, Yorks.
    Died of Wounds: 11 Aug 1944, Normandy Campaign, France, aged 36.
    Buried: Ranville War Cemetery, 8, B, 10.

Commemorated:	**7 DWR WW2 War Memorial, Col 4.**
	Barclay History RoH, page 370.
DWR Enlistment Book:	OVER 32, page 78.

"MEMORIES ARE A GOLDEN CHAIN THAT BINDS US UNTIL WE MEET AGAIN"

MEER, Frederick, 14439308 Pte, 1/7th DWR.
Son of Frederick and Rosina Meer, Radford, Notts.

Died of Wounds:	30 Oct 1944, Normandy Campaign, Belgium, aged 18.
Buried:	Leopoldsburg War Cemetery, 5, C, 12.
Commemorated:	**7 DWR WW2 War Memorial, Col 4.**
	Barclay History RoH, page 370.
DWR Enlistment Book:	OVER 33, page 90.

"THERE IS A FACE THAT'S EVER BEFORE US A SMILE WE'LL ALWAYS REMEMBER"

MILEHAM, Arthur, 14623176 LCpl, 1/7th DWR.
Son of Harold and Lily Mileham, Goole, Yorks.

Killed in Action:	7 Aug 1944, Normandy Campaign, France, aged 19.
Buried:	Banneville la Campagne War Cemetery, 14, C, 3.
Commemorated:	**7 DWR WW2 War Memorial, Col 4.**
	Barclay History RoH, page 370.
DWR Enlistment Book:	OVER 32, page 61.

"IN MIND A CONSTANT THOUGHT IN HEART A SILENT SORROW"

MILLAR, Harry, 4608860 WO3 (Platoon Sergeant Major), 2/7th DWR.
Son of George and Emma Millar, Halifax, husband of Man Millar, Halifax, Yorks.

Died:	30 Jan 1941 (drowned), Home Duties, aged 50.
Buried:	Halifax (Mount Pellon Christ Church) Cemetery 3B, 41.
Commemorated:	**7 DWR WW2 War Memorial, Col 4.**
	Barclay History RoH, page 372.
	Fenton Album, page 5 (inter war TA camp photograph).
DWR Enlistment Book:	EB 8, page 173 (enlisted Halifax, 11 May 1926 & re-enlisted).

MILLINGTON John Albert, 14206603 Pte, 1/7th DWR.
Son of Arthur and Ellen Millington, Moss Side, Manchester, Lancs.

Died of Wounds:	18 Jun 1944, Normandy Campaign, France, aged 21.
Buried:	Bayeux War Cemetery, 14, L, 2.
Commemorated:	**7 DWR WW2 War Memorial, Col 4.**
	Barclay History RoH, page 370.
DWR Enlistment Book:	OVER 31, page 20.

"HOW DEAR HE WAS WE LOVED HIM SO IT BROKE OUR HEARTS TO LET HIM GO. GOOD-BYE, SON"

MOORE, Roland William, 4979979 Pte, HQ Coy Sigs 1/7th DWR.
SON OF Harry and Gertrude Moore, Worksop, Notts, husband of Dorothy Moore, Skegness, Lincs.

Killed in Action:	25 Jul 1944, Normandy Campaign, France, aged 27.
Buried:	Ranville War Cemetery, 8, B, 19.
Commemorated:	**7 DWR WW2 War Memorial, Col 4.**
	Barclay History RoH, page 370.
DWR Enlistment Book:	OVER Numbers, page 160.

MORRISEY, James, 50211 Capt, RAMC attached 2/7th DWR, awarded MID, *LG 11 Nov 1945*.
Son of James and Sarah Morrisey, husband of Winifred Morrisey, Blunellsands, Liverpool, Lancs.

Killed in Action:	11 Jun 1940, France & Belgium Campaign, 1939/40, aged 39.
Buried:	Veules les Roses Communal Cemetery, 1, 5.
Commemorated:	**7 DWR WW2 War Memorial, Col 1.**
Commissioned:	RAMC.

"MAY HIS SOUL REST IN PEACE"

MUNDY, James, 4614681 Pte, 1/7th DWR.
Son of James and Eliza A Mundy, Stalybridge, Cheshire.

Killed in Action:	26 Jun 1944, Normandy Campaign, France, aged 26.
Buried:	Jerusalem War Cemetery, Chouain, A, 8.
Commemorated:	**7 DWR WW2 War Memorial, Col 4.**
	Barclay History RoH, page 370.
DWR Enlistment Book:	TED 17, page 70.

"NOT JUST TODAY BUT EVERY DAY IN SILENCE WE REMEMBER. MOTHER"

MURPHY, John, 4532858 Sgt, 1/7th DWR, also W Yorks Regt, awarded BEM, *LG 1 Jan 1944, page 29.*
Son of Peter and Alice Murphy, husband of Elizabeth Ann Murphy, West Harton, South Shields, Co Durham

Killed in Action	18 Jul 1944, Normandy Campaign, France, aged 34.
Buried:	Hottot les Bagues War Cemetery, 8, G, 2.
Commemorated:	**7 DWR WW2 War Memorial, Col 4, D Coy Memorial, Col 1.**
	Barclay History RoH, page 370.
	Fenton Album, page 5 (inter war camp photograph).
DWR Enlistment Book:	UNDER 34, page 30.

"IN LOVING MEMORY OF JOHN BELOVED HUSBAND OF ELIZABETH. HE DIED THAT OTHERS MIGHT LIVE"

MUSHING, Philip, 4614921 Pte, 1/7th DWR.
Son of John and Mary Ann Mushing, Oldham, Lancs, husband of Annie Mushing, Oldham, Lancs.

Killed in Action:	25 Jun 1944, Normandy Campaign, France, aged 32.
Buried:	Hottot les Bagues War Cemetery, 8, G, 7.
Commemorated:	**7 DWR WW2 War Memorial, Col 4.**
	Barclay History RoH, page 370.
DWR Enlistment Book:	TED 14, page 94.

"IN EVERLOVING MEMORY. A DEAR HUSBAND & FATHER EVER IN OUR THOUGHTS. LOVING WIFE AND SON"

MYNERS, Kenneth Austin, 11234125 Sgt, ACC att 1/7th DWR, awarded CinC Cert for Gallantry.
Son of Edward and Phillippa Cordelia Myners (nee Mutton), Truro, Cornwall, husband of Velma Doreen Myners, Falmouth, Cornwall.

Killed in Action:	4 Dec 1944, Normandy Campaign, Netherlands, aged 28.
Buried:	Jonkerbos War Cemetery, 7, D, 2.
Commemorated:	**7 DWR WW2 War Memorial, Col 4.**
DWR Enlistment Book:	No trace.

"PEACE, PERFECT PEACE"

NEALE, Donald, 4615786 Pte, 1/7th DWR.
Adopted son of Arthur and Amelia Storey, Stourton, Leeds, Yorks.

Died:	3 Nov 1942, Home Duties, aged 22.
Buried:	Rothwell (Leeds) Cemetery, Grave 474.
Commemorated:	**Not listed on 7 DWR WW2 Memorial.**
DWR Enlistment Book:	TED 15, page 79 [shows discharge date as 25 Jun 1941].

"TREASURED MEMORIES OF A DEARLY LOVED SON AND BROTHER WHO DIED IN HOSPITAL"

NEALE, William George, 5049863 Cpl, 1/7th DWR [CWGC shows 5099863].
Husband of Dorothy May Neale, Uttoxeter, Staffs.
    Killed in Action: 25 Jun 1944, Normandy Campaign, France, aged 25.
    Buried: Hottot les Bagues War Cemetery, 8, G, 6.
    Commemorated: **7 DWR WW2 War Memorial, Col 4** [shows name as NEAL].
        Barclay History RoH, page 370.
    DWR Enlistment Book: OVER Numbers, page 96.
"DEAR HUSBAND THOU HAST LEFT US, HERE OUR LOSS WE DEEPLY FEEL"

NICHOLLS, Allan, 4612252 Sgt, Sp Coy, 1/7th DWR [CWGC shows 1612252].
Son of Leonard Nicholls and step-son of Frances L Nicholls, Wakefield, Yorks.
    Died of Wounds: 22 Oct 1944, Normandy Campaign, Belgium, aged 30.
    Buried: Lier Belgian Military Cemetery, 2, A, 5.
    Commemorated: **7 DWR WW2 War Memorial, Col 4.**
        Barclay History RoH, page 370.
    DWR Enlistment Book: EB 12, page 43.
"THERE WERE OTHERS, YES, I KNOW BUT HE WAS OURS, WE LOVED HIM SO. MUM, DAD AND EMMA."

NORBURN, Wilfred, 4618825 Pte, 2/7th DWR.
Son of Thomas and Mildred Mabel Norburn, Rotherham, Yorks.
    Killed in Action: 11 Jun 1940, France & Belgium Campaign, 1939/40, aged 22.
    Buried: Sainte Marie Cemetery Le Havre, 67, S, 18.
    Commemorated: Rotherham War Memorial.
        7 DWR WW2 War Memorial, Col 4.
        Barclay History RoH, page 372.
    DWR Enlistment Book: TED 18, page 83.
"A SMILING FACE, A HEART OF GOLD, NO BETTER SON THIS WORLD COULD HOLD"

NORBURY, John, 4614956 Pte, 2/7th DWR.
Son of James Henry and Mary Ellen Norbury, Springhead, Lancs.
    Killed in Action: 11 Jun 1940, France & Belgium Campaign, 1939/40, aged 19.
    Buried: Veules les Roses Cemetery, 3, 1.
    Commemorated: **7 DWR WW2 War Memorial, Col 4.**
        Barclay History RoH, page 372.
    DWR Enlistment Book: TED 14, page 97.
"RESTING WHERE NO SHADOWS FALL. LOVING MOTHER, FATHER, SISTERS AND BROTHERS"

O'BRIEN, Patrick Michael, 4690371 Pte, C Coy, 1/7th DWR.
Husband of Naomi Cecily O'Brien, Prudhoe, Northumberland.
    Killed in Action: 28 Oct 1944, Normandy Campaign, Netherlands, aged 24.
    Buried: Bergen op Zoom War Cemetery, 9, A, 18.
    Commemorated: **7 DWR WW2 War Memorial, Col 4.**
        Barclay History RoH, page 370.
    DWR Enlistment Book: OVER 35, page 134.
"IN GOD'S TIME WE WILL MEET AGAIN. HIS WIFE AND DAUGHTERS"

ODDY, Ronald, 4619009 Pte, 2/7th DWR.
Son of Mrs H A Oddy.
    Died as POW: 6 Sep 1940, France & Belgium Campaign, 1939/40.
    Buried: Poznan Old Garrison Cemetery, 7, A, 1.
    Commemorated: **7 DWR WW2 War Memorial, Col 4.**
         Barclay History RoH, page 372.
    DWR Enlistment Book: TED 19, page 1.

O'LEARY, Bernard, 4609252 LCpl, 2/7th DWR.
Son of Denis and Ellen O'Leary, Boothtown, Halifax, Yorks.
    Died of Wounds: 2 Jul 1940, France & Belgium Campaign, 1939/40, aged 33.
    Buried: Rouen (St Sever) Cemetery Extension, S, 4, Q, 14.
    Commemorated: **7 DWR WW2 War Memorial, Col 4.**
         Barclay History RoH, page 372.
    DWR Enlistment Books: EB 9, page 51 & Depot 1919-32, page 99, enlisted Pontefract.
"ON HIS SOUL, SWEET JESUS, HAVE MERCY, MAY HE REST IN PEACE. AMEN"

OLLERENSHAW Harry, 4609203 Sgt, Sp Coy, 1/7th DWR
Husband of Hilda Ollerenshaw, Mossley, Lancs.
    Killed in Action: 29 Nov 1944, Normandy Campaign, Netherlands, aged 36.
    Buried: Bergen op Zoom War Cemetery, 9, A, 21.
    Commemorated: **7 DWR WW2 War Memorial, Col 4.**
         Barclay History RoH, page 370.
    DWR Enlistment Book: EB 9, page 41, enlisted Mossley.
"THE LOVE, IN LIFE, I HAD FOR YOU IN DEATH GROWS STRONGER STILL"

PAUL, Thomas, 4388417 Pte, 1/7th DWR.
Son of Thomas and Elizabeth Jane Paul, South Shields, Co Durham.
    Killed in Action: 25 Jul 1944, Normandy Campaign, France, aged 33.
    Buried: Ranville War Cemetery, 8, B, 15.
    Commemorated: **7 DWR WW2 War Memorial, Col 4.**
         Barclay History RoH, page 370.
    DWR Enlistment Book: UNDER 34, page 28.
"DEEPLY MOURNED BY HIS MAM, DAD, BROTHERS AND SISTER. HE DIED THAT WE MIGHT LIVE"

PHILLIPS, James, 14647587 Pte, 1/7th DWR.
Son of Thomas and Annie Phillips, Thornhill, Dewsbury, Yorks.
    Killed in Action: 10 Aug 1944, Normandy Campaign, France, aged 19.
    Buried: Ranville War Cemetery, 8, B, 14.
    Commemorated: **7 DWR WW2 War Memorial, Col 4.**
         Barclay History RoH, page 370.
    DWR Enlistment Book: OVER 33, page 26.

PICKERING, Leslie, 4617523 Tpr, 2/7th DWR, later 115 RAC & 8 RTR RAC.
    Killed in Action: 6 Sep 1944, Coriano Ridge, Italy,
    Buried: Coriano Ridge War Cemetery, 19, H, 9.
    Commemorated: **7 DWR WW2 War Memorial, Col 3.**
    DWR Enlistment Book: OVER 31, page 8.

PICKLES, Thomas Edward, 4268905 Cpl, 2/7th DWR.
    Killed in Action: 11 Jun 1940, France & Belgium Campaign, 1939/40, aged 24.

Buried:	Sainte Marie Cemetery, Le Havre, 67, T, 4.
Previously Interred:	Sotteville sur Mer Temp Burial Ground, 5, 9 (until Oct 1947).
Commemorated:	**7 DWR WW2 War Memorial, Col 4.**
	Barclay History RoH, page 372.
DWR Enlistment Book:	No trace.

PLACE, Harry, 3783914 Pte, 1/7th DWR.
Son of Walter and Rebecca Place, Burnley, Lancs.

Died:	15 May 1943, Home Duties, aged 18.
Buried:	Burnley Cemetery, NE, 11026.
Commemorated:	**7 DWR WW2 War Memorial, Col 4.**
	Barclay History RoH, page 370.
DWR Enlistment Book:	UNDER 30, page 72 & OVER 30, page 72.

"HIS LIFE A BEAUTIFUL MEMORY, HIS SILENCE OUR GREATEST SORROW"

POLLARD, Maurice, 14405175 Pte, 1/7th DWR.
Son of Harry and Doris May Pollard, Carr Vale, Derbyshire.

Killed in Action:	19 Jun 1944, Normandy Campaign, France, aged 19.
Buried:	St Manvieu War Cemetery, Cheux, 4, J, 9.
Commemorated:	**7 DWR WW2 War Memorial, Col 4.**
	Barclay History RoH, page 370.
DWR Enlistment Book:	OVER 32, page 78.

"NOT GONE FROM MEMORY NOR FROM LOVE BUT GONE TO HIS FATHER'S HOME ABOVE"

POWELL, Charles, 4607649 Cpl, 1/7th DWR.
Son of John and Elizabeth Powell, husband of Beatrice Powell, Ovenden, Halifax, Yorks.

Killed in Action:	30 Oct 1944, Normandy Campaign, Netherlands, aged 38.
Buried:	Bergen op Zoom War Cemetery, 7, C, 10.
Commemorated:	**7 DWR WW2 War Memorial, Col 4, D Coy Memorial, Col 3.**
	Barclay History RoH, page 370.
DWR Enlistment Book:	EB 7, page 130 & Depot 1919-32, page 78, enlisted Leeds, 1924.

"HE DIED THAT WE MIGHT LIVE"

PRICE, Albert, 5250790 WO2 (CSM), 1/7th DWR.
Son of Alfred George and Anne Price, Birmingham, husband of Marjorie May Price, Erdington, Birmingham.

Died:	13 Sep 1945, Normandy Campaign, Germany, aged 29.
Buried:	Munster Heath War Cemetery, 3, D, 24.
Commemorated:	**7 DWR WW2 War Memorial, Col 4.**
	Barclay History RoH, page 370.
DWR Enlistment Book:	OVER 35, page 206.

"YOU LEFT US SUDDENLY WITH MEMORIES WE ARE PROUD TO OWN. WIFE MARJORIE & SON DAVID"

QUIRKE, Thomas, 4609616 Bdsm, 2/7th DWR.

Killed in Action:	11 Jun 1940, Veules les Roses Cemetery, 1, 9, aged 30.
Commemorated:	**7 DWR WW2 War Memorial, Col 4.**
	Barclay History RoH, page 372.
DWR Enlistment Book:	EB 9, page 124 & EB 1936, discharged 12 Mar 1936, re enlisted.

RACE, Thomas Frederick, 1458534 Pte, 1/7th DWR.
Son of Mr and Mrs L Race, Sharlston, Yorks, husband of Hilda Race.
    Killed in Action: 26 Jun 1944, Normandy Campaign, aged 19.
    Buried: Hottot les Bagues War Cemetery, 8, G, 11.
    Commemorated: **7 DWR WW2 War Memorial, Col 4.**
    Barclay History RoH, page 370.
    DWR Enlistment Book: OVER 32, page 76.
"RESTING WHERE NO SHADOWS FALL IN PERFECT PEACE HE AWAITS US ALL"

REDMOND, Alexandra, 14206700 Pte, 1/7th DWR.
Son of John and Margaret Redmond, Pemberton, Wigan, Lancs.
    Died of Wounds: 19 Jun 1944, Normandy Campaign, France, aged 21.
    Buried: Bayeux War Cemetery, 12, J, 16.
    Commemorated: **7 DWR WW2 War Memorial, Col 4.**
    Barclay History RoH, page 370.
    DWR Enlistment Book: OVER 31, page 21.
"ETERNAL REST GIVE UNTO HIM, O LORD; AND LET PERPETUAL LIGHT SHINE UPON HIM"

REYNOLDS, John (Jack), 88766 2Lt, 2/7th DWR (also B Coy 1/6th DWR).
Son of Charles W and Alice Reynolds, husband of Margaret Reynolds, Codrington, Glos.
    Died of Wounds as POW: 9 Jul 1940, France & Belgium Campaign, 1939/40, aged 27.
    Buried: Abbeville Communal Cemetery Extension, 9, D, 5.
    Commemorated: **7 DWR WW2 War Memorial, Col 1.**
    Barclay History RoH, page 372.
    Commissioned: 6 Jun 1939.
"GREATER LOVE HATH NO MAN THAN THIS"

REYNOLDS, William, 4618923 Pte, 2/7th DWR.
    Killed in Action: 11 Jun 1940, France & Belgium Campaign, 1939/40, aged 22.
    Buried: No known grave.
    Commemorated: Dunkirk Memorial, Col 61.
    7 DWR WW2 War Memorial, Col 4.
    Barclay History RoH, page 372.
    DWR Enlistment Book: TED 18, page 83.

RHODES, Robert Henry, 154080 Pte, 1/7th DWR.
Son of Robert and Kathleen mary Rhodes, Alderhsot, Hants.
    Killed in Action: 21 Oct 1944, Normandy Campaign, aged 28.
    Buried: Wuustwezel Churchyard Cemetery, 4.
    Commemorated: **7 DWR WW2 War Memorial, Col 4.**
    Barclay History RoH, page 370.
    DWR Enlistment Book: UNDER 34, page 44.
"GOD'S WILL BE DONE R.I.P."

ROBERTS, Harold, 14423956 Pte, 1/7th DWR.
Son of Harold and Mary Roberts Knottingley, Yorks.
    Killed in Action: 30 Oct 1944, Normandy Campaign, Netherlands, aged 19.
    Buried: Bergen op Zoom War Cemetery, 7, C, 17.
    Commemorated: **7 DWR WW2 War Memorial, Col 4; D Coy Memorial, Col 3.**
    Barclay History RoH, page 370.
    DWR Enlistment Book: OVER 32, page 14.

"SO BRAVE AND YOUNG HE MET HIS FATE. REWARD HIM, O LORD, AT THY HEAVENLY GATE"

ROBERTS, Wilfred, 4618940 Pte, 2/7th DWR.
Son of Ernest and Ellen Agnes Roberts.
Killed in Action:	11 Jun 1940, France & Belgium Campaign, 1939/40, aged 23.
Buried:	No known grave.
Commemorated:	Dunkirk Memorial, Col 62.
	7 DWR WW2 War Memorial, Col 4.
	Barclay History RoH, page 372.
DWR Enlistment Book:	TED 18, page 95.

ROBINSON, Herbert, 4620158 Pte, 2/7th DWR.
Son of Thompson and Margaret Robinson, Shiney Row, Co Durham.
Died:	21 Mar 1941, Home Duties, aged 24.
Buried:	Penshaw Cemetery (Durham), 4, 1, 39.
Commemorated:	**7 DWR WW2 War Memorial, Col 4.**
	Barclay History RoH, page 372.
DWR Enlistment Book:	TED 20, page 16.

ROBINSON, John, 4609778 WO2 (CSM), 1/7th DWR, awarded CinC's Certificate for gallantry.
Son of William and Hannah Robinson, husband of Ivy Edna May Robinson, St Budeaux, Plymouth, Devon.
Killed in Action:	10 Aug 1944, Normandy Campaign, France, aged 34.
Buried:	Ranville War Cemetery, 8, B, 18.
Commemorated:	**7 DWR WW2 War Memorial, Col 4.**
	Barclay History RoH, page 370.
DWR Enlistment Book:	EB 9, page 156 & Depot 1919-32, page 107.

"THOUGHTS GO BACK TO BYGONE DAYS LIFE MOVES ON BUT MEMORIES STAY"

ROCHESTER, Raymond, 14661188 Pte, 1/7th DWR.
Son of Fred and Mary Emma Rochester, York.
Killed in Action:	27 Jun 1944, Normandy Campaign, France, aged 19.
Buried:	Hottot les Bagues War Cemetery, 10, G, 10.
Commemorated:	**7 DWR WW2 War Memorial, Col 4; D Coy Memorial, Col 2.**
	Barclay History RoH, page 370.
DWR Enlistment Book:	OVER 33, page 35.

RODEN, Benjamin John, 4619266 LSgt, 1/7th DWR.
Killed in Action:	15 Apr 1945, Normandy Campaign, Netherlands, aged 26.
Buried:	Arnhem Oosterbeek War Cemetery, 8, B, 19.
Commemorated:	**7 DWR WW2 War Memorial, Col 4.**
	Barclay History RoH, page 370.
DWR Enlistment Book:	OVER 35, page 136.

RODGERS, Harold Norman, 4618827 Pte, 2/7th DWR.
Son of Tom and Louisa Rogers, Sheffield, Yorks.
Killed in Action:	11 Jun 1940, France & Belgium Campaign, 1939/40, aged 22,
Buried:	No known grave.
Commemorated:	Dunkirk Memorial, Col 62.
	7 DWR WW2 War Memorial, Col 4.
	Barclay History RoH, page 372.

DWR Enlistment Book: TED 18, page 83.

ROSS. John Thomas, 4612998 Pte, 1/7th DWR.
Son of William K and Annie Ross, Stockton on Tees, Co Durham.
    Died of Wounds: 26 Jun 1944, Normandy Campaign, France, aged 30.
    Buried: Bayeux War Cemetery, 12, C, 23.
    Commemorated: **7 DWR WW2 War Memorial, Col 4.**
    Barclay History RoH, page 370.
    DWR Enlistment Book: EB 12, page 167.
"IN LOVING MEMORY OF MY DEAR SON JOHN THOMAS DEEPLY MOURNED BY MOTHER"

SAWYER, Frank, 4923248 Sgt, Sp Coy, 1/7th DWR.
Son of A;bert Char;es and Edith Sarah Emily Sawyer, Rushall, Walsall, Staffs.
    Killed in Action: 1 Dec 1944, Normandy Campaign, Netherlands, aged 25.
    Buried: Jonkerbos War Cemetery, 19, D, 6.
    Commemorated: **7 DWR WW2 War Memorial, Col 4.**
    Barclay History RoH, page 370.
    DWR Enlistment Book: OVER 35, page 168.
"THOUGH SEAS DIVIDE US WHERE YOU LIE THE MEMORIES OF YOU WILL NEVER DIE"

SCHOLES, Frank Colin, 74249 Capt, 1/7th DWR, awarded MID, *LG 22 Mar 1945, page 1559.*
Son of Richard and Ellen Maud Scholes, husband of Hilda Scholes, Rawdon, Yorks.
    Killed in Action: 18 Jun 1944, Normandy Campaign, France, aged 25.
    Buried: Hottot les Bagues War Cemetery, 10, E, 2.
    Commemorated: **7 DWR WW2 War Memorial, Col 1.**
    Barclay History RoH, page 370.
    Commissioned: 1939.
"IN PROUD AND EVER LOVING MEMORY"

SCOTT, John, 4616540 John, 2/7th DWR.
Son of Albert and Margaret Scott, Holmfield, Yorks.
    Died as POW: 4 Jul 1940, France & Belgium Campaign, 1939/40, aged 20.
    Buried: Rouen (St Sever) Cemetery Extension, S, 4, Q, 18.
    Commemorated: **7 DWR WW2 War Memorial, Col 4.**
    Barclay History RoH, page 372.
    DWR Enlistment Book: TED 16, page 55.
"NO VERSE CAN SAY, NO WEALTH REPAY. LIFE STILL MOVES ON BUT OUR MEMORIES STAY"

SEDDON, Edward, 14206703 Pte, 1/7th DWR.
    Died: 2 Jan 1945, Normandy Campaign, evacuated to UK.
    Buried: Wigan Cemetery, S, 198 [CWGC Vol 5, p 74, not on Website].
    Commemorated: **7 DWR WW2 War Memorial, Col 4.**
    Barclay History RoH, page 370.
    DWR Enlistment Book: OVER 31, page 22.

SELLARS, William Thomas George, 14293272 LCpl, 1/7th DWR.
Son of William Frederick and Frances Sellars, husband of Doris May Sellars, Charlton, London.
    Killed in Action: 17 Jun 1944, Normandy Campaign, France, aged 31.
    Buried: Hottot les Bagues War Cemetery, 8, J, 8.
    Commemorated: **Not listed on 7 DWR WW2 Memorial.**
    Barclay History RoH, page 367.

DWR Enlistment Book: OVER 32, page 17.
"TO THE WORLD HE WAS ONLY ONE OF US, TO US HE WAS THE WORLD. LOVING WIFE AND MOTHER"

SHAW, Arthur, 14403885 Pte, 1/7th DWR.
Son of Arthur and Catherine Shaw, Osmondthorpe, Leeds, Yorks.
    Killed in Action: 18 Jun 1944, Normandy Campaign, France, aged 19.
    Buried: Hottot les Bagues War Cemetery, 10, E, 7.
    Commemorated: **7 DWR WW2 War Memorial, Col 4.**
    Barclay History RoH, page 370.
    DWR Enlistment Book: OVER 32, page 38.
"ETERNAL REST GIVE UNTO HIM, O LORD; AND LET PERPETIAL LIGHT SHINE UPON HIM. R.I.P."

SHAW, Dennis, 14661190 Pte, 1/7th DWR.
Son of George and E Shaw, Sheffield Yorks.
    Killed in Action: 18 Jun 1944, Normandy Campaign, France, aged 19.
    Buried: Bayeux War Cemetery, 14, H, 19.
    Commemorated: **7 DWR WW2 War Memorial, Col 4; D Coy Memorial, Col 1.**
    Barclay History RoH, page 370.
    DWR Enlistment Book: OVER 33, page 38.
"MEMORIES WE SHALL ALWAYS TREASURE OF HAPPY DAYS WE SPENT TOGETHER"

SHAW, Frank, 4615616 Cpl, 1/7th DWR.
Son of Henry and Clara Ann Shaw, Huddersfield, Yorks.
    Killed in Action: 17 Oct 1944, Normandy Campaign, Belgium, aged 24.
    Buried: Leopoldsburg War Cemetery, 2, D, 6.
    Commemorated: **7 DWR WW2 War Memorial, Col 4.**
    Barclay History RoH, page 370.
    DWR Enlistment Book: EB 6, page 63 [shows forename David].
"AT THE GOING DOWN OF THE SUN AND IN THE MORNING WE WILL REMEMBER HIM R.I.P."

SHAW, Harry, 14727465 Pte, DWR [Barclay History shows Unit as Inf Trg Centre].
Son of Charles and Harriet Ann Shaw, Glasshoughton, Castleford, Yorks.
    Died: 31 Aug 1944, place not known, aged 18.
    Buried: Castleford New Cemetery, W, 197.
    Commemorated: **7 DWR WW2 War Memorial, Col 4.**
    Barclay History RoH, page 377.
    DWR Enlistment Book: OVER 35, page 90.

SHAW, John Henry, 1114934 Pte, 1/7th DWR.
Son of John and Hanah Shaw, husband of Mary Ellen Shaw, Hunthwaite, Notts.
    Killed in Action: 31 Oct 1944, Normandy Campaign, Netherlands, aged 38.
    Buried: Bergen op Zoom Canadian War Cemetery, 6, C, 8.
    Commemorated: **7 DWR WW2 War Memorial, Col 4.**
    Barclay History RoH, page 370.
    DWR Enlistment Book: UNDER 34, page 42.
"WORTHY OF EVERLASTING REMEMBRANCE"

SHAW, Terence Ambler, 4615946 Pte, 1/7th DWR.
Son of Arthur Marsden and Lucy Shaw, Marsh, Huddersfield, Yorks.

Killed in Action:	11 Jun 1940, France & Belgium Campaign, 1939/40, aged 26.
Buried:	Blosseville sur Mer Churchyard, Mil 1, 2.
Commemorated:	**7 DWR WW2 War Memorial, Col 5.**
	Barclay History RoH, page 372.
DWR Enlistment Book:	TED 15, page 95 [shows names as Francis Arthur].

"YOUNGEST SON OF THE LATE ARTHUR AND LUCY SHAW, HUDDERSFIELD, YORKS, ENGLAND"

SHEA, Henry Edward, 4617101 Cpl, 1/7th DWR.
Son of Henry Edward and Emma Shea, Halifax, Yorks.

Killed in Action:	25 Jun 1944, Normandy Campaign, France, aged 26.
Buried:	Hottot les Bagues War Cemetery, 8, G, 4.
Commemorated:	**7 DWR WW2 War Memorial, Col 5.**
	Barclay History RoH, page 370.
DWR Enlistment Book:	TED 17, page 11.

"REMEBERED WITH HONOUR"

SHORROCKS. William James C, 2083114 Pte, 1/7th DWR.
Husband of Elizabeth Alice Shorrocks, Standish, Lancs.

Killed in Action:	10 Aug 1944, Normandy Campaign, aged 23.
Buried:	Ranville War Cemetery, 3, B, 3.
Commemorated:	**7 DWR WW2 War Memorial, Col 5.**
	Barclay History RoH, page 370.
DWR Enlistment Book:	UNDER 30, page 101 & OVER 30, page 101.

"THE TEST OF BEAUTIFUL LIVES IS THE EMEMORY LEFT BEHIND"

SIMISTER John, 4399768 Cpl, 1/7th DWR.

Killed in Action:	28 Sep 1944, Normandy Campaign, Belgium, aged 29.
Buried:	Leopoldsburg War Cemetery, 5, C, 17.
Commemorated:	**7 DWR WW2 War Memorial, Col 5.**
	Barclay History RoH, page 370.
DWR Enlistment Book:	UNDER 30, page 91 & OVER 30, page 91.

SIMPSON, Arthur, 4613347 Pte, 2/7th DWR.
Son of George Henry and Emma Simpson, Slaithwaite, Yorks.

Died of Wounds:	30 Jun 1940, France & Belgium Campaign, 1939/40, aged 23.
Buried:	Forges les Eaux Communal Cemetery, Mil 23.
Commemorated:	**7 DWR WW2 War Memorial, Col 5.**
	Barclay History RoH, page 372.
DWR Enlistment Book:	TED 13, page 35.

"TO HAVE, TO LOVE, AND THEN TO PART IS THE DEEPEST SORROW OF A PARENT'S HEART"

SLATCHER, Charles Frederick, 4613061 LCpl, 1/7th DWR.
Son of Charles Frederick and Lily Slatcher, Carlton, Notts.

Killed in Action:	18 Jun 1944, Normandy Campaign, France., aged 32.
Buried:	Hottot les Bagues War Cemetery, 10, E, 8.
Commemorated:	**7 DWR WW2 War Memorial, Col 5** [shows initial F].
	Barclay History RoH, page 370.
DWR Enlistment Book:	TED 13, page 7.

"MAY THE SUNSHINE HE MISSED ON LIFE'S HIGHWAY BE FOUND IN GOD'S GARDEN OF REST"

SMALLEY, Granville William Henry, 14705862 Pte, 1/7th DWR.
    Died of Wounds: 12 Dec 1944, Normandy Campaign, aged 19.
    Buried: No known grave.
    Commemorated: Blackpool (Carleton) Crematorium, Panel 4.
        7 DWR WW2 War Memorial, Col 5; D Coy Memorial, Col 3.
        Barclay History RoH, page 370.
    DWR Enlistment Book: OVER 33, page 82.

SMITH, John Henry, 4618828 Pte, 2/7th DWR.
Son of James and Betsy Smith, Attercliffe, Sheffield, Yorks.
    Killed in Action: 11 Jun 1940, France & Belgium Campaign, 1939/40, aged 22.
    Buried: Sainte Marie Cemetery, Le Havre, 67, S, 15.
    Commemorated: **7 DWR WW2 War Memorial, Col 5.**
        Barclay History RoH, page 372.
    DWR Enlistment Book: TED 18, page 83.
"DEEP IN OUR HEARTS HIS MEMORY IS KEPT ALWAYS"

SMITH, Kenneth, 92004 2Lt, HQ Coy, 2/7th DWR [CWGC shows 97004].
Son of Harry and Nora Smith, husband of Winifred Grace Smith, Greetland, Halifax, Yorks.
    Killed in Action: 21 May 1940, France & Belgium Campaign, 1939/40, aged 29.
    Buried: Abbeville Communal Cemetery Extension, 8, C, 5.
    Commemorated: Rotherham War Memorial.
        7 DWR WW2 War Memorial, Col 1.
    Commissioned: 6 Sep 1939 (from the ranks).
"EVERY MEMORY THAT LINGERS, A SWEET THOUGHT OF HAPPINESS LENDS"

SMITH, Robert Hayes, 253669 Lt, A Coy 1/7th DWR, awarded CinC's Certificate for Gallantry, 1944.
Son of Alfred and May Hayes Smith, Manningham, Bradford, Yorks.
    Killed in Action: 15 Aug 1944, Normandy Campaign, France, aged 20.
    Buried: Ranville War Cemetery, 8, B, 13.
    Commemorated: **7 DWR WW2 War Memorial, Col 5.**
        Barclay History RoH, page 370.
        Iron Duke: 060-1945, page 51.
    Commissioned: Nov 1942, from R Scots.

> SMITH.—In August, 1944, killed in action in France, Lt. Robert Hayes Smith, The Duke of Wellington's Regiment, aged 20. Lt. Smith was educated at Malvern College, and for a year before joining the Royal Scots served with the Bradford Home Guard. He received his commission in The Duke of Wellington's Regiment on his 19th birthday, and he went out to France a few days after D-Day. The following is an extract from a letter written by his padre and published in the *Bradford Telegraph*:—" We were all very fond of him for his own sake, and as an officer he really had done a magnificent job, and seemed to posses a head well beyond his years. Bob was commanding the company during one of their most difficult advances through a minefield and I know he did the job extremely well.
> "At the time he was killed he was leading a patrol, well forward. He was shot in the head and died instantaneously. I am quite sure of this, as I went to see his company just afterwards. As his body was lying so far forward it was impossible to bury him that day, but I went myself two days later and brought his body back to a place called Cuverville, a few miles east of Caen. Here we buried him, where several others of the Battalion are also buried."

Extract from the Regimental Journal, the Iron Duke, 1945
"BELOVED ONLY SON OF A. AND M. SMITH, BRADFORD, ENGLAND"

SPEARING, Walter Thomas, 4621088 Pte, 2/7th DWR.
Son of Charles and Emma Maud Spearing, Shepherd's Bush, London.
    Died of Wounds: 1 Oct 1940, France & Belgium Campaign, 1939/40.
    Buried: Kensal Green (All Souls') Cemetery, 185, 36, 50801 (Screen Wall).

Commemorated:	**7 DWR WW2 War Memorial, Col 5.**
	Barclay History RoH, page 372.
DWR Enlistment Book:	TED 21, page .

SPENCE, Jack, 4616496 Pte, 2/7th DWR.
Son of May Spence, Marsden, Yorks.

Reported Missing:	presumed killed 11 Jun 1940, France & Belgium Campaign, 1939/40, aged 20.
Buried:	No known grave.
Commemorated:	Dunkirk Memorial, Col 62.
	7 DWR WW2 War Memorial, Col 5.
	Barclay History RoH, page 372.
DWR Enlistment Book:	TED 16, page 50.

STEAD Fred, 14579362 Pte, 1/7th DWR.

Killed in Action:	28 Jul 1944, Normandy Campaign, France, aged 20.
Buried:	Ranville War Cemetery, 1, D, 21.
Commemorated:	**7 DWR WW2 War Memorial, Col 5.**
	Barclay History RoH, page 370.
DWR Enlistment Book:	OVER 32, page 16.

STEPHENSON, George, 14553987 Pte, 1/7th DWR, from DLI.
Son of Mr and Mrs J G Stephenson, South bank, Middlesbrough, Yorks.

Killed in Action:	18 Jun 1944, Normandy Campaign, France, aged 19.
Buried:	No known grave.
Commemorated:	Bayeux memorial, Panel 15, Col 1.
	7 DWR WW2 War Memorial, Col 5.
	Barclay History RoH, page 370.
DWR Enlistment Book:	DLI Book 39, page 79.

STOCKTON, Reginald, 4617677 Pte, 2/7th DWR.
Son of James Edward and Lizzie Stockton, Sowerby Bridge, Yorks.

Killed in Action:	11 Jun 1940, France & Belgium Campaign, 1939/40, aged 21.
Buried:	Veules les Roses Cemetery, 3, 10.
Commemorated:	**7 DWR WW2 War Memorial, Col 5.**
	Barclay History RoH, page 372.
	Halifax Courier, 13 Jul 1940 (reported missing).
DWR Enlistment Book:	TED 17, page 68.

"GREATER LOVE HATH NO MAN THAN THIS, THAT A MAN LAY DONW HIS LIFE FOR HIS FRIENDS"

STOREY, Thomas Edward, 14721738 Pte, HQ Coy (MT) 1/7th DWR.
Son of Edward and Annie Elizabeth Storey, Liverpool, Lancs.

Died:	7 Jan 1947, Normandy Campaign, Germany, aged 20.
Buried:	Hamburg Cemetery, 1A, K, 2
Commemorated:	**Not listed on 7 DWR WW2 Memorial.**
DWR Enlistment Book:	OVER 36, page 173.

"FATHER, IN THY GRACIOUS KEEPING LEAVE WE NOW OUR LOVED ONE SLEEPING"

STRAW, Isaac Ronald, 14579366 Pte, 1/7th DWR.
Son of Bertie and Mary Vera Straw, Masbrough, Rotherham, Yorks.

Killed in Action:	26 Sep 1944, Normandy Campaign, Belgium, aged 19.

Buried:	Turnhout Communal Cemetery, 3, 8.
Commemorated:	Rotherham War Memorial.
	DWR WW2 War Memorial, Col 5, D Coy Memorial, Col 1.
	Barclay History RoH, page 370.
DWR Enlistment Book:	OVER 32, page 16.

"IN LOVING MEMORY OF OUR ONLY SON RONALD WHO GAVE HIS LIFE FOR HIS KING AND COUNTRY"

SYKES, George Clarence, 4612649 Cpl, 2/7th DWR.

Reported Missing:	Died 18 Jun 1940, France & Belgium Campaign, 1939/40, aged 25.
Buried:	Sainte Marie Cemetery, Le Havre, 67, T, 8.
Previously Interred:	Sotteville sur Mer Temp Burial Ground, 6, 1 (until Oct 1947).
Commemorated:	**7 DWR WW2 War Memorial, Col 5.**
	Barclay History RoH, page 372.
DWR Enlistment Book:	EB 12, page 109., enlisted 10 Apr 1933.

TANNER, Wilfred Gordon, 4394944 Pte, 1/7th DWR.

Son of Eleanor Tanner, husband of Mabel Tanner, Kilburn, Middlesex.

Killed in Action:	7 Aug 1944, Normandy Campaign, France, aged 31.
Buried:	Banneville la Campagne War Cemetery, 14, CA, 18.
Commemorated:	**7 DWR WW2 War Memorial, Col 5.**
	Barclay History RoH, page 370.
DWR Enlistment Book:	UNDER 30, page 92 & OVER 30, page 92.

"THEY MISS HIM MOST WHO LOVED HIM BEST"

TAYLOR, Bernard, 4546429 Pte, 1/7th DWR.

Killed in Action:	11 Aug 1944, Normandy Campaign, France, aged 20.
Buried:	Ranville War Cemetery, 8, B, 9.
Commemorated:	**7 DWR WW2 War Memorial, Col 5.**
DWR Enlistment Book:	UNDER 30, page 76 & OVER 30, page 76.

TAYLOR, Cyril, 4622018 Pte, 1/7th DWR.

Son of Ernest and Mary Emma Taylor, Cornholme, Todmorden, Yorks.

Killed in Action:	16 Jul 1944, Normandy Campaign, France, aged 29.
Buried:	Hottot les Bagues War Cemetery, 8, G, 1.
Commemorated:	**7 DWR WW2 War Memorial, Col 5.**
	Barclay History RoH, page 371.
DWR Enlistment Book:	TED 22, page 2.

"HE GAVE HIS TO-DAY FOR OUR TOMORROW. MAKE US WORTHY OF HIS GREAT SACRIFICE"

TAYLOR, Cyril Henry, 1740136 Pte, 1/7th DWR.

Son of Henry Sturgess and Isobel Annie Taylor, Belper, Derbyshire.

Killed in Action:	29 Oct 1944, Normandy Campaign, Netherlands, aged 24.
Buried:	Bergen op Zoom War Cemetery, 7, C, 11.
Commemorated:	**7 DWR WW2 War Memorial, Col 5.**
	Barclay History RoH, page 370.
DWR Enlistment Book:	UNDER 30, page 97 & OVER 30, page 97.

"NOT JUST TODAY BUT EVERY DAY IN SILENCE WE REMEMBER. MOTHER AND DAD. BELPER"

TEBB, Robert Wallace, 4614100 Pte, 2/7th DWR.
Son of Wallace and Hilda Tebb, Charlton, London.
    Killed in Action: 11 Jun 1940, France & Belgium Campaign, 1939/40, aged 19.
    Buried: Blosseville sur Mer Churchyard Military, 1, 5.
    Commemorated: **7 DWR WW2 War Memorial, Col 5.**
    Barclay History RoH, page 372.
    DWR Enlistment Book: TED 14, page 12.
"HE GAVE HIS TO-DAY FOR YOUR TO-MORROW"

TERRY, Terence Norman, 14423965 Pte, 1/7th DWR.
Son of Albert George and Sarah Elizabeth Terry, Wakefield, Yorks.
    Died of Wounds: 3 Oct 1944, Normandy Campaign, Belgium, aged 19.
    Buried: Leopoldsburg War Cemetery, 5, C, 19.
    Commemorated: **7 DWR WW2 War Memorial, Col 5; D Coy Memorial, Col 3.**
    Barclay History RoH, page 371.
    DWR Enlistment Book: OVER 32, page 77.
"DEEP IN OUR HEARTS A MEMORY IS KEPT OF ONE WE LOVED AND CAN NEVER FORGET"

THOMSON, Hugh Steel, 2056127 LCpl, 1/7th DWR.
    Killed in Action: 2 Apr 1945, Normandy Campaign, Netherlands, aged 33.
    Buried: Jonkerbos War Cemetery, 2, F, 3.
    Commemorated: **7 DWR WW2 War Memorial, Col 5; D Coy Memorial, Col 3.**
    Barclay History RoH, page 371.
    DWR Enlistment Book: UNDER 34, page 37.

TILLY, Arthur James, 4624486 Cpl, 1/7th DWR [WW2 Memorial shows spelling Tilley].
Son of A H and Catherine Tilly.
    Killed in Action: 27 Jun 1944, Normandy Campaign, France, aged 31.
    Buried: Hottot les Bagues War Cemetery, 10, G, 9.
    Commemorated: **7 DWR WW2 War Memorial, Col 5; D Coy Memorial, Col 1.**
    Barclay History RoH, page 371.
    DWR Enlistment Book: TED 24.

TITTERTON, Leonard, 258675 Lt, 1/7th DWR.
Son of Ernest and Christiana Titterton, husband of Mary Titterton, Headingley, Leeds, Yorks.
    Killed in Action: 23 Mar 1945, Normandy Campaign, Germany, aged 26.
    Buried: Reischwald Forest War Cemetery, 52, D, 15.
    Commemorated: **7 DWR WW2 War Memorial, Col 1.**
    Barclay History RoH, page 371.
    Commissioned: Jan 1943.
"AT THE GOING DOWN OF THE SUN AND IN THE MORNING WE WILL REMEMBER THEM"

TOOTILL, James Kingsley, 7905327 Pte, 1/7th DWR
Son of James and Lily Tootill, Bradshaw, Lancs.
    Killed in Action: 18 Jun 1944, Normandy Campaign, France, aged 24.
    Buried: Hottot les Bagues War Cemetery, 10, F, 4.
    Commemorated: **7 DWR WW2 War Memorial, Col 5.** [shows initials G R].
    Barclay History RoH, page 371.
    DWR Enlistment Book: OVER 31, page 8.
"HE GAVE HIS ALL FOR HIS KING AND COUNTRY, AN UNFINISHED LIFE"

TOWNEND Norman, 4613459 Pte, 1/7th DWR.
Husband of Margaret Isabel Townend, Bedlington, Northumberland.
    Killed in Action: 18 Jun 1944, Normandy Campaign, France, aged 27.
    Buried: Hottot les Bagues War Cemetery, 9, G, 9.
    Commemorated: **7 DWR WW2 War Memorial, Col 5.**
                                          Barclay History RoH, page 371.
    DWR Enlistment Book: TED 13, page 46.
"SILENT THOUGHTS BRING MANY A TEAR FOR ONE I LOST AND LOVE SO DEAR. R.I.P."

TREMEER, Arthur George 4610578 Sgt, 1/7th DWR, awarded CinC's Certificate for gallantry, 1945.
Son of Felix George and Louis Sarah Ann Tremeer, husband of Gladys Irene Tremeer, St Marychurch, Torquay, Devon.
    Killed in Action: 4 Dec 1944, Normandy Campaign, Netherlands, aged 30.
    Buried: Jonkerbos War Cemetery, 19, D, 7.
    Commemorated: **7 DWR WW2 War Memorial, Col 5.**
                                          Barclay History RoH, page 371.
    DWR Enlistment Book: EB 10, page 116.
"HE GAVE HIS LIFE FOR FREEDOM, GOD'S GREATEST GIFT TO MAN"

TURNER, Wilfred, 4618805 Pte, 2/7th DWR.
Son of John L and Martha Ann Turner, Southowram, Halifax, Yorks.
    Killed in Action: 4 Oct 1940, France & Belgium Campaign, 1939/40, aged 23.
    Buried: Rouen (St Sever) Cemetery Extension, S, 4, S, 28.
    Commemorated: **7 DWR WW2 War Memorial, Col 5.**
                                          Barclay History RoH, page 371.
                                          Halifax Courier, 13 Jul 1940.
    DWR Enlistment Book: TED 18, page 81.
"FOR EVER IN OUR THOUGHTS"

WAINWRIGHT, William, 4973370 LCpl, 1/7th DWR, from Sherwood Foresters.
Son of William and Charlotte Ann Wainwright, of Newbold, Chesterfield, Derbyshire, husband of Emma Wainwright, Newbold Moor, Chesterfield.
    Killed in Action: 18 Jun 1944, Normandy Campaign, France, aged 29.
    Buried: Hottot les Bagues War Cemetery, 10, E, 5.
    Commemorated: **7 DWR WW2 War Memorial, Col 5.**
                                          Barclay History RoH, page 371.
    DWR Enlistment Book: OVER Numbers, page 165.
"THE SOULS OF THE RIGHTEOUS ARE IN THE HANDS OF GOD"

WALKER, Edgar, 4626568 Pte, 1/7th DWR.
Son of Herbert and Louisa Walker, Huddersfield, husband of Alma Walker, Longwood, Huddersfield.
    Killed: 12 Sep 1944, looters, Havre, Normandy Campaign, France, aged 35.
    Buried: Sainte Marie Cemetery, Le Havre, 67, Q, 15.
    Commemorated: **7 DWR WW2 War Memorial, Col 5.**
                                          Barclay History RoH, page 371.
    DWR Enlistment Book: TED 26.
"SWEET IS HIS MEMORY DEAR HIS NAME DEEP IN MY HEART HE WILL EVER REMAIN"

WALKER, John, 3189550 LCpl, 1/7th DWR.
Son of Thomas and Marion Walker, husband of Elizabeth King Walker, Jedburgh, Scotland.
    Died: 3 Feb 1947, aged 24.

> **Buried:** Jedborough (Castlewood) Cemetery, 2, 877.
> **Commemorated:** **Not listed on 7 DWR WW2 Memorial.**
> **DWR Enlistment Book:** UNDER 34, page 133.

"DEATH IS BUT A PATH THAT MUST BE TROD IF MAN WOULD EVER PASS TO GOD"

WALKER, Norman Henry, 14574731 Pte, 1/7th DWR.
Son of Herbert and Violet Annie Walker, Wansford, Yorks.
> **Killed in Action:** 19 Jul 1944, Normandy Campaign, France, aged 19.
> **Buried:** St Manvieu War Cemetery, Cheux, 3, B, 3.
> **Commemorated:** **7 DWR WW2 War Memorial, Col 5; D Coy Memorial, Col 1.**
> Barclay History RoH, page 371.
> **DWR Enlistment Book:** OVER 32, page 14.

"A HEARTACHE, A TEAR, A MEMORY SO DEAR; EACH DAY OF MY LIFE, I WISH YOU WERE HERE"

WARD, Kenneth, 14406347 Pte, 1/7th DWR.
Son of Wilson and Mabel Ward, Christchurch, Hants.
> **Killed in Action:** 19 Jun 1944, Normandy Campaign, France, aged 19.
> **Buried:** Hottot les Bagues War Cemetery, 8, G, 3.
> **Commemorated:** Rotherham War Memorial.
> **7 DWR WW2 War Memorial, Col 5.**
> Barclay History RoH, page 371.
> **DWR Enlistment Book:** OVER 32, page 37.

"KEN. A DARLING SON & BROTHER REMEMBERED BY MUM, DAD, SISTER, BROTHERS AND SALLY"

WATSON, Thomas Arthur, 4620232 Pte, 1/7th DWR.
Son of Thomas and Amy Agnes Watson.
> **Died:** 29 Oct 1943, Home Duties, aged 27.
> **Buried:** Newcastle (Byker) Cemetery, 7, 159.
> **Commemorated:** **7 DWR WW2 War Memorial, Col 5.**
> Barclay History RoH, page 371.
> **DWR Enlistment Book:** TED 20, page 24.

"AT REST. FOREVER IN OUR THOUGHTS"

WATSON, Walter, 4616257, Pte, 1/7th DWR.
> **Killed in Action:** 29 Oct 1944, Normandy Campaign, Netherlands, aged 27.
> **Buried:** Bergen op Zoom War Cemetery, 9, A, 15.
> **Commemorated:** **7 DWR WW2 War Memorial, Col 5.**
> Barclay History RoH, page 371.
> **DWR Enlistment Book:** TED 16, page 26.

WEIR, Robert, 4620206 Pte, 1/7th DWR.
Son of James William and Caroline Ethel Weir, Murton, Co Durham.
> **Died:** 31 Jan 1942, Home Duties, aged 22.
> **Buried:** Murton Cemetery, East Murton, G, K, 2.
> **Commemorated:** **7 DWR WW2 War Memorial, Col 5.**
> Barclay History RoH, page 361 [shows unit as 2 DWR].
> **DWR Enlistment Book:** TED 20, page 21.

"WHAT DEPTH OF LOVE NO TOUNGUE CAN TELL THAT LINGERS IN THE LAST FAREWELL"

WELLINGS, Kenneth, 4614546 Pte, 1/7th DWR.
Son of Mr and Mrs A Wellings, Marsden, Yorks, resided Mossley.
    Died of Wounds: 4 Jan 1945, aged 22.
    Buried: Mossley Cemetery, 31.
    Commemorated: **7 DWR WW2 War Memorial, Col 5.**
        Barclay History RoH, page 371.
    DWR Enlistment Book: TED 14, page 56 (discharged 8 Jun 1944).

WHIPP, Sydney, 34023, Maj, A Coy, 7th DWR, Territorial Decoration, *LG 28 Jan 1943, page 526.*
    Killed in Action: 3 May 1944, RAF Liaison Officer, pre D Day bombing sortie.
    Buried: Cheniers Churchyard Cemetery, Mil 1, Collective Grave 2.
    Commemorated: **7 DWR WW2 War Memorial, Col 1.**
        Barclay History RoH, page 371.
        Iron Duke, obituary, 179-1979, page 160.
    Commissioned: Dec 1925.

WIGGLESWORTH, Frank, 14555655 Pte, 1/7th DWR.
Son of Frank and Louisa Wigglesworth, Featherstone, Yorks.
    Killed in Action: 24 Oct 1944, Normandy Campaign, Netherlands, aged 20.
    Buried: Geel War Cemetery, 3, C, 1.
    Commemorated: **7 DWR WW2 War Memorial, Col 5.**
        Barclay History RoH, page 371.
    DWR Enlistment Book: OVER 32, page 4.
"WORTHY OF REMEMBRANCE"

WILCOCK, Reginald Arthur, 14550916 LCpl, 1/7th DWR.
Son of Arthur and Lillian Wilcock, Nelson, Lancs, husband of Winnie Wilcock.
    Died of Wounds: 29 Oct 1944, Normandy Campaign, Belgium, aged 20.
    Buried: Bergen op Zoom War Cemetery, 9, A, 22.
    Commemorated: Barnoldswick War Memorial; Nelson War Memorial.
        7 DWR WW2 War Memorial, Col 5, D Coy Memorial, Col 1.
        Barclay History RoH, page 371.
    DWR Enlistment Book: OVER 32, page 77.
"IN LOVING MEMORY OF OUR DEAR SON, REG. HE GAVE HIS LIFE THAT WE MIGHT LIVE"

WILKINSON, Bernard Baker, S Coy (DR), 498062, 1/7th DWR.
Son of John and Mary Ann Wilkinson, husband of Lucy Irene Wilkinson, Clarendon Park, Leicester.
    Killed in Action   25 Jun 1944, Normandy Campaign, France, aged 29.
    Buried: St Manvieu War Cemetery, Cheux, 1, G, 1.
    Commemorated: **7 DWR WW2 War Memorial, Col 5.**
        Barclay History RoH, page 371.
    DWR Enlistment Book: OVER Numbers, page 165.
"IN MEMORY OF MY DEAR HUSBAND, LOVING WIFE AND CHILD IRENE AND MARGARET"

WILKINSON, John Robert Revel, 4616482 Pte, 2/7th DWR.
Son of Alfred and Emma Wilkinson, Slaithwaite, Yorks.
    Killed in Action: 17 Jun 1940, France & Belgium Campaign, 1939/40, France, aged 20.
    Buried: Rouen (St Sever) Cemetery Extension, S, 4, Q, 5.
    Commemorated: **7 DWR WW2 War Memorial, Col 5.**
        Barclay History RoH, page 372.
    DWR Enlistment Book: TED 16, page 49.

"IN LOVING MEMORY OF OUR DEAR SON. WE SHALL NEVER FORGET. MOTHER AND DAD"

WILLISCROFT, Benjamin Thomas, 14529347 Pte, 1/7th DWR, [D Coy Memorial shows initial W].
Son of Mrs E E Williscroft, Rugeley, Staffs.
Killed in Action:	24 Oct 1944, Normandy Campaign, Belgium, aged 20.
Buried:	Geel War Cemetery, 3, 2, C.
Commemorated:	**7 DWR WW2 War Memorial, Col 5; D Coy Memorial, Col 1.**
	Barclay History RoH, page 371.
DWR Enlistment Book:	OVER 35, page 138.

"A BEAUTIFUL MEMORY DEARER THAN GOLD OF A SON WHOSE WORTH CAN NEVER BE TOLD"

WILSON, George, 14665943 Pte, 1/7th DWR.
Son of William E and Agnes Wilson, Seacroft, Leeds.
Killed in Action:	15 Jun 1944, Normandy Campaign, France, aged 19.
Buried:	No known grave.
Commemorated:	Bayeux Memorial, Panel 15, Col 1.
	7 DWR WW2 War Memorial, Col 5.
	Barclay History RoH, page 371.
DWR Enlistment Book:	OVER 33, page 24.

WINSTANLEY, Arthur, 4619024, Pte, 2/7th DWR.
Son of Arthur and Adelaide Winstanley, Painthorpe, Yorks.
Killed in Action:	10 Jun 1940, France & Belgium Campaign, 1939/40, aged 20.
Buried:	No known grave.
Commemorated:	Dunkirk Memorial, Col 62.
	7 DWR WW2 War Memorial, Col 5.
	Barclay History RoH, page 372.
DWR Enlistment Book:	TED 19, page 3.

WOOD, Cyril, 4547763 Pte, 1/7th DWR.
Son of Owen and Rose Ann Wood, Lidget Green, Bradford.
Killed in Action:	28 Sep 1944, Normandy Campaign, Belgium, aged 21.
Buried:	Leopoldsburg War Cemetery, 5, C, 15.
Commemorated:	**7 DWR WW2 War Memorial, Col 5.**
	Barclay History RoH, page 371.
DWR Enlistment Book:	UNDER 30, page 78 & OVER 30, page 78

"DEEP IN MY HEART YOUR MEMORY IS KEPT I LOVED YOU TOO DEARLY TO EVER FORGET"

WOOD, Edwin, 4546683 Pte 1/7th DWR.
Son of Harry and Miriam Wood, Siddall, Halifax.
Killed in Action:	19 Jul 1944, Normandy Campaign, France, aged 19.
Buried:	St Manvieu War Cemetery, Cheux, 3, C, 1.
Commemorated:	**7 DWR WW2 War Memorial, Col 5; D Coy Memorial, Col 2.**
	Barclay History RoH, page 371.
DWR Enlistment Book:	UNDER 30, page 77 & OVER 30, page 77.

"UNTIL WE MEET AGAIN. THIS HALLOWED SPOT WILL BE FOR EVER ENGLAND"

WOODHEAD, Lionel, 4613568 Cpl, 1/7th DWR.
Son of Fred and Annie Taylor Woodhead, Golcar, Yorks, husband of Doris Evelyn Woodhead, Golcar.

Killed in Action:	19 Jun 1944, Normandy Campaign, France, aged 38.
Buried:	Hottot les Bagues War Cemetery, 10, E, 10.
Commemorated:	**7 DWR WW2 War Memorial, Col 5.**
	Barclay History RoH, page 371.
DWR Enlistment Book:	TED 13, page 57.

"WHEN THE RACE OF LIFE IS RUN FATHER, GRANT THY WEARIED ONE REST FOR EVERMORE"

WOOTTON, Wilfred, 4612292 WO2, CSM S Coy, 1/7th DWR.

Son of George and Mary Harriet Wootton, husband of Nellie Wootton, New Bank, Halifax.

Killed in Action:	25 Jun 1944, Normandy Campaign, France, aged 30.
Buried:	St Manvieu War Cemetery, 1, G, 2.
Commemorated:	**7 DWR WW2 War Memorial, Col 5.**
	Barclay History RoH, page 371.
DWR Enlistment Book:	EB 12, page 49 (enlisted 3 Oct 1932).

"AND WITH THE MORN THOSE ANGEL FACES SMILE, WHICH I HAVE LOVED… AND LOST AWHILE"

WRIGHT, Harold, 4615124 Pte, 2/7th DWR.

Killed in Action:	11 Jun 1940, France & Belgium Campaign, 1939/40, aged 19.
Buried:	No known grave.
Commemorated:	Dunkirk Memorial, Col 62.
	7 DWR WW2 War Memorial, Col 5.
	Barclay History RoH, page 372.
DWR Enlistment Book:	TED 15, page 13.

WRIGHT, William, 4616213 Pte, 2/7th DWR.

Son of William and Edith Mary Wright, Stalybridge

Died:	14 Jan 1940, Home Duties, aged 18.
Buried:	Stalybridge (St Paul's) Cemetery, Range 34, Grave 44.
Commemorated:	St Paul's Churchyard Memorial.
	7 DWR WW2 War Memorial, Col 5.
	Barclay History RoH, page 372.
DWR Enlistment Book:	TED 16, page 22.

"HIS FATHER WILLIAM BLINDED IN THE 1914-18 WAR AND MOTHER EDITH ARE BURIED WITH HIM"

YEARDLEY, Colin Parkin, 4618814 Pte, 2/7th DWR.

Son of Hagar Yeardley, High Green, Yorks.

Killed in Action:	11 Jun 1940, France & Belgium Campaign, 1939/40, aged 22.
Buried:	Veules les Roses Cemetery, 1, 11.
Commemorated:	**7 DWR WW2 War Memorial, Col 5.**
	Barclay History RoH, page 372.
DWR Enlistment Book:	TED 18, page 82.

"O REST IN THE LORD"

THE UNITS

Title changes 1860 to 1945

6th West Yorkshire Rifle Volunteer Corps
2nd Volunteer Battalion (Duke of Wellington's Regiment) West Riding Regiment
7th Battalion Duke of Wellington's (West Riding Regiment) (Territorial Force)
7th Battalion Duke of Wellington's Regiment (West Riding) (Territorial Army)

WW2

1/7th Battalion Duke of Wellington's Regiment (West Riding) (Territorial Army)
&
2/7th Battalion Duke of Wellington's Regiment (West Riding) (Territorial Army)
(later converted to 115th Regiment Royal Armoured Corps)

1. 7th Battalion.

The 7th Battalion traces its history back to the 6th West Yorkshire Rifle Volunteer Corps but was an offshoot of the 2nd Volunteer Battalion of the Regiment when the original three Volunteer Battalions were developed into the Territorial Force. The new Territorial Force Divisions were created to mirror the Regular Army Divisional structure, each of which had four infantry Battalions in each of their Brigades at that time.

The 7th Battalion was one of four Territorial Force Battalions, numbered 4th (Halifax), 5th (Huddersfield), 6th (Skipton) and 7th (Colne Valley) formed from the three old Volunteer Battalions in 1908. The 7th Battalion was formed from a Cadre of the 5th Battalion (formerly 2nd Volunteer Battalion), taking over some of the 5th Battalion's Drill Halls and having others constructed. Eventually the Companies were housed in Milnsbridge (Headquarters and Golcar Company), Marsden, Mossley, Slaithwaite, Springhead, Thongsbridge and Uppermill.

In both World Wars the battalion was ordered to double its size by splitting in two and increasing the numbers in each unit from volunteers or conscripts. These became the 1st 7th (1/7th) and 2nd 7th (2/7th), etc. The First and Second Line Battalions served in different Brigades and Divisions. In the Second World War the 1/7th Battalion formed part of 147th Infantry Brigade and the 2/7th Battalion was, initially, part of 137th Infantry Brigade.

THE CAMPAIGNS

1. 2/7th Battalion - France and Belgium Campaign 1939-1940.

2. 1/7th Battalion - Normandy Campaign 1944-1945.

3. 115 Regiment RAC - Normandy Campaign 1944-1945.

1. 2/7th Battalion, 1939-40.

**The Campaign:
2/7th Battalion**

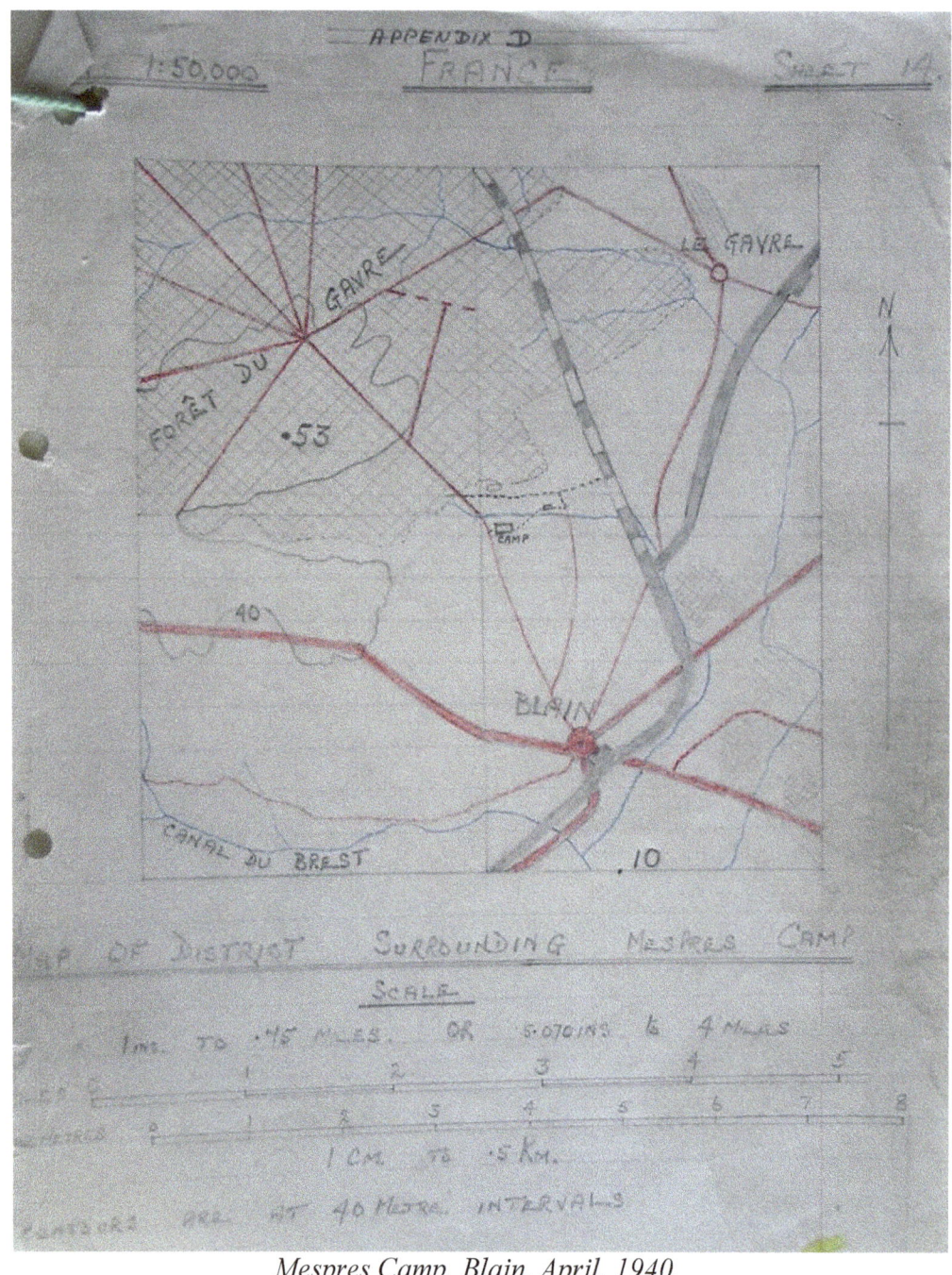

Mespres Camp, Blain, April, 1940.

St Valery en Caux, June, 1940.
(Sotteville lies to the East of 7 DWR's final position before withdrawal)

The 2/7th Battalion, commanded by Lt Col W A Hinchcliffe, was mobilised at Milsnbridge Drill Hall on the outbreak of war, being formed from a cadre of the existing 7th Battalion. It became part of 137th Bde, under Brigadier Gawthorpe, of 46th Infantry Division, commanded by Major General Curtis.

The Division was warned off for service abroad in late March, 1940, to carry out work on the lines of communication, initially for a period of three months. On 28th April, the Battalion, now commanded by Lt Col G Taylor, entrained at Huddersfield and embarked on an Isle of Man steamer for Cherbourg and, on 29th April, the battalion entrained and arrived at Mespres Camp, Forest of Gavre, near Blain, some 20 miles from St Nazaire, where the Companies were billeted in a medieval castle or Nissen huts and tents outside the town. The men spent the next six weeks working on ammunition and petrol dumps as well as organizing local air defences.

On 10 May, 1940, the Germans struck in the west, bypassing the Maginot Line and rapidly breaking through the French defences around Sedan and crossing the Meuse. The Divisional Commander offered the services of the 46th Division to Lord Gort, the Commander in Chief of the BEF, as a result 46 Div was ordered forward and left Blain on 18th May headed for Bethune, via Amiens. The 137th Brigade was split into two trains, with the two 'Dukes' Battalions in the rear train of the Division. The route was Le Mans, Rouen, Dieppe, Eu, Abbeville but at Abbeville, by 20 May, the Division had been split up due to the increasing disorganisation of the French rail network by bombing and detours, the Brigade's second train was unable to get beyond Abbeville and was cut off from the rest of the Brigade, which managed to reach Dunkirk.

Forced to leave the train, the 2/7th Battalion helped to extricate an ambulance train before setting off for Dieppe on foot but the French railwaymen gave them a lift in some cattle trucks attached to a train all the way to Dieppe, arriving on 27th May. The following day the 2/7th Battalion took over the defensive line Dieppe - Arques la Battaille, along the River Bethune, as part of Beauman Force (Beauman Division from 29th May), coming under dive bomber attack that day. On the 29th May, a reconnaissance party found the Battalion train had been looted but the band's instruments were recovered, the band played in the town square to bolster the morale of the civilians

Meanwhile, the 2/6th Battalion, also part of Beauman Force, was sent by rail from Bruz to Louviers, with orders to defend the River Seine crossings in the area Les Andelys - Venables.

On 9th June the 2/6th and 2/7th Battalions were ordered to join 51st Highland Division. A withdrawal to Veules les Roses was ordered for the 2/7th Battalion, which ended up on the defensive perimeter to the east of St Valery en Caux, fighting a rearguard action to allow as many men as possible to be withdrawn from the coastal town and, on 11th June, under attack from German tanks and artillery, further orders, to destroy all transport and equipment and evacuate through St Valery, arrived.

The Unit War Diary outlines the details of the final battle:

11 Jun Veules les Roses	Battalion still had no casualties and moved off to Manneville in good order at 0131 hrs. No enemy were encountered along the coastal roads to Veules les Roses which was reached at dawn. Orders were given by commander 152 Bde to take up defensive position from the sea at Veules to road Blosseville - le Bourg Dun inclusive. Inform[atio]n of enemy and own troops very vague. Hint of possible second Dunkirk. Roads packed with British and French MT and some French tanks. Troops continued to stream along road Dieppe to St Valerie. Our transport somewhat disorganised and split by this traffic. CO recced Veule end of the long frontage and Adjutant went along the front to the Blosseville - Le Bourg Dun road. On return Adjutant took Company Commanders along the frontage while the CO reported to HQ 51 Division. CO returned with orders that French Alpine troops had taken up a position NW of Veules thus shortening our front. Air raid on Veules at noon. Incendiary and HE bombs were dropped. Only communication with Bde HQ was by liaison Officer who reported at noon stating that Bde had been ordered away and the Battalion now came under the command of 153 Inf Bde. A conference was called at Bde HQ in Blosseville at 1730 hrs. CO and Adjutant attended. Defence was lucidly co-ordinated by Brigadier at the conference. No artillery or MG support on the Veules front. A bridgehead was being held from Veules les Roses to St Valerie where intense fighting was in progress. Watched from Bde HQ at 1800 hrs and AFVs were seen to be operating. Not known definitely if the Navy would take us off that night. Intention was to hold off enemy until darkness which would cover embarkation. Battalion disposition was, right Y Company,, middle W Company, left Z Company. X Company was in reserve near to Battalion HQ in Veules les Roses. MT in wood behind French position. Whilst CO and Adjutant were at Bde HQ activity had broken out along the Veules front. Left forward Company reported heavy SS fire for half an hour. Mortar bombardment followed at 1800 hours.. An attack was made on battalion front by some 40 light and medium tanks down main road from Dieppe. Air and firework activity had broken out around Battalion HQ, accompanied by long range MG fire. Battalion HQ site in sunken road in orchard which came under intense mortar and MG fire. Fire was intense and literally pinned down communications. Forward Companies successful in holding off initial attacks by tanks. At least five being put out of action.

	Companies then experienced a lull which was followed by bombardment and mass attack by AFVs, some 200, at about 2100 hrs. These pierced our lines and drove in the direction of Battalion HQ and the coast line and appeared to have swung left towards St Valerie along the main road running SW within the bridgehead. This move by-passed the village defile and road blocks which were probably reported by air recce. At about 2145 hrs when the action was dying down the CO issued orders to Companies to withdraw in darkness to beach near St Valerie in small parties. Battalion HQ and part of HQ made ready to withdraw to beach. Tanks then heard and seen approaching up the field to the top of the sunken road near Battalion HQ which rapidly evacuated. Remainder of HQ KSLI details and part of X Company remained hidden in the middle portion of lane until AFVs patrol moved on. Village streets of Veules difficult to negotiate owing to buildings being on fire and the enemy had succeeded in placing some light artillery on high wooded ground to NW of village. As illumination subsided men from lane withdrew in small parties. Officers collected various small parties and withdrew them through the woods onto the Veules beach.
13 Jun	At dawn boats came ashore from many vessels off the coast and evacuation commenced. Enemy began to harass operations with fireworks dropped from fighter planes. AA fire from several vessels drove off these planes. As daylight improved and the mist lifted enemy artillery near St Valerie opened fire on the ships. Navy dealt with this fire before any serious casualties occurred. Beach eventually evacuated. Survivors were landed safely in England. Unfortunately, the CO, Lt Col G Taylor, had not been seen since he left the Battalion HQ.

Eventually the bulk of the battalion was successfully taken off the beaches by boats and returned to England on a small ferry requisitioned by the Royal Navy. This was commemorated by the rare presentation of a commemorative plaque by British Railways, see below. The Battalion lost three Officers and 62 Other Ranks killed or died of wounds (some as far away as Rouen and Forges les Eaux), with 13 ORs wounded and 97 Prisoners of War. 23 men with no known grave are commemorated on the Dunkirk Memorial.

The Battalion was reorganized in Manchester and was engaged in training and coastal defence, in Norfolk and the south coast until the summer of 1943, when 137 Infantry Brigade was selected to be converted into the Armoured role, the 2/7th Battalion becoming 115 Regiment Royal Armoured Corps.

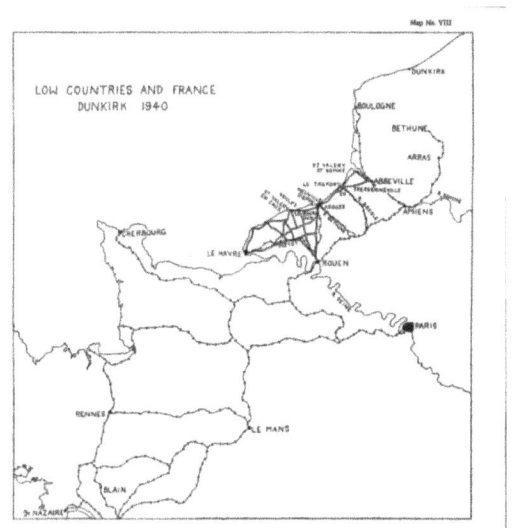

2/7th DWR route from Blaine to St Valery (Barclay History, page 256)

HONOURS AND AWARDS
2/7th Battalion

ACKROYD, Jack Raynor ('Smack On'), 4603885 WO2, 2/7th DWR
(from 2 DWR), r. Ripponden.
Military Medal, France & Belgium Campaign 1939-40, WW2.
"The King has been graciously pleased to approve the following awards in recognition of gallant and distinguished services in the Field."
LG: 11 Oct 1945, page 5008. MIC: recommended by 51st Highland Division POW Pool (68/Gen/8169). Iron Duke: 1946, page 30, Iron Duke: 1970, page 128, Iron Duke: 161-1973, page 31.

BEVERLEY, Douglas, 4616375 LSgt, 2/7th DWR.
Mentioned in Despatches, France & Belgium Campaign 1939-40, WW2.
"The King has been graciously pleased to approve that the following be mentioned in recognition of gallant and distinguished services in the Field".
LG: 31 Jan 1946, page 750. MIC: BM/996 68/Gen/7276/41. Iron Duke: 152-1970, page 34.

BRIGGS, Tom, 178321 2Lt, 2/7th DWR (formerly Sgt, DWR), r. Kirkheaton.
Military Cross, France & Belgium Campaign 1939-40, WW2.
"The King has been graciously pleased to approve the following awards in recognition of gallant and distinguished services in the Field."
LG: 11 Oct 1945, page 5007. Iron Duke: 1946, page 30.

CARR, George, 4609593 Cpl, 2/7th DWR.
Mentioned in Despatches, France & Belgium Campaign 1939-40, WW2.
"For gallant and distinguished services in the Field."
LG: 11 Oct 1945, page 5509.

CODE, Sidney Edward, 4606156 WO1, 2 DWR, 4 DWR, 5 DWR & 2/7th DWR
(later 141 Regt RAC & RHQ DWR).
Member, the Most Excellent Order of the British Empire, WW2.
"The King has been graciously pleased on the occasion of His Majesty's Birthday, to give orders for the following promotions in, and appointments to, the Most Excellent Order the British Empire. To be additional members of the Military Division of he said Most Excellent Order."
LG: 2 Jun 1943, page 4247. Iron Duke: 1962, page 169.
Mentioned in Despatches, NW Europe, WW2.
"The King has been graciously pleased to approve the following be mentioned in recognition of gallant and distinguished services in North West Europe - 4606156 WO1 S E Code."
LG: 4 Apr 1946, page 1673 (serving with 141 Regt RAC). Iron Duke: 191-1983, page 144.

DOYLE, W E, 769470 Sgt (later Bandmaster), 2/7th DWR.
Mentioned in Despatches, France and Belgium Campaign, 1939-40, WW2.
"For gallant and distinguished service in the Field."
LG: 11 Oct 1945, page 5009. POW, 1428, Hohen Fels.

DRAPER, Sydney, 4612226 LCpl, 2/7th DWR.
Mentioned in Despatches, France & Belgium Campaign 1939-40, WW2.
"The names of the undermentioned have been brought to notice in recognition of distinguished services rendered in connection with operations in the Field, March to June, 1940."
LG: 20 Dec 1940, page 7188.

DYSON, John Oldfield, 117095 2Lt, 2/7th DWR, r. Mossley.
Mentioned in Despatches, France & Belgium Campaign 1939-40, WW2.
"The names of the undermentioned have been brought to notice in recognition of distinguished services in the Field, March to June, 1940."
LG: 20 Dec 1940, page 7188. MIC: 68/Gen/6974, dated 20 Dec 1940.

EATON-SMITH, Barry Davidson, 90252 Capt (later Maj), 2/7th DWR.
Member, the Most Excellent Order of the British Empire, Italy (POW France), WW2.
"The King has been graciously pleased to give orders for the following promotions in, and appointments to, the Most Excellent Order of the British Empire in recognition of gallant and distinguished services in Italy. To be additional Members of the said Most Excellent Order."
LG: 20 Sep 1945, page 4673. MIC: 68/Gen/8146, 5 PD Italy.
Mentioned in Despatches, France & Belgium Campaign 1939-40, WW2.
"The King has been most graciously pleased to approve that the following be mentioned for gallant and distinguished service in the Field."
LG: 11 Oct 1945, page 5009. MIC: 68/Gen/8169, 51 H Div POW Pool.

EVERS, Thomas, 235378 Maj (later Lt Col), 2/7th DWR (formerly Pte, 9 DWR)
Member, the Most Excellent Order of the British Empire, WW2.
"The King has been graciously pleased, on the occasion of the Celebration of His Majesty's Birthday, to give orders for the following promotions in, and appointments to, the Most Excellent Order of the British Empire. To be Additional Members of the Military Division of the said Most Excellent Order."
LG: 14 Jun 1945, page 2944. Iron Duke: 161-1973, page 31.

FARRAR, Eric Mitchell, 4616054 Cpl, 2nd Line TA Bn, 2/7th DWR (later POW).
Mentioned in Despatches, France & Belgium Campaign 1939-40, WW2.
"The King has been graciously pleased to approve that the following be mentioned for gallant and distinguished service in the Field."
LG: 11 Oct 1945, page 5009. MIC: 678/Gen/8169, 51st HD POW Pool.

FIRTH, Frank, 88986 Capt (QM), 2/7th DWR (formerly Sgt).
Member, the Most Excellent Order of the British Empire, WW2.
"The King has been graciously pleased to give orders for the following promotions in, and appointments to, the Most Excellent Order of the British Empire in recognition of gallant and distinguished services in the Field. To be additional Members of the Military Division of the said Most Excellent Order."
LG: 11 Oct 1945, page 4989. MIC: 68/Gen/8160, dated 11 Oct 1945, 51st HD POW Pool. Iron Duke: 1946, page 30.
Territorial Efficiency Medal.
"The King has been graciously pleased to confer the Efficiency Decoration upon the following Officers of the Territorial Army."
LG: 11 Oct 1945, page 4989. Iron Duke: 157-1971, page 126. Iron Duke: 158, 1972, page 39.

GAMBLE, William Henry, 4610782 LCpl, 2/7th DWR.
Mentioned in Despatches, France & Belgium Campaign 1939-40, WW2.
"The names of the undermentioned have been brought to notice in recognition of distinguished services rendered in connection with operations in the Field, March to June, 1940, - 4610782 LCpl W Gamble."
LG: 20 Dec 1940, page 7188. Iron Duke: 1941, page 86.

GERRARD, Robert Anthony Herbert, 42195 Capt, 2/7th DWR (from 2 DWR, also 1 DWR).
Mentioned in Despatches, France and Belgium Campaign, 1939-40, WW2.
"For recognition of distinguished services in the Field. Since died."
LG: 11 Oct 1945, page 5009. MIC: 68/Gen/8169 dated 11 Oct 1945, 51 HD POW Pool.

HARPIN, Douglas Arnold, 4616484 WO2 (later WO3 PSM), 2/7th DWR.
Mentioned in Despatches, France and Belgium Campaign, 1939-40, WW2.
"The King has been graciously pleased to approve that the following be mentioned for gallant and distinguished service in the Field."
LG: 11 Oct 1945, page 5009. MIC: 68/Gen/8169, dated 11 Oct 1945, 51 HD POW Pool. Iron Duke: 236-1998, page 50.

HAYNES, Ronald, 4616385 Pte, 2/7th DWR, r. Sowerby Bridge.
Military Medal, France & Belgium Campaign 1939-40, WW2.
"The King has been graciously pleased to approve the following awards in recognition of gallant and distinguished services in the Field."
LG: 11 Oct 1945, page 3316. MIC: 68/Gen/869, dated 11 Oct 1945, 51st H Div POW Pool. Iron Duke: 1946, page 30.

HINCHCLIFFE, William Arthur, 23241 Col, 2/7th DWR.
Efficiency Decoration (Territorial).
"The King has been graciously pleased to confer the Efficiency Decoration upon the undermentioned officers under the terms of the Royal Warrant dated 23rd September, 1930."
LG: 22 Mar 1935, page 1984.
Efficiency Decoration (Territorial).
"The King has been graciously pleased to confer the award of 'three clasps' to the Territorial Efficiency Decoration upon the following officers."
LG: 16 Mar 1951, page 1416.
Member, the Most Excellent Order of the British Empire, Chairman, National Assistance Board Appeal Tribunal, Huddersfield.
"The Queen has been graciously pleased on the occasion of the celebration of Her Majesty's Birthday to give orders for the following promotions in, and appointments to, the Most Excellent Order of the British Empire. To be Ordinary Members of the Civil Division of the said Most Excellent Order."
LG: 12 Jun 1965, page 5487. Iron Duke: 147-1968, page 96.

HOYLE, Sam Robinson, 79923 2Lt, (later Lt Col) 2 DWR (from 2/7th DWR, later CO 7 DWR).
Military Cross, Burma, WW2.
"The King has been graciously pleased to approve the following awards in recognition of gallant and distinguished services in the Field."
LG: 11 Oct 1945, page 5007. MIC: 68/Gen/8169. Iron Duke: Feb 1946, page 30.
Efficiency Decoration (Territorial) and 1st Clasp.
"The King has been graciously pleased to confer the award of the Territorial Efficiency Decoration and 1st Clasp to the following Officers."
LG: 13 Apr 1951, page 2061. Iron Duke: 095-1952, page 99.

JOHNSON, William Arthur Clifford, 90232 Maj, 2 DWR
(from Cdt Sgt, Worksop College Contingent Jnr Div OTC, commissioned into 2/7th DWR).
Mentioned in Despatches, Burma, WW2.
"The King has been graciously pleased to approve the following be mentioned in recognition of gallant and distinguished services in Burma."
LG: 19 Sep 1946, page 4700. MIC: 68/Gen/8197, dated 19 Sep 1946. Iron Duke: 221-1993, page 31.

LAWTON, William Tyas, 75866 Capt, 2/7th DWR (later POW, also RMP).
Mentioned in Despatches, Normandy, WW2.
"The King has been graciously pleased to approve that the following be mentioned in recognition of gallant and distinguished services in the Field."
LG: 6 Jun 1946, page 2741. MIC: 68/Gen/7276/42/22 Spec Ops, dated 6 Jun 1946.

LEES, Ernest ('Jigger') 4602645 Sgt, 2/7th DWR
(previously 7 DWR pre WW1. to York & Lancaster Regt, 1916, MM awarded).
Military Medal, France & Flanders, WW1 - 203878 Sgt, 1/5th York & Lancaster Regt.
Citation not currently available.
LG: 17 Jun 1919, page 7682.
Mentioned in Despatches, France & Belgium Campaign 1939-40, WW2.
"The names of the undermentioned have been brought to notice in recognition of distinguished services rendered in connection with operations in the Field, June, 1940."
LG: 20 Dec 1940, page 7188. MIC: 68/Gen/6974, dated 20 Dec 1940. Iron Duke: 112-1959, page 53. Medals: held in Bankfield Museum, donated in 1959.

LOWE, Percy Bruce, 102513 Maj, 2/7th DWR
(formerly Pte, commissioned Aug 1939, later OC 521 Field Press Censor Section).
Member, the Most Excellent Order of the British Empire, North Africa, WW2.
"From early in the North African campaign, Major Lowe was employed as press censor liaison Officer with Advanced Army and Army Group Headquarters. His work consisted of feeding press censors with guidance on what was releasable for publication on current operations and in interpreting to the HQ Staff the needs of the Press. Under the high pressure in which war correspondents work, the security of their Despatches was greatly dependent upon the efficiency of Major Lowe. It is largely owing to his efforts that no breaches of security occurred in press reports throughout the North African, Sicilian and Italian campaigns. He was untiring in his zeal and in obtaining and disseminating up-to-the minute information for the assistance of censors and correspondents both in the forward ad rear areas. Towards the end of the Italian campaign, Major Lowe took over the duties of the Chief Field Press Censor, to which post he applied successfully the same qualities of sound judgment and common sense which enabled the maximum amount of news to be published consistent with security. His team of censors consisted of American, British, South African, Canadian, French, Polish, Indian and Brazilian Officers, and it is greatly to the credit of Major Lowe that the team worked in complete harmony."
LG: 13 Dec 1945, page 6065. MIC: 68/Gen/8203, dated 13 Dec 1945 (Italy Cease Fire). Iron Duke: 1946, page 92.
Mentioned in Despatches, Italy, WW2.
"The King has been graciously pleased to approve that the following be mentioned in recognition of gallant and distinguished services in Italy."
LG: 29 Nov 1945, page 5813. MIC: 68/Gen/8098, dated 29 Nov, 1945 (4 PD, Italy). Iron Duke: 1946, page 92.
Efficiency Medal (Territorial).
"The following Officers are awarded the Efficiency Medal (Territorial)."
LG: 23 May 1947, page 2294.
Efficiency Decoration (Territorial) and first Clasp.
"The King has been graciously pleased to confer the Efficiency Decoration (Territorial) and first Clasp."
LG: 21 Apr 1950, page 1926. Iron Duke: 191-1983, page 146.

MORRISEY, James, 50211 Capt, RAMC att 2/7th DWR, r Caernarvonshire.
Mentioned in Despatches, France & Belgium Campaign 1939-40, WW2.
Citation not currently available.
LG: 11 Oct 1945, page 5010. CWGC Records.

OAKES, James S, 4607732 RQMS, 2/7th DWR.
Mentioned in Despatches, France & Belgium Campaign 1939-40, WW2.
"The names of the undermentioned have been brought to notice in recognition of distinguished service in the Field, March to June, 1940 - 4607723 WO2 (RQM) J S Oakes)."
LG: 20 Dec 1940, page 7188. Iron Duke: 1941, page 86. Iron Duke: 152-1970, page 35.

ROYDS, Richard Heaton (Dick), 65517 Capt, 2/7th DWR, r. Halifax.
Military Cross, France and Belgium Campaign, 1939-40, WW2.
"The King has been graciously pleased to approve the following awards in recognition of gallantry in France and Flanders."
LG: 20 Dec 1940, page 7174. Iron Duke: 1941, pages 81 & 86. Iron Duke: 245-2001, page 50.

SLANE, John Bernard, 4602107 WO2 (later RQMS), 2 DWR (from Spec Res to 8 DWR, WW1; also 1 DWR, and 2/7th DWR WW2).
Mentioned in Despatches, France & Belgium Campaign 1939-40, WW2.
"The King has been graciously pleased to approve that the following be mentioned for gallant and distinguished service in the Field."
LG: 11 Oct 1945, page 5009. MIC: 68/Gen/8169, dated 11 Oct 1945.

SMITH, Herbert Frederick, 4605999 (88986, on MIC) WO1, 2/7th DWR, r. Mossley.
Mentioned in Despatches, France & Belgium Campaign 1939-40, WW2.
"The King has been graciously pleased to approve the following be mentioned for gallant and distinguished service in the Field: 4605999 WO1 H F Smith."
LG: 11 Oct 1945, page 5009. MIC: 68/Gen/8169, dated 11 Oct 1945, POW Pool 51 Highland Div.

STANCLIFFE, Ronald, 4616619 Pte, 2/7th DWR, r. Halifax.
Military Medal, France and Belgium Campaign 1939-40, WW2.
"The King has been graciously pleased to approve the following awards in recognition of gallant and distinguished services in the Field.
LG: 11 Oct 1945, page 5008. MIC: 68/Gen/ 8169, dated 11 Oct 1945, 51st Highland Div POW Pool. Iron Duke: 1946, page 30.

TAYLOR, George, 2637 Lt Col, 2/7th DWR
Mentioned in Despatches, France and Belgium Campaign 1939-40, WW2.
"For gallant and distinguished service in the Field."
LG: 11 Oct 1945, page 5009. MIC: 68/Gen/8169, dated 11 Oct 1945, 51st Highland Div POW Pool. Iron Duke: 1948, page 50, Iron Duke: 1983, page 228.
Distinguished Service Order, France and Belgium Campaign 1939-40, WW2.
"His Majesty the King has been graciously pleased to approve the following awards in recognition of gallant and distinguished services in the Field (prior to September, 1945).
LG: 25 Sep 1947, page 4516. MIC: 68/Gen/7276/49, dated 25 Sep 1947, submitted by Maj Gen Fortune.
Efficiency Decoration (Territorial).
"The King has been graciously pleased to confer the Efficiency Decoration upon the following Officers of the Territorial Army."
LG: 30 May 1947, page 2423.
Efficiency Decoration (Territorial).
"The Queen has been graciously pleased to confer the award of the 1st [to] 4th Clasps to the Territorial Efficiency Decoration upon the following Officers."
LG: 25 Feb 1955, page 1157. Iron Duke: 1948, page 50. Iron Duke: 103-1983, page 227.

WALKER, Cuthbert Horsbrugh, Lt Col, 11 Border Regt (later CO 2/7th DWR, 1940-1941).
Military Cross, France & Flanders, WW1 - Capt Border Regt.
Citation not currently available.
LG; 18 Jun 1917, page 9374. Iron Duke: 072-1949, page 88.

WATHEN, Alfred Hubert Graham (Bob), 20733 Lt Col, 1 DWR (also CO 2/7th DWR)
Mentioned in Despatches, France and Belgium Campaign, 1939-40, WW2.

"The names of the undermentioned have been brought to notice in recognition of distinguished services rendered in connection with operations in the Field, March to June ,1940 - Lt Col A H G Wathen."
LG: 20 Dec 1940, page 7188. MIC: 68/Gen/6974, dated 20 Dec 1940. Iron Duke: 166-1974, page 132.
Officer, the Most Excellent Order of the British Empire, Coronation Honours List.
"The Queen has been graciously pleased, on the occasion of Her Majesty's Coronation, to give orders for the following promotions in, and appointments to, the Most Excellent Order of the British Empire. To be additional Officers of the Military Division of the said Most Excellent Order."
LG: 1 Jun 1953, page 2949. Iron Duke: 1953, page 95.

WHITELEY, Edward Sunderland, 4616081 Pte, 2/7th DWR.
Military Medal, France and Belgium Campaign 1939-40, WW2.
"The King has been graciously pleased to approve the following awards in recognition of distinguished services in the Field."
LG: 4 Nov 1941, page 6359. MIC: 68/Gen/6986/12 (BEF escape). Iron Duke: 272-2012, page 48.

WILKINSON, E G, Rev Lt, RAChD att 2/7th DWR (att for France & Belgium Campaign, 1939/40, 1940).
Mentioned in Despatches. France and Belgium Campaign 1939-40, WW2.
Citation not currently available.
LG: Not Known.
Mentioned in Despatches.
Citation not currently available.
LG: Not Known.
Mentioned in Despatches.
Citation not currently available.
LG: Not Known. Iron Duke: 162-193, page 50.

MAPRES CAMP, BLAIN
APRIL 1940

Constructing the Depot at Blain, April 1940.

Offloading ammunition and stores into the Depot.

Stockpiles for the BEF.

SOTTEVILLE sur MER

Site of the Calvary at Sotteville sur Mer.

Here on the plain of Sotteville during the battle of 11th and 12th June, 1940, 65 French and British soldiers fell whom we commemorate.

Courtesy of Major H Savary.

2. 1/7th Battalion, 1944-45.

THE CAMPAIGN:
1/7th Battalion

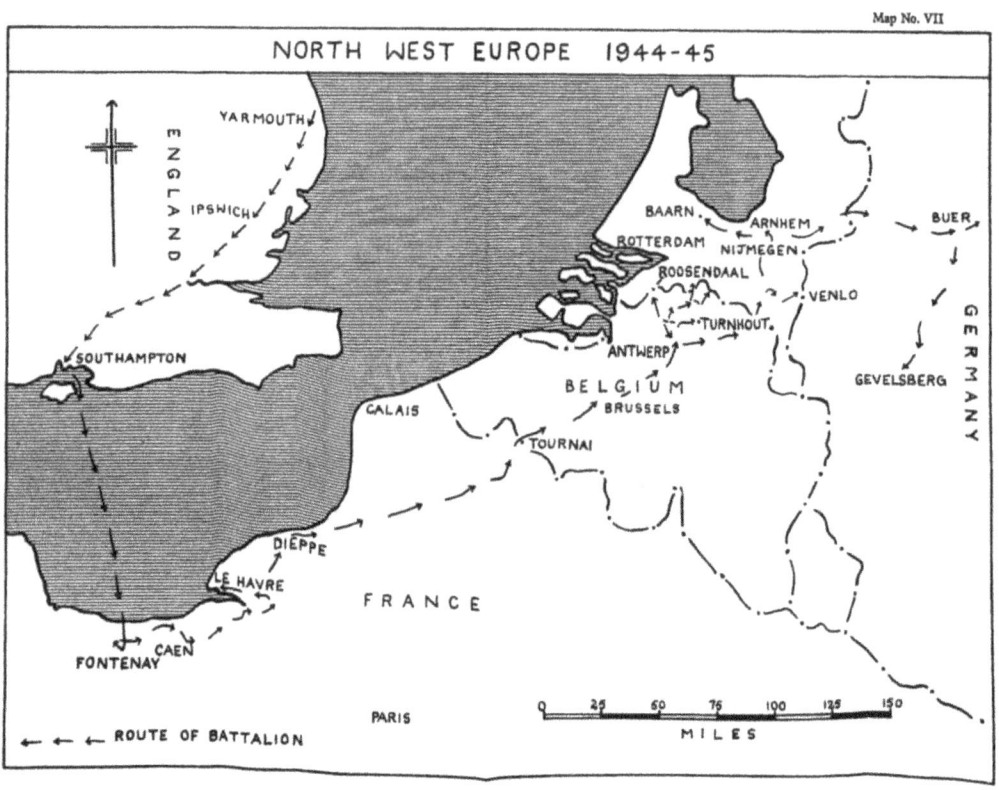

1/7th DWR – Route map, Normandy Campaign
Gold Beach to Gevelsberg, 1944-45.

The Normandy Campaign, two years in the planning, was unleashed on the beaches of Normandy on 6th June, 1944, by the Allied Armies but it wasn't until the 11th June that the 1/6th and 1/7th Battalions of the Duke of Wellington's Regiment landed, moved to Cristot and prepared to go into action in the operations to liberate Caen, tying down the German armoured divisions, which would have been better employed in a counter thrust against the beachhead and the build-up of supplies required for a successful campaign against a powerful enemy.

On 18th June, 1944 (Waterloo Day) the 1/7th Battalion was in action, ordered to attack Point 102, just south of Cristot, at 1400 hrs. However, at 1300hrs, the 1/6th Battalion, in the le Parc de Boislonde, was counter-attacked by elements of 12 SS Panzer Division, which forced the 6th Battalion back. Shorly afterwards, their QM and 100 men arrived in the 7th Battalion area and were quickly absorbed into the Companies, as a counter attack was hastily planned and the objective taken at 1700 hrs.

The Battalion was relieved from the Parc on 23rd Jun and orders were issued the next day for a Divisional attack on Fonteney le Pesnel and Rauray. The Battalion attacked, with artillery and tank support, at 2100 hrs and fought through the night securing most of Fontenay by midnight. At 1530 hrs the Battalion supported a Regimental tank attack on St Nicholas' Ferme, which was taken by 1900 hrs.

As German resistance crumbled due to the efforts of Patton's sweep around their flank and their desperation to escape from the Falaise pocket being closed by the Poles, Canadians and American forces gathering near Chambois, the Battalion followed up and were next in a major action at Vimont on 9th

August, successfully attacking Vimont but suffering a number of casualties, mostly due to anti personnel mines.

The Battalion advanced over the River Vie and attacked St Crispin on 21st August, all objectives taken by 0900hrs, with two prisoners take. On 28th August the Battalion moved to a rest area at Bourdon until 3rd September, when the Battalion crossed the River Seine in amphibious vehicles, the Motor Transport section being delayed by their original bridge being damaged.

On 4th September, British troops met a delegation of Germans and demanded the surrender of Le Havre, which was refused. Planning began for the siege and assault of the port, the Battalion plan was received on 7th September, an RAF bombing raid on the town was carried out the next day, followed by a further air raid directly on the Battalion's objective on the 10th. The Battalions attack was delayed and, on moving off the lead vehicles carrying them towards their objectives were disabled by mines delaying them further, allowing another unit to take over the lead, entering the town first. The objective was then changed to the Rotunda but while on the start line under failing light this was cancelled but the Battalion reached the objective with no opposition by 2130 hrs. the following day the Battalion's position (which was on Henry V's Field of the Cloth of Gold) was cluttered with French civilians searching through their shattered houses the result of the RAF raids. One man, a stretcher bearer, was killed whilst rendering first aid to one of the civilians, the Battalion being involved in reorganizing and mopping up, then left Le Havre for a rest area nearby.

The Battalion move to Belgium commenced on 21st September, where a great welcome was received from the grateful inhabitants, particularly in Brussels. The move through Brussels was led by the Adjutant who had the foresight to ask a local how best to get through the shattered streets. He was advised to follow the No 10 tram, which he did, stopping at each tram stop along the way, of course, but successfully reaching the countryside beyond. The Escaut Canal was crossed without interference from the enemy, reported by locals to be 20 miles away, although a patrol captured 4 prisoners, with more coming in over the following days.

Contact with an alert enemy was regained on the banks of the Turnhout Canal on 25th September. The enemy had been ordered to halt the Allied advance "at all costs" but did not appear to be very well trained. Many of them were killed or wounded by the British firing small arms and mortars over the canal, whilst a great many more were killed in numerous counter attacks once British troops had crossed the waterway at various places. Even so, the greatest loss at this time appears to have been large numbers of DWR cap badges, in Turnhout, all lost to "enemy action". A horrified Regimental Quartermaster Sergeant was probably very suspicious.

The Battalion supported 1 Leicesters to capture the Dépôt de Mendicité, a large prison, workhouse and lunatic asylum complex which the Canadians had tried to seize. A fierce fight from 28th to 29th September left the 49th Division in control of the objective and 10 Polish Armoured Division was clear to pass through with their armour by 1740 hrs. For the next few days the Battalion was tasked with clearing and holding ground taken by the Polish troops, taking a number of prisoners.

On 12th September, the Battalion moved to Poppel where they came under sustained shelling and mortar fire, suffering some casualties. By the 17th October their own patrolling and harassing mortar and artillery fire led to a quieter life and a number of prisoners over the following days.

From 22nd to 24th October Battalion attached to Clarke Force and attacked Schanker, many enemy killed wounded and taken prisoner, only 1 man wounded in B Company. Returned to command of 147th Brigade at 1730, remained in the front line until relived on 27th October.

The same day the Battalion received orders to seize and hold a bridgehead over the anti tank ditch in front of Roosendaal in Holland, was embussed and moved to Nieumoor to carry out a reconnaissance of the obstacles in front of the town. Patrols were sent out to gauge the state of the defences, they were soon in contact with strong German forces, coming under fire from small arms, artillery and self propelled guns from elements of the German 6th Parachute Division and 9th Panzer Division. By 30th October the Battalion had infiltrated the front line under cover of darkness and liberated Roosendaal, where it remained at rest and training until 8th November. The Regimental cap badge can be seen carved on the rear of the 49th Division Memorial in the town square. During the rest of the month reinforcements arrived and rehearsals for the operations to cross the River Maas were conducted.

On 29th November the Battalion crossed the Maas, which had already been crossed by the 50th Division, into an area known as the Island (low lying land between the Maas and the Lower Rhine (still held by the Germans) and occupied the village of Haalderen, coming under machine gun and artillery fire. By 3rd December, German pressure to destroy the Nijmegen Bridge was increasing and, during the early morning of the 4th, a major German attack by German paratroops was mounted to seize Haalderen and destroy the bridge. They were repulsed with heavy casualties and many prisoners were taken in desperate fighting in the village. Relieved on the 6th December and moved to rest area at Bemmel, where close defence of the Nijmegen Bridge occupied the Battalion, as well as at Elst and Wettering, for the winter.

The Battalion returned to Haalderen on 5th March, 1945, the enemy being strongly harassed and attacked until relieved on the 18th, to continue bridge defence at Bemmel. Following Orders for Op Destroyer, the Battalion was back in Haalerderen on 1st April, with a Divisional attack on 4th April successfully pushing the German troops across the Lower Rhine and off 'The Island', with Arnhem finally liberated on 12th April, after the failed airborne assault in September, 1944.

The Germans had withdrawn to the Grebbe Line, Ede-Utrecht, with the 49th Division moving towards Rotterdam. Fighting around the area De Klomp and Ederveen came to a halt, more or less, when a truce was agreed on this front on 28th April. By 8th May, the Battalion was tasked with disarming Germans of the 6th Para Division, while besieged by masses of cheering Dutch civilians. The Battalion took part in a victory parade through Baarn, the salute being taken by the Brigade Commander.

On 25th May the Battalion crossed the border into Germany and arrived at Gevelsberg on 29th May, to be engaged in security duties, with demobilization commencing from 2nd July, 1945.

The Territorials were not reconstituted until 1947, and with only one infantry battalion. The 7th Battalion was selected and reformed at Milnsbridge, commanded by Lt Col S R Hoyle. The 5th Battalion became 578 (Mobile) Heavy Anti Aircraft Regiment RA (5 DWR) TA.

HONOURS AND AWARDS:
1/7th Battalion

ARMITAGE, Jack, 4615780 LCpl (later Sgt), 1/7th DWR.
Mentioned in Despatches, for Normandy, NW Europe, WW2.
Citation not currently available.
LG: 22 Mar 1945, page 1559. Unit WD: MID award, Mar 1945, page 16. Iron Duke: 061-1945, page 100.

BAILEY, R, 5049767 LSgt, 1/7th DWR.
Mentioned in Despatches, for NW Europe, WW2.
Citation not currently available.
LG: 4 Apr 1946, page 1694.

BAKER, Charles Thomas, 14661145 Pte, 1/7th DWR, r. York.
Distinguished Conduct Medal, for Haalderen, Dec 1944, NW Europe, WW2.
"At Haalderen 7566 at 0315 hrs 4th December, 1944, the enemy launched a full scale attack on the positions of 7 DWR in an attempt to secure the Nijmegen bridge. The enemy companies were first sighted and engaged by a Bren gun team of three men. Their fire drew the fire of at least four Spandaus and one man was killed immediately. The enemy then attacked the post with grenades and cup dischargers and isolated it from the rest of the platoon. Pte Baker was one of the two remaining soldiers. Incensed by the death of his comrade, Pte Baker took charge, held his fire so his exact location would not be pin-pointed in the darkness. When the enemy section was within five to ten yards of the position, he opened fire and completely wiped out the enemy force, killing six Germans. He then engaged the remainder of the enemy battalion which had overrun other posts and was advancing along the road and caused further considerable casualties, only ceasing fire when his ammunition was completely exhausted. The enemy then attempted to search for the post, but the men went to ground in the ruins of a house until a counter-attack cut off the enemy who had penetrated deeply into the Battalion position. From then onwards they blocked the road and by noises and shouts prevented the enemy withdrawing. When the enemy force was finally rounded up, Pte Baker and his comrade crawled from their weapon pit still carrying the gun and an armful of empty magazines. Pte Baker's great heroism and initiative when cut off and great determination to deny his post until the last not only resulted in the death of many Germans, but was one of the outstanding factors in the destruction of the enemy attempt on the Nijmegen Bridge. The fact that Pte Baker is only 19 years old makes his feat more remarkable."
LG: 5 Apr 1945, page 1810. Unit WD: MM award, Mar 1945, page 16. Iron Duke: 1945, page 98 & 1983, page 185.

BAX, T (Tris) B, 187058 Capt, 1/7th DWR (att DCLI).
Mentioned in Despatches, NW Europe, WW2.
Citation not currently available. (awarded with DCLI when acting as Intelligence Officer).
LG: 8 Nov 1945, page 5446. Iron Duke: 217-1991, page 117.

BELL, Matthew, 1506652 Cpl, 1/7th DWR.
Military Medal, WW2.
Announcement: "The King has been graciously pleased to approve the following awards in recognition of gallant and distinguished services in North West Europe."
LG: 5 Apr 1945, page 1810.
Citation: "At Haalderen, 7566, on the night 3rd-4th December, this Non-Commissioned Officer was a member of a reconnaissance patrol which was bringing back valuable information about a German position. One man was killed and another wounded on a mine near the enemy position and the Germans opened fire. After making sure no identity had been left on the dead man, LCpl Bell and his patrol commander crawled back through the minefield under fire to deliver their information. Later on the 4th

December, LCpl Bell's courage was further in evidence when a strong enemy attack, designed to destroy the Nijmegen Bridge, developed on his platoon position to which he had returned. Part of LCpl Bell's section was overwhelmed by weight of numbers and LCpl Bell was ordered to withdraw to a new position on the flank where more damage could be inflicted on the enemy. This change of position was hotly contested by the enemy but LCpl Bell alone covered the withdrawal. When the men reached their position LCpl Bell's own withdrawal was followed by the Germans. As he reached his new position LCpl Bell turned and shot the leading German dead at point blank range. LCpl Bell and his men then kept up a determined fire all night against the Germans who finally gave up all attempts to silence the post. The Non-Commissioned Officer's determination to defend his post to the last was a great factor in the demoralisation of the enemy who were crushingly defeated and his personal courage was all the more remarkable as it was his first time in action."
Unit WD: MM award, Mar 1945, page 16. Iron Duke: 1945, page 99.

CANNON, John Rowland, Lt 157323, 1/7th DWR (formerly 157323 WO3 PSM, Lincoln Regt, commissioned into DWR 29 Nov 1940, to Home Guard 20 Apr 1942, returned to Lincolns 1 Apr 1949), r. Boston. Lincs.
Military Cross, for Klomp, NW Europe, WW2.
"On 20th April, 1945, the Battalion was holding the Ede Line (MR 5885) with the enemy on the Grebbe Line 5,000 yards away. A policy of deep daylight patrolling supported by armour was decided upon. Lt Cannon's platoon, supported by a troop of tanks, was ordered to recce the strongpoint at Klomp which was believed to be heavily mined and defended. This necessitated a 4,000 yard advance by road, in daylight in full view of the enemy, before infantry dismounted from the tanks and worked along the hedges into Klomp. Surprise seemed impossible. After a preliminary recce with his orderly, Lt Cannon led his platoon into Klomp and a fierce small arms engagement took place, while the tanks in reserve were engaged by anti tank fire. More than six Germans were killed before the opposition, which was at least company strong, became too heavy. Lt Cannon then reported to the Commanding Officer by 38 set and was ordered to withdraw his platoon and not lose any casualties. This was a most desperate operation as the enemy tried to stalk the platoon through a wood and through houses and outflank it while it was withdrawing. Lt Cannon moved through machine gun and bazooka fire to organise the withdrawal of each section. This was done so successfully and unhurriedly that the platoon and tanks were withdrawn complete, the last two minutes through mortar fire. Lt Cannon was the last to leave the area.
Lt Cannon's patrol produced the complete information required for the attack on the strongpoint which was later cancelled. The success of the operation was due to Lt Cannon's leadership and bravery, which were all the more praiseworthy when it was known that some negotiations for a cease fire were in progress."
LG: 11 Oct 1945, page 5004. MIC: 68/Gen/8091 dated 11 10 1945. Iron Duke: 1945, page 144.

CHAFER, William Kenneth, 894082 Cpl, 1/7th DWR.
Military Medal, Haalderen, NW Europe, WW2.
Announcement: "The King has been graciously pleased to approve the following awards in recognition of gallant and distinguished services in North West Europe."
LG: 12 Jul 1945, page 3595. MIC: 68/Gen9091 dated 12 Jul 1945.
Citation: "At Haalderen (7566) on 2nd April, 1945, on the breakout from the Nijmegen salient, this Non-Commissioned Officer was in charge of a section of No 18 Platoon, D Company, 7th DWR. He was ordered to assault a house which was strongly held by a determined enemy, armed with bazooka, Spandaus and machine pistols. As he closed to the house he was shown up by a white Very light but he managed to get in and clear the house and immediately came under strong enemy fire from a house opposite. A bazooka was fired, wounding himself and two men, and his 2IC was killed clearing the house, which left him with two men. He climbed upstairs alone and engaged the house opposite with Sten gun fire and, in spite of considerable enemy fire, bazooka and Spandau, which was being directed at him, he held on to this house, firing his weapon from behind a thin, broken wall and held on until assistance came nearly half an hour later. This Non-Commissioned Officer's personal disregard for his

own danger in spite of the fact that he himself was wounded was an inspiration to his platoon and was in no small way a contribution to the final success of the action."
LG: 12 Jul 1945, page 3595. Iron Duke: 1945, page 146.

CHARLESWORTH, William Arthur, 4611895 Sgt, 1/7th DWR.
Mentioned in Despatches, NW Europe, WW2.
"The King has been graciously pleased to approve the following be mentioned in recognition of gallant and distinguished services in North West Europe."
LG: 9 Aug 1945, page 4053. MIC: 68/Gen/8103 dated 9 Aug 1945.

CHASE, Stephen Henry, 133397 Capt, RAChD att 1/7th DWR.
Military Cross, NW Europe, WW2.
"On 26th June, 1944, at Fonteney le Pesnel, during an attack on St Nicholas Farm, one Company had been held up in an open field by heavy fire from infantry and two or more Panther and Mark IV German tanks. The Company withdrew slightly, on orders, to the cover of houses and hedges, leaving behind some casualties in the open field. The Rev S H Chase, attached to the Battalion, was forward with the Company. In spite of heavy fire he crawled forward alone into the open field and successfully evacuated a wounded man into the cover of his Company. A short while later, in company with one stretcher bearer, he went forward with a stretcher to bring in any other wounded. He only returned when he had satisfied himself that the remaining casualties were already dead. His devotion to duty and complete disregard for his own safety have been an inspiration to the Battalion."
LG: 19 Oct 1944, page 4788. Unit WD: MC award, Mar 1945, page 16. Iron Duke: 1945, pages 33 & 95; Iron Duke: 1946, page 83; Iron Duke: 1976, page 73.

COLLEY, James William, 4914608 Sgt, 1/7th DWR.
Mentioned in Despatches, NW Europe, WW2.
"The King has been graciously pleased to approve that the following be mentioned in recognition of gallant and distinguished service in North West Europe - 4914608 Sgt J W Colley."
LG: 8 Nov 1945, page 5446. MIC: 68/Gen.8157, dated 9 Nov 1945.

DENTON, Walter Leslie, 137307 Capt, 1/7th DWR, r. Harrogate.
Military Cross, Fonteney & Haalderen, NW Europe, WW2.
"Capt Denton has been Adjutant of the 7th DWR for two years and his strong personality and ability have enabled four commanding officers to take over at short notice without any loss of efficiency to the Battalion. Capt Denton trained the HQ Staff of the Battalion to an outstanding pitch of efficiency so that when the Battalion HQ suffered extreme casualties in the first month after D Day there were always replacements available and the headquarters functioned admirably.
Except for one period of leave, Capt Denton has been in action with the Battalion since D plus 4. His great attention to detail, his calmness and is own astonishing vitality have been of the greatest importance to his commanding officers and to the Company commanders in some very difficult actions. On many occasions, Capt Denton has been on duty more than 24 hours without a break. During the confusion of the battle of Fonteney-le-Pesnil in June, 1944, the Battalion was ordered to carry out a most difficult attack at less than an hour's notice. The Commanding Officer decided to brief one Company himself and sent the Adjutant to find B Company and brief them. This journey was undertaken in the heaviest mortaring experienced in the campaign, but Capt Denton was able to explain his mission, and the attack, vital to this operation, went in successfully and in co-ordination with the other Company. Capt Denton for four more days was the only officer with the Commanding Officer at Battalion Headquarters and acted as Adjutant and Intelligence Officer.
At Haalderen, on December 4th, 1944, Capt Denton organised the defences of Battalion Headquarters with the enemy only 100 yards away and, when the Commanding Officer was away with the Companies and cut off, he organised an attack which drove the enemy out of a house.

On the conclusion of every consolidation, Capt Denton has been among the first round Companies and his calmness and well known personality have been of great moral value to the Battalion, especially when Battalion Headquarters has been the target for artillery. Capt Denton's staff work has been of the highest order and his persistence in attending to detail, which might have made an officer stale over so long a period, has been of enormous assistance to the Battalion as a substitute was never available. Capt Denton's devotion to duty has been outstanding and his own constant disregard for his own safety when he could have sheltered in the command post has won him a high place in the affections of the men."
LG: 24 Jan 1946, page 638. MC: 68/Gen/8212. Iron Duke: 1946, pages 81, 91. Iron Duke: 221-1993, page 70.

DRIVER, George Francis, 184148 Lt (later Capt), 1/7th DWR.
Mentioned in Despatches, NW Europe, WW2.
"The King has been graciously pleased to approve that the following be mentioned in recognition of gallant and distinguished service in North West Europe."
LG: 22 Mar 1945, page 1559. Unit WD: MID award, Mar 1945, page 16. MIC: 68/Gen/8002, dated 22 Mar 1945.

DRIVER, John Edward, 96766 Maj, 1/7th DWR (formerly Pte, Loyal Regt, commissioned 1939, later 30 (DWR) Bn Home Guard & 5/7th DWR).
Mentioned in Despatches, NW Europe, WW2.
Citation not currently available.
LG: 4 Apr 1946, page 1694. MIC: 68/Gen/8212, dated 4 Apr 19146. Iron Duke: 164-1974, page 41.
Efficiency Decoration (Territorial).
"The King has been graciously pleased to confer the Efficiency Decoration (Territorial) upon the following Officers."
LG: 21 Apr 1950, page 1937.
Member, the Most Excellent Order of the British Empire;
"The Queen has been graciously pleased to give orders for the following promotions in, and appointments to, the Most Excellent Order of the British Empire. To be ordinary Members of the Military Division of the said Most Excellent Order."
LG: 31 Dec 1960, page 8895.
Efficiency Decoration (Territorial).
"The Queen has been graciously pleased to confer the award of the 1st Clasp to the Territorial Efficiency Decoration upon the following Officers."
LG: 17 Jan 1961, page 360. Iron Duke: 163-1973, page 116; 164-1974, page41.

DUNCAN, Robert Anthony, 289289 Lt, 1/7th DWR (from 147th Regt RAC).
Legion d'Honneur, NW Europe, WW2.
Chevalier en l'Ordre National de la Légion d'Honneur.
"I offer you my warmest congratulations on this high honour in recognition of your acknowledged military engagement and your steadfast involvement in the Liberation of France during the Second World War."
Awarded in 2014 by French President, presented by the French Ambassador in Bangkok, Thailand, on 29 Feb 2016.

DYSON, Herbert, 4616989 Pte, 1/7th DWR.
CO's Certificate, North West Europe, WW2.

ELSON, David, 4615004 Pte, 1/7th DWR.
Mentioned in Despatches, NW Europe, WW2.
"The King has been graciously pleased to approve that the following be mentioned in recognition of gallant and distinguished services in North West Europe."

LG: 4 Apr 1946, page 1694. MIC: 68/Gen, 8212, dated 4 Apr 1946.

EVANS, Kenneth Morgan, 261636 Lt, 1/7th DWR (formerly King's Regt), r. Liverpool.
Military Cross, for Haalderen, NW Europe, WW2.
"Lt Evans was in command of 18 platoon, the left forward platoon of D Company, at Haalderen, 7566, on the night of 3rd - 4th December. At 2000 hrs he led a night patrol which discovered a new enemy position. During his return one man was killed and another wounded on an enemy minefield but, with extreme courage and coolness under enemy fire, he found a route back for the rest of his patrol and reached his Company HQ with valuable information and without further casualties. At 0300 hrs next morning a strong enemy Company Group assaulted Lt Evans' platoon as part of an attack to seize Haalderen and, eventually, the Nijmegen Bridge, and two sections were finally overwhelmed. Lt Evan's platoon HQ and one section post continued to deny their position to the enemy throughout the night and finally the Germans gave up all attempts to silence the post. At 0700 hrs Lt Evans was joined by a relieving platoon which sealed off the penetration with the result that 110 POW were taken inside the Battalion area. When the position was finally cleared, Lt Evans was found in a most aggressive spirit with six dead enemy strewn outside his post, but with all his ammunition expended. Lt Evans' great acts of courage on this night were an inspiring example to his men (the majority of whom had just arrived on draft from the United Kingdom) and who fought off superior numbers long enough to give the Battalion warning of the attack. This Officer's successful determination to hold his post at all costs was the principal act in the Battalion's defeat of the enemy attack on Haalderen, the loss of which would most seriously have endangered the Nijmegen Bridge."
LG: 5 Apr 1945, page 1809. Unit WD: MC award, 24 Dec 1944; roll of awards, 13 Mar 1945. Iron Duke: 061-1945, page 96.

FANCOURT, Gerard Vivien, 104371 Maj, 1/7th DWR (from E Yorks Regt), r. Bradford.
Military Cross, Haalderen, NW Europe, WW2.
"The King has been graciously pleased to approve the following awards in recognition of gallant and distinguished services in North West Europe."
LG: 12 Jul 1945, page 3592.
"At Haalderen (7566) on 2nd April, 1945, Major Fancourt was in command of C Company which had the important task of opening up the heavily mined main axis for the subsequent breakout of the Nijmegen Salient. The enemy positions facing this Company were in strong houses and had been occupied for six months. The ground was known to be heavily mined and only one approach gave any chance of success without heavy casualties on mines - that down the main road - which was guarded by several Spandaus and a known DF position. Major Fancourt's plan called for the leapfrogging of his three platoons down 2,000 yards advance to his objective - a most skilful operation in the half-light with no possibility of manoeuvre because of the mines. The first objective was taken after a short struggle. As Major Fancourt was with the leading platoon he was able to guide the succeeding platoon on to its next objective. Heavy cross-fire then broke out from further strongpoints in the left-hand Company objective, almost abreast of Major Fancourt's position. Major Fancourt, despite the casualties to his Company through the enemy fire, decided to push on to his next objective, which was 1,000 yards beyond, with the risk of being isolated. He then led his Company through the fire and quickly secured his objective. His quick decisions to maintain his objective ultimately helped the Company on his left, drove another enemy post into immediate surrender and allowed the following RE to clear the mines from the road far quicker than might have been expected. Major Fancourt's skilful planning and his own personal calm in a most difficult operation in an enemy minefield was a great example to his Company, which was so determined to advance that it succeeded in securing the follow-up Battalion's objective.
Iron Duke: 1945, page 144. Iron Duke: 1946, page 83. Iron Duke: 260-2006, page 44.

FISHER, G O, 5049810 Sgt, 1/7th DWR.
French Croix de Guerre avec Bronze Star, WW2.
Citation not currently available.

LG: Not Known. Barclay History, page 347. Battalion Journal, page 48.

FLETCHER, John William, 14661166 Cpl, 1/7th DWR.
Commanding Officer's Certificate, for Normandy, NW Europe, WW2.
Battalion Journal, Victory Edition, 1945.

HALL, Donald Cecil, 1438009 Pte, 1/7th DWR (att 7 DWR from RASC).
Mentioned in Despatches, for NW Europe, WW2.
Citation not currently available.
LG: 22 Mar 1945, page 1564. Iron Duke: 262-2007, page 47.

HAMILTON, Charles Denis, 90293 Lt Col, 1/7th DWR (from 8 DLI).
Distinguished Service Order, for Haalderen, NW Europe, WW2.
Announcement: "The King has been graciously pleased to approve the following awards in recognition of gallant service in North West Europe."
LG: 5 Apr 1945, page 1809.
Citation: "At about 0300 hrs on 4th December, 1944, approximately one battalion of German parachute infantry suddenly attacked [1/7th] DWR at Haalderen on a narrow front. Owing to the weight of the attack the forward defences were penetrated and approximately a company of infantry reached the centre of the Battalion position, while some reached within 200 yards of Battalion HQ. Lt Col Hamilton, who was acting CO of the Battalion, quickly regained control of the situation. He personally organised two stops near Battalion HQ with his only reserves, the carrier platoon and personnel of Battalion HQ. It was extremely difficult to find out the exact situation and confused fighting was going on all over the Battalion area and round Battalion HQ between small parties of the DWR and the enemy.

Lt Col Hamilton then ordered the perimeter Companies to hold firm, arranged for a counter-attack by the dismounted carrier personnel to eject the enemy from the houses round the central cross roads of the position; and another from a flank Company to close the gap through which the enemy had penetrated. These arrangements were all successful. The position then was that the enemy were bottled up inside the Battalion area, while any reserves the enemy had were pinned down by heavy and accurate DF fire brought down by artillery, heavy mortar and MGs.

As soon as dawn broke, Lt Col Hamilton carried out a further recce with the commander of a Company of another unit which had been sent to his assistance; he gave instructions to this Company to counter-attack the bulk of the enemy. As soon as this got under way, Spandau fire broke out from a house near Battalion HQ. Lt Col Hamilton immediately returned to organise the destruction of this party, which was soon carried out. This post contained six Spandaus.

Within eight hours of the first attack the enemy's very determined attempt to capture the village of Haalderen, as a first step to the destruction of the Nijmegen bridge, had been defeated with the loss to him of fifty killed, one hundred and ten POWs and an unknown number of killed and wounded by DF fire outside the Battalion area.

This success at the cost of very light casualties to his own men was very largely due to Lt Col Hamilton's leadership. Throughout a very confused action he had maintained control over the situation and calmly made his arrangements for the destruction of the enemy. His recces during the night and after first light were carried out in considerable personal danger, and his coolness at all times was an inspiration to his Battalion. It was under his direction that the action was soon brought to a highly successful conclusion."
Unit WD: DSO award, 24 Dec 1945. Iron Duke: 1944, page 45, Iron Duke: 1945 page 95. Iron Duke: 1946, page 83.
Knight Bachelor, for services to the Arts.
"The Queen has been graciously pleased to signify her intention of conferring the honour of knighthood upon the undermentioned, for services to the Arts."
LG: 1 Jan 1976, page 2.

"The Queen was pleased on Tuesday 17th February, 1976, at Buckingham Palace, to confer the Honour of Knighthood upon Sir Charles Dennis Hamilton DSO TD. Her Majesty's approval of these knighthoods was signified on 1st January, 1976."
LG: Not Known. Iron Duke: 1975, page 89. Iron Duke: 207-1988, page 10.

HAWKINS, William Leslie, 1078129 LCpl, 1/7th DWR.
Military Medal, Haalderen, NW Europe, WW2.
"At Haalderen (7566) at 0300 hrs on 4th December, 1944, the Germans launched a strong attack on the 7 DWR positions with the intention of demolishing the Nijmegen Bridge. Two enemy Companies penetrated the outer defences and were advancing across the flank of 13 platoon, C Company, which opened fire and caused considerable casualties. The Germans then detached a force to silence the platoon which was attacked by the fire of bazookas, Spandaus, grenades and light mortars. After a number of men had been killed and wounded, LCpl Hawkins volunteered to crawl out of the back of the house the platoon was occupying and counter attack with his 2inch mortar. Although the ground around was completely open and mostly under flood, LCpl Hawkins worked his way around the house until he could see the Germans, who were firing at the house from a distance of 50 yards. LCpl Hawkins fired his mortar at a low angle at point blank range and, with his first shot, silenced one Spandau. When he had fired all the ammunition he could carry, 12 rounds, LCpl Hawkins withdrew and the enemy ceased their fire. The brilliant stand of his platoon completely demoralised the enemy, 110 of whom were taken prisoner within 100 yards of the platoon. It was only through this newly appointed junior Non-Commissioned Officer's initiative and supreme courage in taking on what seemed a suicide task that the platoon was able to continue its amazing resistance in face of greatly superior numbers."
LG: 5 Apr 1945, page 1810. MIC: 68/Gen/8039, dated 5 Apr 1945. Unit WD: MM award, 31 Mar 1945, page 16. Iron Duke: 1945, page 98.

HIGGINBOTTOM, Harry, 4616295 Sgt, 1/7th DWR.
Mentioned in Despatches, for Normandy, NW Europe, WW2.
"The King has been graciously pleased to approve that the following be mentioned in recognition of gallant and distinguished services in North West Europe."
LG: 22 Mar 1945, page 1559. Unit WD: MID award, Mar 1945, page 16.

HIGGS, L, 5049828 Sgt, 1/7th DWR, r. Hednesford.
Military Medal, for Poppel, NW Europe, WW2.
"In October, 1944, on the Dutch-Belgian frontier, north of Poppel, this Non-Commissioned Officer's Company was holding a defensive position in thickly wooded country in very close contact with the enemy to the north and east. On 17th October, orders were given for an identification to be obtained on this front. In consequence, Sgt Higgs was detailed as leader of a fighting patrol to obtain these identifications. The enemy, from his position in the thick woods, had close and excellent observation of our movements. Sgt Higgs, with great skill, led his patrol into the woods and immediately by surprise captured two sentries. The enemy reacted quickly and attempted to cut off the fighting patrol but Sgt Higgs withdrew his patrol with the prisoners without loss. A further patrol was necessary to penetrate deeper into the woods, in conjunction with a platoon attack on the right. Sgt Higgs immediately volunteered and, by skilful scoutcraft, captured two more prisoners. He continued deeper into the woods and located the enemy platoon position, which was attacked. Once again he was attacked by the enemy who tried to cut off his patrol. Five enemy were killed and Sgt Higgs, without loss again and with two prisoners, succeeded in withdrawing to his Company area. The great personal courage of the Non-Commissioned Officer and his excellent handling of his patrol accounted for five enemy killed and four prisoners without loss to his patrol. The information obtained was of great value for identification purposes and also for the later success of a platoon attack on the enemy post in the depths of the forest."
LG: 1 Mar 1945, page 1182. Unit WD: MM award, 15 Dec 1944 & Mar 1945, page 16. Iron Duke: 1945, pages 20, 33 & 98.

HILL, Charles Herbert, 117116 Capt, 1/7th DWR, r. Battersea.
Commander-in-Chief's Certificate, for Gallantry, N W Europe, WW2.
Unit WD: C-in-C's Cert award, 15 Dec 1944 & Mar 1945, page 16.

HODGE, William Arthur, 285989 Lt, 1/7th DWR (from Royal Armoured Corps), r. Babington.
Military Cross, for Haalderen, NW Europe, WW2.
Announcement: "The King has been graciously pleased to approve the following awards in recognition of gallant and distinguished services in North West Europe."
LG: 5 Apr 1945, page 1809. MIC: 68/Gen/8039, dated 5 Apr 1945.
Citation: "At Haalderen, 7766, at 0315 hrs on 4th December, 1944, an enemy battalion launched an attack on the 7th DWR position with the intention of demolishing the Nijmegen Bridge. One Company penetrated as far as the centre of the Battalion position and the situation seemed critical. The Commanding Officer ordered Lt Hodge, who was in temporary command of the carrier platoon, to place a stop of two carrier sections in the centre of the village and, with the remainder of the platoon to counter-attack another enemy force about forty strong which was advancing on Battalion HQ. The situation at this time was most confused with Battalion HQ cut off from the rest of the Battalion. However, all communications were working and if the Battalion HQ could be safeguarded it seemed possible to launch a counter-attack at dawn. Lt Hodge immediately set off through the flooded orchard in the darkness to counter-attack a school 150 yards away from Battalion HQ. Little information was available and at least three Spandaus were firing from the school. Under the cover of the fire from three Bren guns, Lt Hodge led his small force of 12 men against the school, planning to throw two 77 Grenades to stop the covering fire as he went in with the assault. Both grenades failed to explode so Lt Hodge dashed into the school throwing 36 Grenades into the first room.
His bold decision resulted in the enemy force being partly wiped out, not without loss to the assault group. The remaining Germans withdrew to another house and defied further attempts at elimination. Lt Hodge, realising that the information about the school's recapture was vital and also wishing to bring up flamethrowers or an anti tank gun against the enemy then crawled 100 yards through the German positions to his Company Commander who phoned Battalion HQ, enabling the counter-attack to be launched at dawn against the main enemy force. Lt Hodge's personal leadership, outstanding courage and remarkable speed in counter-attacking without any information undoubtedly stopped the German penetration and thus allowed the Commanding Officer to plan two counter-attacks which completely wiped out the enemy forces and ensured the security of the Nijmegen Bridge.
Unit WD: MC award, Mar 1945, page 16. Iron Duke: 1945, page 96.

HOLLINGSWORTH, Wesley, 4543765 Sgt, 1/7th DWR.
Mentioned in Despatches, NW Europe, WW2.
Citation not currently available.
LG: 10 May 1945, page 2462. Unit WD: MID award, 27 May 1945.

HORNE, John (Jackie) Ernest, CSM, 1/7th DWR
(also 1/6th DWR and DWR OCA), r. Huddersfield.
Member, the Most Excellent Order of the British Empire.
"The Queen has been graciously pleased, on the occasion of the celebration of Her Majesty's Birthday, to give orders for the following promotions in, and appointments to, the Most Excellent Order of the British Empire (Civil Division). To be Ordinary Members of the Civil Division of the said Most Excellent Order."
LG: 12 Jun 1976, page 3028. Iron Duke: 1976, page 44. Iron Duke: 214-1990, page 114. Iron Duke: 218-1992, page 34.

HORNE, Walter, 333686 Lt, 1/7th DWR
(formerly 4616429 Sgt Walter Horne, DWR), r. Crook, Co Durham.
Military Cross, for Roosendaal, NW Europe, WW2.

Announcement: "The King has been graciously pleased to approve the following awards in recognition of gallant and distinguished services in North West Europe."
LG: 1 Mar 1945, page 1176.
Citation: "On 30th October, 1944, this Officer's platoon was engaged with the enemy who were holding a portion of the anti-tank ditch defences north of Telberg, near Roosendaal. The approaches to the enemy defences were over bare, open fields and throughout the day efforts to approach nearer to the ditch were subject to observed enemy small arms, mortar and artillery fire. As part of larger operations, 2Lt Horne's platoon was ordered to gain a footing by night as near the ditch as possible to protect the right flank and keep the enemy engaged. An enemy minefield was suspected as covering the enemy position. That night, in bright moonlight, 2nd Lt Horne led his platoon across open fields, located, and found a passage through, the minefield and passed his platoon through to their objective. On arrival near the objective it was found to be held by an enemy post. This was captured. The platoon was subjected to close and heavy fire from at least four MGs and one 2cm mortar from a dug-in enemy platoon 30 to 40 yards distant on the ditch defences. 2Lt Horne ordered his platoon to withdraw from such an exposed position to another position a short distance back which was less exposed. Under conditions of bright moonlight, noise and the enemy minefield, this was a hazardous operation. With great courage patience and skill, 2Lt Horne conducted the withdrawal personally, passing through the minefield twice and exposing himself to heavy fire at short range in the moonlight. With the aid of 77 Grenades he covered his sections out and withdrew every man to the new positions. Lt Horne, by his actions, showed great courage under fire, skill and patient leadership and achieved with conspicuous success his task of fully engaging the enemy's attention during a difficult and anxious period of the operations."
LG: 1 Mar 1945, page 1176. Unit WD, MC award, 15 Dec 1944. Unit WD: MC award, Mar 1945, page 16. ID, 1945, pages 20, 33 & 96, Iron Duke: 1979, page 138.

HOUNSFIELD, Kenneth Denholm, 258669 Lt, 1/7th DWR, r. Thurstonland.
Mentioned in Despatches, NW Europe, WW2.
"The King has been graciously pleased to approve that the following be mentioned in recognition of gallant and distinguished service in North West Europe."
LG: 22 Mar 1945, page 1559. MIC: 68/Gen/8002, dated 22 Mar 1945.

ILLINGWORTH, John Knox, 160871 Capt, 1/7th DWR, r. Romily, Stockport.
Military Cross, for Arnhem, NW Europe, WW2.
"On 17th April, as part of the operation to break out of Arnhem (7478) 7th DWR were ordered to pursue the enemy to the Grebbe Line and, if possible, trap an enemy force before it could escape. The carrier platoon, commanded by Capt Illingworth, led the advance as mobile troops. Through Capt Illingworth's boldness and complete mastery of his platoon, a distance of eight miles through three villages, a large forest and along roads which were mined and blocked, necessitating detours, was covered by the Battalion in two hours, several enemy being killed and captured. That this operation was a complete success was due entirely to Capt Illingworth's great leadership and taking chances because of the stakes involved.
After Wageningen had been captured, Capt Illingworth was ordered to patrol to Renkum to locate the enemy on the Grebbe Line itself. Because of the uncertainty of mines, Capt Illingworth chose to lead a patrol of four carrier crews. After a mile his carrier was blown up and Capt Illingworth was thrown 20 yards on to his head, the carrier falling on one side and trapping two men. Although wounded in the head and most severely shaken, Capt Illingworth organised the rescue of the wounded and salvaged the equipment. Still bleeding most profusely, Capt Illingworth then started out on foot with his remaining men to continue the patrol and refused to turn back. It finally required a personal order from the Commanding Officer before he returned and had his wounds treated at the RAP. Even then, Capt Illingworth declined to be evacuated, despite several stitches in his head and after a week's rest was back at duty. Capt Illingworth's bravery and calm was of the highest order on this day and, fired by example, his platoon, which lost its remaining Officer a few minutes after Capt Illingworth's accident, continued to patrol most vigorously that day and night."

LG: 11 Oct 1945, page 5004. MIC: 68/Gen/8091, dated 11 Oct 1943. Iron Duke: 1945, page 145.
French Croix de Guerre avec Gilt Star, WW2.
Citation not currently available.
LG: Not Known. Medals: held in the National Army Museum, 1994.

JONES, Frank William, 4807727 Pte, 1/7th DWR.
Commander-in-Chief's Certificate, for Normandy, NW Europe, WW2
"For gallantry."
Battalion Journal, Victory Edition, 1945, page 35.

KALAHAR, Albert John, 4624378 Pte, 1/7th DWR, r. Leicester.
Military Medal, for Mendicite, Sep 1945, NW Europe, WW2.
Announcement: "The King has been graciously pleased to approve the following awards in recognition of gallant and distinguished services in North West Europe."
LG: 1 Mar 1945, page 1182. MIC: 68/Gen/8023, dated 1 Mar 1945.
Citation: "On 28th September, 1944, during an attack on the Depot de Mendicite (9710) the platoon, in which Pte Kalahar was a No 1 Bren gunner, was given orders to work round the right flank of a strongly held farmhouse in order to take up a position as fire platoon for an attack by the remainder of the Company, which was under heavy fire from front and flank. On the platoon approaching its allotted fire positions, the section to which Pte Kalahar belonged found it necessary, because of the enemy fire, to be supported on to its fire position by the Bren. This support drew concentrated fire on to Pte Kalahar. Without orders, he moved, still under fire, to an alternative position. During this move he was knocked from his gun by a bullet wound to his shoulder. He crawled back to his gun, got into position and continued to fire until the remainder of his section and platoon were in position. Throughout this period Pte Kalahar was under fire and he refused to leave his post until, much later, he was given a direct order by his platoon commander to leave his gun.
Pte Kalahar's behaviour, apart from being an example of bravery and gallantry, was instrumental in the successful accomplishment of his platoon's task."
LG: 1 Mar 1945, page 1182. Unit WD: MM award, Mar 1945, page 16. Iron Duke: 1945, pages 18, 33 & 99.

KAVANAGH, Aveling Barry Martin, Maj 95620, 1/7th DWR, later 1 DWR, r. Kensington.
Military Cross, Roosendaal, NW Europe, WW2.
Announcement: "The King has been graciously pleased to approve the following awards in recognition of gallant and distinguished services in North West Europe."
LG: 12 Apr 1945, page 1942.
Citation: "On 30th October, 1944, this Officer's Company was engaging the enemy, holding a sector of the anti-tank ditch defences on the perimeter of Roosendaal (D2321). The approaches to the ditch were over bare, open ground and, throughout the day, efforts to close the ditch resulted in heavy casualties from observed fire of small arms, mortars, artillery and two SP guns which repeatedly shelled the Company. Major Kavanagh's Company was given the important and difficult task of forcing the ditch soon after darkness to protect the flank of a larger operation later, thus drawing off enemy reserves. The first platoon met an enemy minefield which necessitated a complete change of plan and direction. Major Kavanagh swiftly issued these fresh orders and another platoon led off in another direction. In bright moonlight this platoon, together with major Kavanagh's command party, advanced across the fields, found a passage through the minefields and arrived on the objective where a pill box and its garrison on the anti tank ditch were captured. Because of the urgency and the fact that orders had been given so quickly without detailed reconnaissance, Major Kavanagh went back himself for the rest of the Company. During the consolidation the Company was subjected to heavy MG fire from close range and ten minutes later by a considerable heavy calibre artillery concentration in which several men were killed and wounded in the open. Due to Major Kavanagh's remarkable calmness and personal courage, the Company maintained its position and casualties were successfully evacuated. Orders were then received

from Battalion Headquarters that, as the ditch had been forced in strength elsewhere, its task was complete and the Company should be withdrawn. This difficult undertaking under close fire and return through an unmarked gap in a minefield was accomplished through Major Kavanagh's ceaseless example and his cool disregard of all enemy fire. Eventually, the Company returned to its start line, where it was reorganised and took part, three hours later, in the final storming, at 5.00 am, of the inner defences of Roosendaal, in which the Company took several prisoners and broke the enemy resistance. All these operations were carried out at short notice because of the necessity to force the town before the enemy reinforcements could arrive. That the two attacks by 7th DWR this night were so successful was in no small measure due to the remarkable tenacity of D Company who, though tired after fourteen days of ceaseless fighting, were inspired by the patience, leadership, skill in planning and complete disregard of personal safety of Major Kavanagh."

LG: 12 Apr 1945, page 1942. MIC: 68/Gen/8039, dated 12 Apr 1945. Unit WD: MC award, 31 Mar 1945, page 16. Iron Duke: 1945, page 97.

Bar to MC, Korea, 1953.

Announcement: The Queen has been graciously pleased to approve the following awards in recognition of gallant and distinguished services in Korea during the period 1st to 27th July, 1953.

LG: 8 Dec 1953, page 6653. ID 1954, page 26.

Citation: For nine months Major Kavanagh has commanded a rifle Company with success. Under his guidance the Company reached a high standard of morale and fighting efficiency.

For many days before the Chinese attack on the Hook position, his Company was subjected to very heavy shelling and repeated probing by enemy fighting patrols. Although often exposed to danger, he moved freely around his position, encouraging his men, tending to the evacuation of the wounded and supervising the building of his defences. During the main attack, which was accompanied by intense artillery and mortar fire, the Company, under Major Kavanagh's leadership fought with great tenacity and bravery. Throughout the battle, Major Kavanagh directed the fire of his own and other supporting weapons with superb skill and boldness. For displaying the highest qualities of leadership, sense of duty and personal courage in this action and throughout the Korean campaign, Major Kavanagh has maintained the highest traditions of the British Army."

Mentioned in Despatches, WW2.

Citation not currently available.

LG: 22 Mar 1945, page 1559. Unit WD: MID award, 31 Mar 1945, page 16.

Officer, the Most Excellent Order of the British Empire,

"The Queen has been graciously pleased, on the occasion of the celebration of Her Majesty's Birthday, to give orders for the following promotions in, and appointments to, the Most Excellent Order of the British Empire. To be ordinary Officers of the Military Division of the said Most Excellent Order."

LG: 12 Jun 1965, page 5476. Iron Duke: 224-1994, page 37.

KILNER, Bernard Major, 74995 Maj, 1/7th DWR (later 1 DWR, Korea).

Mentioned in Despatches, Normandy, NW Europe, WW2

"The King has been graciously pleased to approve the following be mentioned in recognition of gallant and distinguished services in North West Europe - Capt B M Kilner (74995).

LG: 4 Apr 1946, page 1694. Iron Duke: 189-1982, pages 35 & 65.

Efficiency Medal (Territorial).

"The following Officers are awarded the Efficiency Medal (Territorial)."

LG: 23 Jan 1947, page 443.

Efficiency Decoration (Territorial).

"The King has been graciously pleased to confer the Efficiency Decoration (Territorial) upon the following Officers."

LG: 21 Apr 1950, page 1937. Iron Duke: 189-1982, page 65.

KILNER, Roy, 73544 Maj, 1/7th DWR (att 82nd West African Div Recce).

Military Cross, Burma, WW2.

"The King has been graciously pleased to approve the following awards in recognition of gallant and distinguished services in Burma."
LG: 7 Feb 1946, page 847. MIC: 68/Gen/8111, dated 7 Feb 1946.
Mentioned in Despatches, Burma, WW2.
"The King has been graciously pleased to approve that the following be mentioned in recognition of gallant and distinguished services in Burma - Major (temp) R Kilner MC (73544)."
LG:9 May 1946, page 2214. MIC: 68/Gen/8213 dated 9 May 1946.

KIRKHAM, Frank, 14389985 Cpl, 1/7th DWR.
CO's North West Europe Certificate, N W Europe, WW2.
Unit Journal, Victory Edition, 1945.

LAPPIN, John, 247723 Lt (later Capt), 1/7th DWR
(From RA & 6 R Berks Regt), r. Henley on Thames.
Military Cross, for Fontenay, NW Europe, WW2.
"On 13th July, 1944, this Officer was in command of a fighting patrol of six Other Ranks when contact was made with an enemy platoon in a prepared position near Tessel Bretteville, Normandy. Led by Lt Lappin, the patrol attacked the enemy position and killed several men, but was forced to withdraw to some buildings approximately 300 yards away, when the enemy opened up on both flanks with automatic weapons and counter-attacked with two sections. In order to obtain identification his Company Commander ordered him to attack the enemy position again with the aid of artillery and mortar support. Lt Lappin personally corrected the registration of the artillery and mortar targets, running forward under fire to observe the shots and returning to give corrections over a telephone installed in the buildings to which he had withdrawn. When the second attack commenced he led his patrol within twenty yard of the artillery concentration and when it lifted he rushed over the first line of the enemy defences and succeeded in killing five more of the enemy. Again compelled to withdraw owing to superior enemy firepower and counter-attack, he personally covered the withdrawal of his patrol without loss of casualties. His personal courage and leadership were an inspiration to his men and resulted in heavy loss to the enemy."
LG: 19 Oct 1944, page 4786. Unit WD: MC award, Mar 1945, page 16. Iron Duke: 1945, pages 33 & 96. Iron Duke: 1979 p 137, Iron Duke: 229-1995 p 118, Iron Duke: 1996 p 86. Medals: held in Bankfield Museum.

LAWTON, Eric, 4616045 Sgt (later CSM), 1/7th DWR.
Mentioned in Despatches, NW Europe, WW2.
"The King has been graciously pleased to approve that the following be mentioned in recognition of gallant and distinguished services in North West Europe."
LG: 4 Apr 1946, page 1694. MIC: 68/Gen/8212, dated 4 Apr 1946.

LE CORNU, John, 333688 Lt, 1/7th DWR, (formerly 4546284 Sgt).
Military Cross, for Haalderen, NW Europe, WW2.
"The King has been graciously pleased to approve the following awards in recognition of gallant and distinguished services in North West Europe.
LG: 5 Apr 1945, page 1809. MIC: 68/Gen/8039, NW Eur list 99, dated 5 Apr1945.
"2nd Lt Le Cornu was in command of 13 Pl, the reserve of C Company, at Haalderen when, at 0300 hrs on 4th Dec, an enemy company broke into the defences and was advancing towards the centre of the Bn area. Lt Le Cornu's post immediately engaged the enemy at 80 yards range with small arms fire and the attackers scattered. Eighteen enemy, including the company commander and two officers, being found dead here next morning. The enemy then used bazookas and Spandaus which scored direct hits, killing three of the garrison, in a vain attempt to silence the position. Though by this time 2Lt Le Cornu was cut off, he resisted throughout and when, two hours later, the enemy was driven back from the village 2Lt Le Cornu and his post caused further great casualties. When he was finally relieved, his first thought was to

replenish the empty magazines and follow up the enemy, who were finally trapped and 110 taken prisoner. 2Lt le Cornu's alertness, personal courage and determination to hold his post to the last was an outstanding factor in the smashing defeat of the strong German attempt to penetrate the Nijmegen bridge defences."
Unit WD: MC award, 31 Mar 1945, page 16. Iron Duke: 1945, page 97. Iron Duke: 256-2004, page 167.

LE MESSURIER, Hugh Shelley, 112871 Capt (later Lt Col), 1/7th DWR, also 1 DWR.
Mentioned in Despatches, NW Europe, WW2.
"The King has been graciously pleased to approve the following be mentioned in recognition of gallant and distinguished services in North West Europe."
LG: 4 Apr 1946, page 1694. MIC: 68/Gen/8212, dated 4 Apr 1946.
Mentioned in Despatches, Korea, 1953.
"The Queen has been graciously pleased to approve the following be mentioned in recognition of gallant and distinguished services in Korea during the period 1st to 27th July, 1953."
LG: 8 Dec 1953, page 6654. Iron Duke: 1954, page 69.
Legion d'Honneur, NW Europe, WW2.
"112871 Lt Col Hugh Le Messurier was commissioned into the Duke of Wellington's Regiment on 31st December, 1939, just after the outbreak of the second world war; he served in NW Europe with 1/7th Battalion DWR (TA) before going on to complete a full regular career which saw him serve around the world in Egypt, Palestine, Sudan, Bermuda, Korea, Gibraltar, Aden, Rhodesia, Kenya, Cyprus, Northern Ireland, Yugoslavia and of course elsewhere in the UK. He was twice Mentioned in Dispatches - in NW Europe and Korea.
He served in the usual regimental posts of Subaltern, Coy 2IC, Adjt, and Coy Comd (twice) and Battalion 2IC. He held Staff Capt and GSO2 appointments and commanded the Yorkshire Bde Depot in Strensall. He finally left regular service in 1970 after a 30-year career but went on to run the Catterick Training Centre for a further 15 years before finally retiring in 1985."
In 2014, on the 70th Anniversary of D-Day, President Hollande of France announced that surviving veterans would receive the award in recognition of their contribution to the liberation of France:
"I have the pleasure of informing you that the President of the Republic has appointed you to the rank of: Chevalier en l'Ordre National de la Légion d'Honneur.
I offer you my warmest congratulations on this high honour in recognition of your acknowledged military engagement and your steadfast involvement in the Liberation of France during the Second World War."
Awarded in 2014; presented by Colonel G Kilburn, late DWR, on behalf of the French Ambassador, in Apr 2016. Iron Duke: 285-2018, page 37.

LEVY, Alfred, 4622731 Pte. 1/7th DWR.
CO's North West Europe Certificate, For Normandy, NW Europe.
Battalion Journal, Victory Edition, 1945.

LILLEY, Wilfred, 4609003 Pte, 1/7th DWR
Commanding Officer's North West Europe Certificate, for Normandy, France, WW2.
Battalion Journal, Victory Edition, 1945.

LORD, George, 14322363, 1/7th DWR (also KOSB), r. Rochdale.
Military Medal, for Normandy campaign, NW Europe, WW2.
"The King has been graciously pleased to approve the following awards in recognition of gallant and distinguished services in North West Europe."
LG: 24 Jan 1946, page 644.

LOWE, Arthur, 5048347 Pte, 1/7th DWR.
CO's North West Europe Certificate, for Normandy campaign, WW2.

Battalion Journal, Victory Edition, 1945.

LUGG, Edwin Arthur, 14204938 Sgt, 1/7th DWR.
CO's Certificate North West Europe, for Normandy campaign, WW2.
Battalion Journal, Victory Edition, 1945.

LYON, Frank Matthew, 345381 Lt, 1/7th DWR
(formerly 4534864 Sgt, DWR, granted immediate commission, Feb 1945).
Military Cross, for Haalderen, NW Europe, WW2.
Announcement: "The King has been graciously pleased to approve the following awards in recognition of gallant and distinguished services in North West Europe."
LG: 12 Jul 1945, page 3592. MIC: 68/Gen/8091, dated 12 Jul 1845.
Citation: "At Haalderen (7477) on 2nd April, 1945, this Officer was in command of No 15 Platoon of C Company in the initial breakout from the Nijmegen Bridgehead. The platoon had the most difficult task of the operation - to assault an enemy post, which had been built up and occupied for six months and was covered by mines. As anti personnel mines were known to exist in the orchards round the house it was decided to attack frontally down the road which was thought to have only anti tank mines, a plan which called for courage and not manoeuvre. The leading troops were soon under fire of three MGs. Lt Lyon, with another soldier, then attempted to rush the house, both being hit by bullets, Lt Lyon's binoculars saving his life. Lt Lyon withdrew into a nearby ditch, reorganised the section and led another assault which, together with skilfully placed PIAT fire, resulted in the destruction of the post, three enemy being killed and 17 taken prisoner. But for this officer's action a most difficult operation to capture the FDLs might have ensued. His gallantry and skill was all the more praiseworthy as it was his first time in action as an Officer."
Iron Duke: Oct 1945, page 145. Iron Duke: 1946, page 83.

MAGEEAN, Joseph, 4616684 WO2, 1/7th DWR.
Mentioned in Despatches, for Normandy campaign, NW Europe, WW2.
"The King has been graciously pleased to approve that the following be mentioned in recognition of gallant and distinguished services in North West Europe - 4616684 WOII J Mageean."
LG: 4 Apr 1945, page 1694. MIC: 68/Gen/8212, dated 4 Apr 1946, CF NWE.

MAIDEN, Clement, 4612905 CQMS, 1/7th DWR.
Commander-in-Chief's Certificate, for Normandy campaign, NW Europe, WW2.
"For good service."
Battalion Journal, Victory Edition, 1945.

McDONNELL, James, 4611385 Pte, 1/7th DWR.
Commander-in-Chief's Certificate, for Normandy, NW Europe, WW2.
Battalion Journal, Victory Edition, 1945.

McKEON, Frank, 4614544 Pte, 1/7th DWR.
Commanding Officer's North West Europe Certificate, for Normandy, NW Europe, WW2.
Battalion Journal, Victory Edition, 1945.

MEASEY, George, 5106143 Sgt (later CSM), 1/7th DWR.
Distinguished Conduct Medal, for Roosendaal, NW Europe, WW2.
"Sgt Measey has been with the 7th Battalion in action since D Day plus 4 except for a short time when he was wounded. For a good proportion of this period he has been a platoon commander through the shortage of Officers, and several times has acted as Sergeant Major.

When acting as platoon commander in the fighting around the Depot de Mendicité in early September, 1944,, Sgt Measey was wounded in the head but, although in great pain, he completed the engagement before obeying the order to have his wound attended at the RAP.

In September, 1944, at Schanker (7423) the Company, after a first-class assault, were counter-attacked by a self-propelled gun and 40 enemy. Ammunition ran low in one platoon, which was temporarily isolated. Sgt Measey led a relief party with further ammunition through very heavy shelling and his example undoubtedly saved an extremely delicate situation.

In the following week, Sgt Measey led an ammunition party to his forward platoons which were isolated and pinned down in the flat open ground around the anti tank ditch at Roosendaal. Later in the day he personally crawled 300 yards while being sniped to take 2 inch mortar smoke ammunition which was required to allow the platoon to disengage.

During the four and a half months on 'The Island' salient across the Rhine at Nijmegen, Sgt Measey was constantly employed on standing and fighting patrols in the most difficult conditions and, here as on countless occasions, his bravery became a legend and example to the many young soldiers in his Company.

Sgt Measey's courage, calmness, interest in his men and his constant cheerfulness have made him a proud landmark in the Battalion and the guide for many inexperienced soldiers when actions was particularly fierce."

LG: 24 Jan 1946, page 644. MIC: 68/Gen/8212, dated 24 Jan 1946. Iron Duke: 1946, pages 81 & 92.
Commander-in-Chief's Gallantry Certificate, for Normandy campaign, NW Europe, WW2.
Battalion Journal, Victory Edition, 1945.

MEEHAM, Kenneth. 4547293 Pte, 1/7th DWR.
Commander-in-Chief's Gallantry Certificate, for Normandy campaign, N W Europe, WW2.
Unit WD: C-in-C's Cert award, Mar 1945, page 16. Battalion Journal, Victory Edition, 1945, page 48.

MILLINGTON, Albert, 4690503 LCpl, 1/7th DWR (also KSLI), r. Hemsworth.
Military Medal, NW Europe, WW2,
"The King has been graciously pleased to approve the following awards in recognition of gallant and distinguished services in North West Europe."
LG: 23 Aug 1945, page 4265.

MURPHY, John, 4532858 Sgt, 1/7th DWR (from W Yorks Regt), r. South Shields.
British Empire Medal, WW2.
"The King has been graciously pleased to approve the award of the British Empire Medal (Military Division) to the undermentioned - 4532858 Sgt John Murphy, West Yorkshire Regiment.
LG: 1 Jan 1944, page 29. Medals: sold at auction, 1 Dec 2021.
LG shows Regt as West Yorkshire Regt, CWGC shows killed in action with DWR.

MUSGROVE, Thomas, 4617029 Pte, 1/7th DWR.
Commanding Officer's Certificate, Normandy Campaign, NW Europe, WW2
Battalion Journal, Victory Edition, 1945.

NEEDLE, Kenneth Henry, 14555617 Pte, 1/7th DWR.
Mentioned in Despatches, NW Europe, WW2.
"The King has been graciously pleased to approve that the following be mentioned in recognition of gallant and distinguished service in North West Europe - 14555617 Pte K H Needle."
LG: 10 May 1945, page 2462. Unit WD: MID award, 27 May 1945.

OWEN, George William R, 4922656 LCpl, 1/7th DWR.
Commanding Officer's Certificate, for Normandy Campaign, NW Europe, WW2.
Battalion Journal, Victory Edition, 1945.

PARKIN, William Leonard, 4744600 Pte, 1/7th DWR.
Commander-in-Chief's Gallantry Certificate, for Normandy campaign, NW Europe, WW2.
Battalion Journal, Victory Edition, 1945.

PEACH, Arthur (Taffy), 4612925 Pte, 1/7th DWR, r. Cardiff.
Military Medal, for Pt 102, Fonteney, Normandy campaign, NW Europe, WW2.
Announcement: "The King has been graciously pleased to approve the following awards in recognition of gallant and distinguished services in Normandy."
LG: 31 Aug 1944, page 4048. MIC: 68/Gen/7934, dated 31 Aug 1944.
Citation: "On 18th June, 1944, Pte Peach, whilst No 1 Bren gunner during the assault on Point 102, was in a section which came under heavy mortar fire prior to and during the final assault. The Bren gun was destroyed whilst in action and Pte Peach was wounded. The second in command section was killed at the time. Pte Peach then assumed command of the section and, collecting strays of the platoon on the way, organised the mopping up and re-organisation with skill and determination in spite of his wound. His courage and devotion to duty were a great factor in securing the final objectives and re-organising his platoon. He would not leave his group until ordered to return to the Regimental Aid Post for attention."
Unit WD: MM award, Mar 1945, page 16. Iron Duke: 1945, page 100. Iron Duke: 1955, page 104. Iron Duke: 1967, page 133. Iron Duke: 222-1993, page 68. Medal: held in the Queen Victoria pub, Horton Street, Halifax.

PEARCE, William Henry, 4919341 Pte, 1/7th DWR.
Commanding Officer's Certificate, for Normandy campaign, NW Europe.
Battalion Journal, Victory Edition, 1945.

PICKSTONE, Arthur D, 4914289 LCpl, 1/7th DWR, r. Wednesbury.
Military Medal, NW Europe, WW2.
"The King has been graciously pleased to approve the following awards in recognition of gallantry and distinguished services in North West Europe."
LG: 21 Dec 1944, page 5859. MIC: 68/Gen7970, dated 21 Dec 1944. Unit WD: MM award, 31 Mar 1945.
Bar to MM, for Haalderen, NW Europe, WW2.
Announcement: "The King has been graciously pleased to approve the following awards in recognition of gallant and distinguished services in North West Europe."
G: 12 Jul 1945, page 3593. MIC: 68/Gen/8091, dated 12 Jul 1945.
Citation: "At Haalderen (7566) on 10th March, 1945, LCpl Pickstone was in charge of a stretcher bearer party in our FDLs standing by to carry wounded from a water borne operation carried out by 11th RSF, 2,000 yards behind the enemy lines. Four men of the RSF were cut off and two who were wounded attempted to crawl back to our lines. The ground was completely flat and under fire of a dug in Spandau. Without orders, LCpl Pickstone rushed forward across the open ground to rescue the two men. He was hit in the head but continued to move forward until an officer went out to stop him. Meantime the two injured men, inspired by his act of courage, took advantage of the diversion and reached cover, where LCpl Pickstone, still bleeding from the head, finally got to them and helped them in. He then dressed their wounds and refused to be evacuated himself until the operation was complete. LCpl Pickstone's great courage in a hail of bullets was a great inspiration to all men taking part in the operation and had the direct effect of allowing two wounded men to make their way in."
Unit WD: Bar to MM award, 29 May 1945, page 16. Iron Duke: 1945, page 145.

POOLMAN, Arthur F Thomas. 4748627 CQMS, 1/7th DWR.
Commanding Officer's Certificate, for Normandy campaign, NW Europe, WW2.
Battalion Journal, Victory Edition, 1945.

POYNER, Albert, 4925411 WO2, 1/7th DWR.
Mentioned in Despatches, NW Europe, WW2.
"The King has been graciously pleased to approve that the following be mentioned in recognition of gallant and distinguished services in North West Europe - 4925411 WO2 A Poyner."
LG: 4 Apr 1946, page 1694. MIC: 68/Gen/8212, dated 4 Apr 1946.

PYRAH, John Wilby, 90244 Capt (later Maj), 1/7th DWR (from Leeds UOTC).
Mentioned in Despatches, NW Europe, WW2.
The King has been graciously pleased to approve that the following be mentioned in recognition of gallant and distinguished service in North West Europe."
LG: 9 Aug 1945, page 4053. MIC: 68/Gen/8103, dated 9 Aug 1945. Iron Duke: 228-1995, page 72.

QUEST, Joe, 4614266 LCpl, 1/7th DWR, r. Stalybridge, Mossley.
Military Medal, for Haalderen, NW Europe, WW2.
Announcement: "The King has been graciously pleased to approve the following awards in recognition of gallant and distinguished services in North West Europe."
LG: 5 Apr 1945, page 1810. MIC: 68/Gen/8039, dated 05 Apr 1945.
Citation: "At Haalderen (7566) on 4th December this Non-Commissioned Officer was in command of three men in a house strongpoint cut off during a strong enemy attack on the Battalion position. The enemy force, approximately twenty five strong, engaged him with small arms and Spandaus and continually called on him to surrender for 2½ hours, but his only answer was more fire. This brave garrison held out until a counter-attack relieved them. Without orders, he then led his party in search of Germans and located them three houses away. The men strongly attacked the Huns, one of whom surrendered. As several men had been killed on the other side of the house attempting to force an entry, LCpl Quest determined to make the enemy give up. He stood up in full view of the post and called for their surrender. They refused, thinking they expected to be shot on surrender, LCpl Quest laid down his arms and walked unarmed towards the house, demanding the surrender, which was accepted and ten men were taken prisoner. LCpl Quest's devotion to duty kept open a vital line to Battalion HQ by which a counter-attack was ordered, completely overthrowing the enemy, and his coolness in encouraging a surrender probably saved further bloodshed of his comrades."
Unit WD: MM award, Mar 1945, page 16. Iron Duke: 1945, page 100 [name spelt Guest], Iron Duke: 199-1985, page 237.

REDMAN, N V, 235381 Lt, 1/7th DWR (att from S Staffs Regt).
Mentioned in Despatches, NW Europe, WW2.
Citation not currently available.
LG: 4 Apr 1946, page 1694.

RILEY, F E, 14649935 Sgt, 1/7th DWR.
Mentioned in Despatches, NW Europe, WW2.
Citation not currently available.
LG: 4 Apr 1946, page 1694.

RILEY, Wilfred, 14206667 Pte, 1/7th DWR.
French Croix de Guerre with Bronze Star, Normandy, NW Europe, WW2.
Citation not currently available.
LG: Not Known. Barclay, page 347. Battalion Journal, Victory Edition, 1945.

ROBINSON, J, 4609778 CSM, 1/7th DWR.
Commander-in-Chief's Certificate, for Gallantry, N W Europe, WW2.
Unit WD: C-in-C's Cert award, 15 Dec 1944.
Commander-in-Chief's Certificate, for Gallantry, N W Europe, WW2.

Unit WD: C-in-C's Cert award, 31 Mar 1945, page 16. Battalion Journal, pages 9 & 29.

ROSS, Alexander Duncan William, 156490 Capt, 1/7th DWR.
Mentioned in Despatches, NW Europe, WW2.
Citation not currently available.
LG: 4 Apr 1946, page 1694. MIC: 68/Gen/8212, dated 04 Apr, 1946.
Efficiency Medal (Territorial).
"The following Officers are awarded the Efficiency Medal (Territorial)."
LG:17 Jun 1949, page 2993. Iron Duke: 232-1996, page 123.

SARGEANT, R J, 3767467 CSM, 1/7th DWR.
Commanding Officer's Certificate, NW Europe, WW2.
Battalion Journal, Victory Edition, 1945.

SCHOLES, Frank Colin, 74249 Capt, 1/7th DWR.
Mentioned in Despatches, NW Europe, WW2.
"The King has been graciously pleased to approve that the following be mentioned in recognition of gallant and distinguished service in North West Europe - Major F C Scholes (74249) killed in action."
LG: 22 Mar 1945, page 1559. MIC: 68/Gen/8002, dated 22 Mar 1945. Iron Duke: 1944, page 140. Wrong number (245654) in LG, amended in LG of 16 Aug 1945. Iron Duke: 060-1945, page 51.

SIMPSON, Frank William, 4617054 Sgt, 1/7th DWR.
Commanding Officer's Certificate, for NW Europe, WW2.
Battalion Journal, Victory Edition, 1945.

SIMPSON, Henry, 4611795 Sgt, 1/7th DWR, r. Oldham.
Distinguished Conduct Medal, for Haalderen, NW Europe, WW2.
"During a strong enemy attack at Haalderen (7566), a key point in the defence of the Nijmegen Bridge, on the 4th December, 1944, Sgt Simpson was in command of a section of carriers which was ordered to place a stop across a line of buildings to halt the enemy house clearing operations. That this difficult mission was soon completed in the darkness was due to Sgt Simpson's great leadership. Shortly afterwards, Sgt Simpson was told to clear the enemy from a school from which Battalion HQ was threatened. Under the cover of Bren fire, this Non-Commissioned Officer led three riflemen immediately towards the door of the school in face of concentrated fire of six Spandaus. Sgt Simpson was seriously wounded in the leg and fell out. In spite of great pain, he remained on the ground directing the assault, shouting encouragement and refusing to be taken to safety until his men, fired by his great example, rushed the door and forced the Bosche garrison of fourteen men to surrender. This Non-Commissioned Officer's decision to assault a greatly superior force, and inspiration he gave his men when wounded, saved Battalion HQ from encirclement, with the eventual result that a counter-attack was planned which entirely eliminated the enemy force."
LG: 5 Apr 1945, page 1809. Unit WD: DCM award, Mar 1945, page 16. Iron Duke: 1945, page 98. Iron Duke: 230-1996, page 38. Medals: ex Donald Hall collection, 1994.

SIMPSON, James (Jimmy), 14407560 Cpl, 1/7th DWR, r. Bradford.
Military Medal, for Normandy campaign, NW Europe, WW2.
Announcement: "The King has been graciously pleased to approve the following awards in recognition of gallant and distinguished services in North West Europe."
LG: 19 Oct 1944, page 4790. MIC: 68/Gen/7970, dated 19 Oct 1944.
Citation: "On 13th July, 1944, this Non-Commissioned Officer, who is only 19 years of age, was a member of a fighting patrol of six men commanded by No 247723 Lt J Lappin. During two attacks on an enemy platoon in prepared positions near Tessell-Bretteville, Normandy, this Non-Commissioned Officer showed exemplary courage and leadership and personally assisted Lt Lappin to cover the withdrawal of

the patrol after the attack, without loss or casualties. His personal courage, coolness and leadership were an inspiration to the other members of the patrol. Twelve of the enemy were killed during the operation."
Unit WD: MM award, Mar 1945, page 16. Battalion Journal, page 32. Iron Duke: 1945, pages 33 & 99. Iron Duke: 1979, page 230. Iron Duke: 251-2003, page 44.

SMALLWOOD, Geoffrey Malcolm Mercer, 99737 Maj, South Staffordshire Regiment (later att 1/7th DWR), r. Warrenpoint, N Ireland.
Military Cross, NW Europe, WW2.
"The King has been graciously pleased to approve the following awards in recognition of gallant and distinguished services in North West Europe. Major Smallwood has taken part in every action this unit has fought as a Battalion in France. He has commanded his Company with great courage, skill and determination and, at all times, has been an inspiration to his men. On 16th July, 1944, he led his Company to attack the Les Nouillous feature, first phase, and, despite heavy enemy MMG and mortar fire, he captured and held on to his objective. On 6th August, 1944, his Company led the attack on Mesnil Hermie and, on the 20th August, on to Pt 271. Both of these attacks were successful and that on Mesnil Hermie despite very heavy enemy mortar and shell fire.
By his personal courage, leadership and gallantry have these successes been achieved and there is no doubt that, but for the example shown by Major Smallwood, the success of all these operations would have been prejudiced."
LG: 29 Mar 1945, page 1710. Unit WD: MM award, Mar 1945, page 16. Iron Duke: 1945, page 97. Medals: ex Donald Hall collection, 1994.

SMITH, Albert Edward William, 4620707 Cpl, 1/7th DWR.
Mentioned in Despatches, NW Europe, WW2.
Citation not currently available.
LG: 4 Apr 1946, page 1694.

SMITH, C, 13094343 Driver, RASC att 1/7th DWR.
Commanding Officer's North West Europe Certificate, for Normandy campaign, WW2.
Battalion Journal, Victory Edition, 1945.

SMITH, James, 3655204 LCpl, 1/7th DWR, r. Newton le Willows.
Military Medal, for Haalderen, NW Europe, WW2.
Announcement: "The King has been graciously pleased to approve the following awards in recognition of gallant and distinguished services in North West Europe."
LG: 12 Jul 1945, page 3595. MIC: 68/Gen/8091, dated 12 Jul, 1945.
Citation: "At Haalderen (7566) on 2nd April, 1945, this Non-Commissioned Officer was in command of a section of a platoon of D Company which led the breakout of the Nijmegen salient. After the Company had lost the cover of darkness and was in an exposed, flat, ploughed field movement became difficult through the fire of an enemy strongpoint which was holding out. LCpl Smith was ordered to pass through the first house in the west side of the road and clear the second house. When he was called forward little was known of the progress of the first section which was under enemy fire. Nevertheless, this Non-Commissioned Officer took his section into the first house across an area constantly being swept by Spandau fire from two sides. As he took up a preliminary position he saw a German shoot a member of the leading section. Without any regard to his personal safety, he ran forward from his cover and shot the German who was trying to get back into another house. He then managed to contact the leading section commander and find out the situation. This valuable information was passed to the platoon commander by continually crossing an open space including a dyke which he had to wade, throughout the time exposing himself to fire and eventually resulted in the complete destruction of the enemy post."
Unit WD: MID award, Mar 1945, page 16. Iron Duke: 1945, page 146.

SMITH, John Thomas C, 4617122 Pte, 1/7th DWR.
Mentioned in Despatches, NW Europe, WW2.
"The King has been graciously pleased to approve that the following be mentioned in recognition of gallant and distinguished services in North West Europe - 4617122 Pte J T C Smith"
LG: 22 Mar 1945, page 1559. MIC: 68/Gen/9002, dated 22 Mar 1945.

SMITH, Robert Hayes, Lt, 1/7th DWR.
Commander-in-Chief's Certificate, for Gallantry, N W Europe, WW2.
Unit WD: C-in-C's award, 15 Dec 1944. Unit WD: C-in-C's Cert award, Mar 1945, page 16.

SOMERVILLE, Arnold U, 239804 Capt, RAMC att 1/7th DWR.
Mentioned in Despatches, NW Europe, WW2.
Citation not currently available.
LG: 22 Mar 1945, page 1565. Unit WD: MID award, Mar 1945, page 16.

STANIFORTH, Edward, 4609706 Sgt, 1/7th DWR (also York & Lanc Regt), r. Sheffield.
Military Medal, NW Europe, WW2.
"The King has been graciously pleased to approve the following awards in recognition of gallant and distinguished services in North West Europe."
LG: 1 Mar 1945, page 1183.

STEVENS, Victor Clarence, 324893 Lt, 1/7th DWR (from QORWK Regt), r. Bromley, Kent.
Military Cross, for Arnhem, NW Europe, WW2.
"At Arnhem (7477) on the night 14th - 15th April, the Battalion had secured its objectives on the perimeter after a final stiff fight at 2000 hrs, when a German counter-attack by a battle group of three tanks and a company of infantry developed in the half light. As one platoon of D Company appeared to be cut off in a wood during the confused fighting, No 9 Platoon of A Company was placed under command of OC D Company to restore the situation and also to contact a troop of our own armour which seemed to be engaged by German infantry at close quarters. Lt Stevens issued rapid orders to his platoon and led it through fairly heavy shelling to contact the D Company platoon which was still fighting in the wood. Lt Stevens assumed command of the total force and personally led a counter-attack-cum-mopping-up operation to clear the wood and also search for the three tanks which, by this time, had been knocked out. This operation took place in complete darkness in a wood which had for months been mined and wired. It was due to his personality and complete disregard for his own personal safety that the enemy were mopped up after some very close quarter fighting. Later in the night, when his platoon Sergeant was killed and a Runner was severely wounded on a security patrol while the enemy was shelling the area, Lt Stevens went out to organise the rescue of the men, as stretcher bearers were not then available, and then continued with the patrol. Lt Stevens' example and bearing at all times under fire was entirely responsible for the steadiness of the force and the complete failure of the enemy attack."
LG: 23 Aug 1945, page 4264. Iron Duke: 1945, page 145.

STIMSON, Peter George, 4751116 Pte, 1/7th DWR, r. Derby.
Military Medal, for Battle of Haalderen, Dec 1944, NW Europe, WW2.
"The King has been graciously pleased to approve the following awards in recognition of gallant and distinguished services in North West Europe."
LG: 5 Apr 1945, page 1810. Unit WD: MM award, 24 Dec 1944.
"This soldier was a member of 13 Platoon, the reserve platoon of C Company, when an enemy Company broke into the Battalion defences at 0300 hrs on 4th December. The first waves were scattered and almost wiped out by Stimson's post, due to his skilful handling of his LMG. From then onwards, until 0900 hrs, his house was under constant enemy Spandau and bazooka fire and half the garrison of nine were killed or wounded. At about 0500 hrs, Pte Stimson was wounded in the leg but, although in great pain, continued to fire his gun, causing further great enemy casualties. Not until the action was over, and

eighteen enemy dead counted within 80 yards of Stimson's gun, did this soldier inform his platoon commander of his wound. He was later evacuated. Pte Stimson was determined to fire his gun until the last and his great fortitude and skill was a symbol of defiance of this small garrison which ultimately led to the complete overthrow of the enemy attack."
Iron Duke: 1945, page 99.

STONE, W, 4687194 LCpl, 2 DWR (later 1/7th DWR)
Military Medal, Mohmand Operations, 1935, NWFP, India.
"The King has been graciously pleased to approve of the undermentioned rewards for distinguished services rendered in the Field in connections with Mohmand Operations, North West Frontier of India, during the period 15/16 August to 15/16th October, 1935. The Military Medal for bravery in the Field."
LG: 8 May 1936, page 2979.
Commander-in-Chief's Certificate, for Good Service, N W Europe, WW2.
Unit WD: C-in-C's Cert award, 31 Mar 1945. Battalion Journal, Victory Edition, 1945.

TAYLOR, Eric, 14409169 Pte, 1/7th DWR.
Commanding Officer's North West Europe Certificate, for Normandy campaign, NW Europe, WW2.
Battalion Journal, Victory Edition, 1945.

TEMPLE, B, 229814 Capt (QM), 1/7th DWR
(commissioned from CSM, E Yorks Regt), r. Beverley.
Member, the Most Excellent Order of the British Empire, NW Europe, WW2.
Announcement: "The King has been graciously pleased to give orders for the following promotions in, and appointments to, the Most Excellent Order of the British Empire in recognition of gallant and distinguished services in North West Europe. To be additional Members of the Military Division of the said Most Excellent Order."
LG: 24 Jan 1946, page 624.
Citation: "Captain Temple has been Quartermaster of the 7th Battalion since 8th June, 1942, and has twice mobilised for war. The final mobilisation before D Day involved many nights of intensive indenting, checking and distribution of stores and it was due to Captain Temple's great devotion to duty that the Battalion was so perfectly equipped for war. Just before D Day Capt Temple was told by medical authorities that he was unfit for active service and that an operation on his leg was necessary. Captain Temple pleaded to go overseas with the Battalion, despite the risk involved, and realising that he was jeopardising any possibility of pension.
Capt Temple's organisation, his tireless work in the search for stores and his constant journeys with rations which, from June to August, 1944, were often under fire, have always resulted in the Battalion being efficient for any operation and the men were never without food. In addition, he ran a Battalion rest camp at B Echelon for men resting from the line.
Captain Temple's devotion to duty in this campaign and throughout his twenty two years in the Army has been outstanding and he has certainly contributed to the high morale of all ranks in the Battalion."
Iron Duke: 1946, pages 81 & 92.

THOMLINSON, Benjamin Vincent, 69243 Maj, 1/7th DWR
(commissioned from Tpr, Yorkshire Hussars, 1936), r. York.
Mentioned in Despatches, NW Europe, WW2.
"The King has been graciously pleased to approve that the following be mentioned in recognition of gallant and distinguished services in North West Europe. DWR Major (temp) B V Thomlinson (69243)."
LG: 8 Nov 1945, page 5446. MIC: 68/Gen/8157, dated 8 Nov 1945.
Netherlands Knight of the 4th Class of the Militaire Willems Ord, NW Europe, WW2.
"Decorations conferred by The Queen of the Netherlands. Permission to wear granted."
LG: 18 Jul 1947, page 3320.

"He showed exceptional valour, leadership, loyalty and outstanding devotion to duty and great perseverance in action against the enemy, thereby setting in every respect a highly praiseworthy example to everyone in those glorious days."
Wetherby News: medal presented on 18 Dec 1947 by Dutch Ambassador, London, 19 Dec 1947. Iron Duke: MWO, permission to wear, 1985, page 196.
Territorial Efficiency Decoration.
"The following Officers have qualified and are recommended for the award of the Territorial Efficiency Decoration."
"The following Officers have qualified and are recommended for the award of the 1st Clasp to the Territorial Efficiency Decoration."
LG: 18 Mar 1958, page 1760. Iron Duke:235-1997, page 134. Medals: held in Bankfield Museum.

TILLEY, Walter John Leonard, 1775718 Pte, 1/7th DWR.
Commanding Officer's North West Europe Certificate, for Normandy campaign, WW2.
Battalion Journal, Victory Edition, 1945.

TISSINGTON, Charles Frederick ('Tissie'), 94938 Major (later Lt Col), 1/7th DWR
(from Cheshire Regt, 2/7th DWR & later CO 1/6th DWR).
Military Cross, WW2.
Citation not currently available.
LG: Not Known. Iron Duke: 152-1970, page 36.
Territorial Efficiency Decoration.
"The King has been graciously pleased to confer the Efficiency Decoration (Territorial) upon the following Officers:"
LG: 8 May 1953, p 2573; 1st Clasp: 8 May 1953, p 2572.

VALENTINE, Jack, 4749138 CQMS, 1/7th DWR.
Commanding Officer's North West Europe Certificate, for Normandy campaign, WW2.
Battalion Journal, Victory Edition, 1945.

WATKINS, Stanley, 4609410 CSM, 1/7th DWR.
Commander-in-Chief's Certificate for Good Service, for Normandy campaign, NW Europe, WW2.
Battalion Journal, Victory Edition, 1945.

WEALE, Leon Charles, 4620723 LCpl, 1/7th DWR.
Commanding Officer's Certificate for North West Europe, for Normandy campaign, WW2.
Battalion Journal, Victory Edition, 1945.

WEBB, S W, 4979635 Pte (later Sgt), 1/7th DWR.
Mentioned in Despatches, NW Europe, WW2.
"The King has been graciously pleased to approve that the following be mentioned in recognition of gallant and distinguished services in North West Europe - 4979635 Sgt S W Webb."
LG: 8 Nov 1945, page 5446. MIC: 68/Gen/8157, dated 8 Nov 1945.

WHITELEY, Bernard, 4623827 Cpl, 1/7th DWR.
Commanding Officer's North West Europe Certificate, for Normandy campaign, WW2.
Citation not currently available.
Battalion Journal, Victory Edition, 1945.

WHITTLE, James, 4612623 Sgt, 1/7th DWR.
Commanding Officer's North West Europe Certificate, for Normandy campaign, WW2.
Citation not currently available.

Battalion Journal, Victory Edition, 1945.

WILLIAMSON, Stanley, 14569345 Pte, 1/7th DWR.
Military Medal, for Haalderen, NW Europe, WW2.
Announcement: "The King has been graciously pleased to approve the following awards in recognition of gallant and distinguished services in North West Europe."
LG: 12 Jul 1945, page 3595. MIC: 68/Gen/8091, dated 12 Jul 1945.
Citation: "At Haalderen (7566) on 2nd April, 1945, Pte Williamson was a member of a platoon of C Coy which was assaulting an enemy strongpoint, wired and covered by mines, during the initial operation to open the Nijmegen Bridgehead. Pte Williamson and his platoon commander first of all carried out a two man attack on the post in darkness, under the covering fire of the other men. Pte Williamson was hit in the chest, the magazines in his pouches being torn open but, fortunately, he was not wounded. Pte Williamson and his platoon commander then withdrew to a nearby position until a fire plan could be made, and then he went in again with two grenades. This plan succeeded and those enemy not killed were taken prisoner. The great courage and devotion to duty of the Private soldier in a difficult operation in which few men could be deployed because of mines and booby traps brought about the capture of a strongpoint without any casualties to the platoon and opened the way for a most successful further Company operation."
Iron Duke: 1945, page 146.

WILSEY, John Harold Owen, 30965 Lt Col (A/Brig), 1/7th DWR
(from Worcs Regt, later GOC 158 Inf Bde), r Camberley.
Distinguished Service Order, NW Europe, WW2.
"Lt Col Wilsey has been in command of [*1/7th*] DWR since the start of the campaign in Normandy. Except for short periods of rest, the Battalion has been in close contact with the enemy for the whole period, during which the fighting has varied from the heavy battles of early June to active patrolling east of Caen; from the pursuit to the River Seine to the attack on Le Havre, and the recent fighting in northern Belgium and southern Holland.
During all this varied fighting the Battalion has always been successful. That these successes were achieved, and with comparatively light losses, was entirely due to Lt Col Wilsey's leadership and efficiency. There is no doubt that his example has been an inspiration to his Battalion, and he has never spared himself so that he has always got the best out of his Battalion."
LG: 29 Mar 1945, page 1709. Unit WD: DSO award, Mar 1945, page 16. Iron Duke: 1945, page 95.
Commander, the Most Excellent Order of the British Empire, NW Europe, WW2.
"The King has been graciously pleased to give orders for the following promotions in, and appointments to, the Most Excellent Order of the British Empire, in recognition of gallant and distinguished services in North West Europe. To be additional Commanders of the said Most Excellent Order."
LG: 24 Jan 1946, page 615. Battalion Journal, Victory Edition, 31 Jan 1946.
Commander, the Most Honourable Order of the Bath.
"New Years Honours List."
LG: 01 Jan 1953, page 3.

WILSON, Edward Francis, 4626316 CQMS, 1/7th DWR.
Commander-in-Chief's Certificate for Good Service, for Normandy campaign, WW2.
Battalion Journal, Victory Edition, 1945.

WINDER, James, 4617195 CQMS, 1/7th DWR.
Commanding Officer's North West Europe Certificate for Normandy campaign, WW2.
Battalion Journal, Victory Edition, 1945.

WOOD, John, 4614804 Pte, 2 DWR (from 1/7th DWR), r. Mossley.
Mentioned in Despatches, for Chindits, Burma, WW2.

"The King has been graciously pleased to approve that the following be mentioned in recognition of gallant and distinguished service in Burma - 4614804 Pte J Wood."
LG: 19 Sep 1946, page 4700. MIC: 68/Gen/8197.

WOODCOCK, Arnold, 10254 Capt (later Maj), 1/7th DWR.
Mentioned in Despatches, NW Europe, WW2.
"The King has been graciously pleased to approve that the following be mentioned in recognition of gallant and distinguished service in North West Europe - T/Capt A Woodcock (102514)."
LG: 22 Mar 1945, page 1559. MIC: 68/Gen/8002, dated 22 Mar 1945. Iron Duke: 212-1990, page 32.

WRIGHT, Derick R, 5049910 Pte, 1/7th DWR.
Commanding Officer's North West Europe Certificate, for Normandy campaign, WW2.
Battalion Journal, Victory Edition, 1945.

Estate Agent's board advertising the attractions of the Elst region of Holland.

Polar Bear Division advancing into Holland.

1945-04 Holland 1/7th DWR (Polar Bears) Passing 8th Canadian Armoured Div towards Ede

Preparations for the breakout from Haalderen to seize Arnhem, April 1945.

1945-04 Holland Haalderen area 1/7th DWR (Polar Bears) Continuing advance

1/7th Battalion rounding up elements of enemy forces, 1945.

Images - Lt J Lappin's collection.

1945-04 Holland Haalderen area 1/7th DWR (Polar Bears) John Lappin & D Coy Rounding up Dutch SS Prisoners

3. 115 Regt RAC, 1944-1945.

THE FALLEN

SPANTON, George Samuel, 4620178 LCpl, 2/7th DWR (115 Regt RAC).
    Died: 23 Aug 1944, aged 27.
    Buried: Washington Cemetery, K 98.
    Commemorated: **Not listed on 7 DWR WW2 Memorial.**
                                         Barclay History RoH, Page 377.
    DWR Enlistment Book: TED 20, page 18.

THE UNIT

The formation and early operations of the 2/7th Battalion has been covered above. After returning to the UK, 46th Division was sent to Scotland to reform whilst training and was also engaged on coastal defence.

In January, 1941, the Division moved to East Anglia, joining 2nd Corps, and continuing its anti-invasion duties. Later that year it moved to Kent, coming under the command of Lt Gen B L Montgomery, GOC 12th Corps at that time.

In 1942, a decision was taken to create mixed divisions of two Infantry Brigades and one Armoured Brigade and, on 20th July, 1942, the 137th Brigade left the Division for conversion to armour, becoming 137th Armoured Brigade under the auspices of the Royal Armoured Corps. However, the decision was later reversed, and the 137th Infantry Brigade was replaced in 46th Division by 128th Infantry Brigade; the 137th Armoured Brigade coming under command of the War Office and, later, Eastern Command.

137th ARMOURED BRIGADE.

The Brigade was now made up of 113th Regiment Royal Armoured Corps (formerly 2/5th Battalion West Yorkshire Regiment); 114th Regiment Royal Armoured Corps (2/6th Battalion Duke of Wellington's Regiment) and 115th Regiment Royal Armoured Corps (2/7th Battalion Duke of Wellington's Regiment).

The 'Dukes' History, states, *"...in mid-1942 the 137th Infantry Brigade was converted to armour and renamed 137th Armoured Brigade. After conversion to armour the strength of the Regiment gradually declined as the men were posted away on returning to the Royal Armoured Corps at Catterick and Bovington. A new lease of life was granted by an intake of recruits from the Primary Training Centre*, who were immediately put through Regimental courses in all phases of armoured training."* [* 4 ITC, Barnard Castle, where the 'Dukes' and DLI had formed a combined training centre].

"In September, 1943, the [115th] Regiment went into suspended animation, but individual squadrons continued as Tank Delivery Units."

"The connection with the 'Dukes' was not entirely lost, as certain squadrons in the new unit were officially shown as 'Dukes' Squadrons and wore the regimental badges and buttons and the scarlet lanyard. These squadrons did excellent service with the British Army of Liberation from D Day onwards in 1944 and 1945."

137 TANK DELIVERY UNIT.

On 26th September, 1943, the Armoured Brigade was disbanded, the Armoured Regiments forming 137 Tank Delivery Unit, with its Sub Units forming three Corps Delivery Squadrons:

B Squadron (heavy), formed at Wivenhoe, December, 1943, moving to Driffield in December, 1943, and renamed 257 Corps Delivery Squadron in January, 1944, coming under command of 2nd Armoured Delivery Regiment. The unit moved to Eastbourne in May, 1944, and embarked for France on 2nd July, 1944.

F Squadron formed at Wivenhoe, in December, 1943, moving to Shorncliffe in January, 1944, being re-titled 258 Corps Delivery Squadron the same month. Embarked for France in July, 1944.

J Squadron (formerly C Sqn, 114 Regt RAC) formed at Wivenhoe, September, 1943, becoming O Squadron in December and moving to Eastbourne in January, 1944, when it became 259 Corp Delivery Squadron. It moved to Uckfield in April, 1944, and embarked for France on 9th June, 1944.

and also three Forward Delivery Squadrons:

H Squadron formed at Finedon, September, 1943, moved to Wivenhoe in October, 1943. It was renamed as 260 Forward Delivery Squadron in January, 1944. Commanded by Capt J Landless, Duke of Wellington's Regiment, who saw action in the Dunkirk Campaign in the 2/6th Battalion of the 'Dukes'. This Squadron was disbanded in April, 1944.

C Squadron formed at Spinkhill, November, 1943, moving to Eckington in January, 1944, where it was renamed 261 Forward Delivery Squadron, under command 2nd Armoured Delivery Regiment. Embarked for France on 22nd July, 1944, in support of 6th Guards Armoured Brigade.

J Squadron formed at Alresford, December, 1943, being renamed 262 Forward Delivery Squadron in January, 1944, and moving to Diss, in support of 33rd Armoured Brigade. Embarked for France in June, 1944.

At the same time, both the 113rd Regt (2/5th Bn West Yorkshire Regiment) and 115th Regt (2/7th Bn The Duke of Wellington's Regiment) were placed into 'suspended animation'.

The commanding officers of 114th and 115th Regts RAC at this time were Lt Col G H Bolster and Lt Col W Coates, respectively.

The following Delivery Sqns were linked to the two 'Dukes' Battalions:

2/6th	259 Corps Delivery Squadron		disbanded 3 1946
	260 Forward Delivery Squadron		disbanded 4 1944
2/7th	262 Forward Delivery Squadron	became 2 ARG Edn Sch	disbanded 21 10 1945

2nd ARMOURED DELIVERY REGIMENT (ADR).

2nd Armoured Delivery Regiment RAC was formed on 29th January, 1944, at Brackley, commanded by Major W J Wykes MBE. On formation the following Delivery Squadrons were under command:

256 Army Delivery Squadron
260 Forward Delivery Squadron

263 Forward Delivery Squadron
264 Forward Delivery Squadron (from 3rd February, 1944)
265 Forward Delivery Squadron
271 Forward Delivery Squadron

2 AD Regt RAC came under command 2nd Armoured Replacement Group (ARG) RAC, at Brackley, on 6th February, 1944.

260 Squadron was last mentioned in 2 AD Regt's War Diary on 14th April, 1944, when it was disbanded. Capt J Landless moved to OC 264 Fwd Dy Sqn.

THE CAMPAIGN:
115 Regt RAC (2/7th DWR)

2 ADR RAC was ordered to move to Weybridge on 5th May, 1944, where administration and inspections for field conditions were conducted, prior to embarking for active service overseas.

The unit embarked on LSTs at Southampton at 0945 hrs, 14th June, and spent a night off the Isle of Wight. The troops disembarked on Jig Red Beach, Le Hamel, on 16th June, 1944, and proceeded to Harbour Area, Sully, near Bayeux, the same day.

During the campaign the Army, Corps and Forward Delivery Squadrons (ADS, CDS & FDS) received Armoured Fighting Vehicles (AFV), including tanks, armoured cars and self propelled guns, for delivery to the fighting units, as well as replacement crews (many directly from the 2nd Armoured Reinforcement Unit (ARU), responsible for training and drafting reinforcements, in conjunction with 21 RAC Training Regiment). It was not a glamorous job but was vital in keeping the front line units supplied with the materiel required to defeat the enemy. By the end of the war on 8th May, 1945, the Regiment had received 20,251 AFVs and had 1,397 in stock. These numbers were also supplemented by a Canadian ADR and shows how the Germans could not possibly have held out against the Allies in the long run and the statistics are a credit to the men of 2/6th and 2/7th Battalions whose skill and determination kept the fighting units supplied in order to keep up the pressure on the Wehrmacht. The three Squadrons which were directly descended from the two 'Dukes' Territorial Battalions had received 2,661 AFVs and had 168 vehicles on hand at the end of hostilities.

HONOURS AND AWARDS:
115 Regiment (RAC)

DOWNS, Horace, 4739660 CSM (WO2), 2/7th DWR (115 Regt RAC).
Mentioned in Despatches, NW Europe, WW2.
"The King has been graciously pleased to approve that the following be mentioned in recognition of gallant and distinguished services in the Field - 4739660 CSM (WO2) Horace Downs."
LG: 23 Jan 1947, page 442.

PARFITT, George, 96825 Maj, 2/7th DWR (115 Regt RAC), r. Delph, Yorks.
Member, the Most Excellent Order of the British Empire, Burma, WW2.
"The King has been graciously pleased to give orders for the following promotions in, and appointments to, the Most Excellent Order of the British Empire in recognition of gallant and distinguished services in Burma. To be additional Members of the Military Division of the said Most Excellent Order."
LG: 13 Sep 1945, page 4556. Iron Duke: 175-1977, page 218-9.
Efficiency Decoration (Territorial).
"The King has been graciously pleased to confer the Efficiency Decoration (Territorial) upon the following Officers."
LG: 21 Apr 1950 page 1937.

Sherman tanks ready to be supplied to units, 1944.

ADDENDA

In common with the previous two First World Memorials, the following sixteen names are missing from the Second World War Memorial Boards, although they do appear in the lists above. The names have been gleaned from our Regimental History (Barclay) Roll of Honour, published after the war, as well as the Commonwealth War Graves Commission records, as recorded in the DWR Regimental Master Index, which provided the framework for this publication.

For the First World War Memorials we considered links to their home towns for eligibility in adding further memorials alongside the originals, as it was a much more localised conflict. None of those listed below were 'local' men but the practice of enlisting men into their local Regiments had proved foolhardy in the Great War as entire close-knit communities were so badly affected by the appalling losses in the Pals Battalions, in particular, during the Battle of the Somme, especially.

The Trustees will, I am sure, examine the case for a memorial in the Drill Hall for these men who died in the ranks of these local units. Until then, this Roll will forever commemorate their noble sacrifice.

1/7th & 2/7th DWR:

BENTLEY, Cecil Farnsworth Burley, 4618951 Pte, 2/7th DWR.
Son of Harry and Ellen Bentley, Hull, husband of Clarice Irene Bentley, Hull, Yorks.
- **Died:** 11 Oct 1941, aged 21.
- **Buried:** Hull Western Cemetery, 173, 16891.
- **Commemorated:** Commonwealth War Graves Commission, Vol 5, page 67.
  Not listed on 7 DWR WW2 Memorial.
- **DWR Enlistment Book:** TED 18, page 96, discharged 27 Dec 1940.

"PEACEFULLY SLEEPING"

CAMBELL, Herbert Alexander, 326885 Lt, 1/7th DWR, also 11 R Scots Fus.
Son of Edgar and Alice Eva Campbell, husband of Violet Campbell, West Hartlepool, Co Durham.
- **Killed in Action:** 17 Apr 1945, Normandy Campaign, Netherlands, aged 28.
- **Buried:** Arnhem Oosterbeek War Cemetery, 7, A, 1.
- **Commemorated:** **Not listed on 7 DWR WW2 Memorial.**
  Barclay History RoH, page 375.
- **Commissioned:** Aug 1944.

"TREASURED MEMORIES OF MY LOVING HUSBAND. HE DIED THAT WE MIGHT LIVE"

CHAPMAN, Arthur, 4622104 Cpl, 1/7th DWR, att HQ 1st Abn Div.
- **Killed in Action:** 24 Sep 1944, Normandy Campaign, Netherlands.
- **Buried:** Arnhem Oosterbeek War Cemetery, 20, C, 17.
- **Commemorated:** **Not listed on 7 DWR WW2 Memorial.**
  Barclay History RoH, page 375.
- **DWR Enlistment Book:** TED 22, page 11.

DAVIES, Gwyn Wood, 4615594 Sgt, 2/7th DWR.
- **Killed in Action:** 11 Jun 1940, France & Belgium Campaign, 1939/40, aged 25.
- **Buried:** No known grave.
- **Commemorated:** Dunkirk Memorial, Col 61.
  Not listed on 7 DWR WW2 Memorial.
  Barclay History RoH, page 371.
- **DWR Enlistment Book:** TED 15, page 60.

DERMODY, John, 14454064 Pte, 1/7th DWR.
Son of Donald and Mary Dermody, Waun-wen, Swansea, Wales.
    Died: 28 Aug 1946, Normandy Campaign, Germany, aged 20.
    Buried: Reichswald Forest War Cemetery, 59, J, 7.
    Commemorated: **Not listed on 7 DWR WW2 Memorial.**
    DWR Enlistment Book: OVER 36, page 205.
"ETERNAL REST GIVE UNTO HIM, O LORD; AND LET PERPETUAL LIGHT SHINE UPON HIM"

HALLIDAY, Reginald, 4615921, 2/7th DWR.
    Killed in Action: 10 Jun 1940, France & Belgium Campaign, 1939/40, aged 26.
    Buried: No known grave.
    Commemorated: Dunkirk Memorial, Col 62.
    Not listed on 7 DWR WW2 Memorial.
    Barclay History RoH, page 367.
    DWR Enlistment Book: TED 15, page 93.

HARESIGN, Harold, 14546078 Pte, 1/7th DWR (CWGC shows 6 DWR).
Son of Albert and Edith Haresign, Balby, Doncaster, Yorks.
    Killed in Action: 18 Aug 1944, Normandy Campaign, France, aged 19.
    Buried: No known grave.
    Commemorated: Bayeux Memorial, Panel 15, Col 1.
    Not listed on 7 DWR WW2 Memorial.
    Barclay History RoH, page 366.
    DWR Enlistment Book: OVER 31, page 98.

HILTON, Eric, 14687366 LCpl, 1/7th DWR.
Son of Rupert and Ethel Hilton, Middleton, Manchester, Lancs.
    Died: 2 Jun 1946, BLA, Germany, aged 21.
    Buried: Reichswald Forest War Cemetery, 59, J, 8.
    Commemorated: **Not listed on 7 DWR WW2 Memorial.**
    DWR Enlistment Book: OVER 33, page 53.
"THOUGH ABSENT YOU ARE ALWAYS NEAR, STILL LOVED, STILL MISSED, AND VERY DEAR"

HUGHES, Robert, 4618829 Pte, 2/7th DWR.
Son of William Henry and Nellie Hughes, Sheffield' Yorks.
    Reported missing: presumed killed 10-11 Jun 1940, France & Belgium Campaign, 1939/40, aged 22.
    Buried: Sainte Marie Cemetery, Le Havre, 67, T, 12.
    Previously Interred: Sotteville sur Mer Temp Burial Ground, 6, 5 (until Oct 1947).
    Commemorated: **Not listed on 7 DWR WW2 Memorial.**
    Barclay History RoH, page 372.
    DWR Enlistment Book: TED 18, page 83.
"WORTHY OF EVERLASTING REMEMBRANCE. GOODNIGHT BOB, GOD BLESS"

KNIGHT, Clifford Aubrey, 262161 Lt, 1/7th DWR, att 4 Welch Regt.
Son of Edward Ernest and Charlotte Eleanor Knight, husband of Florence Mary Knight, Leyburn, Yorks.
    Killed in Action: 18 Sep 1944, Normandy Campaign, Belgium, aged 29.
    Buried: Bergen op Zoom War Cemetery, 11, B, 4.
    Commemorated: **Not listed on 7 DWR WW2 Memorial.**
    Barclay History RoH, page 376.
    Commissioned: Feb 1943.

LEE, Thomas, 4617114 Pte, 2/7th DWR.
Son of Thomas and Betsy Lee, Siddal, Halifax, Yorks.
    Reported Missing: presumed killed 11 Jun 1940, France & Belgium Campaign, 1939/40, aged 21.
    Buried: No known grave.
    Commemorated: Dunkirk Memorial, Col 62.
    Not listed on 7 DWR WW2 Memorial.
    Barclay History RoH, page 372.
    DWR Enlistment Book: TED 17, page 12.

NEALE, Donald, 4615786 Pte, 1/7th DWR.
Adopted son of Arthur and Amelia Storey, Stourton, Leeds, Yorks.
    Died: 3 Nov 1942, Home Duties, aged 22.
    Buried: Rothwell (Leeds) Cemetery, Grave 474.
    Commemorated: **Not listed on 7 DWR WW2 Memorial.**
    DWR Enlistment Book: TED 15, page 79 [shows discharge date as 25 Jun 1941].
"TREASURED MEMORIES OF A DEARLY LOVED SON AND BROTHER WHO DIED IN HOSPITAL"

SELLARS, William Thomas George, 14293272 LCpl, 1/7th DWR.
Son of William Frederick and Frances Sellars, husband of Doris May Sellars, Charlton, London.
    Killed in Action: 17 Jun 1944, Normandy Campaign, France, aged 31.
    Buried: Hottot les Bagues War Cemetery, 8, J, 8.
    Commemorated: **Not listed on 7 DWR WW2 Memorial.**
    Barclay History RoH, page 367.
    DWR Enlistment Book: OVER 32, page 17.
"TO THE WORLD HE WAS ONLY ONE OF US, TO US HE WAS THE WORLD. LOVING WIFE AND MOTHER"

STOREY, Thomas Edward, 14721738 Pte, HQ Coy (MT) 1/7th DWR.
Son of Edward and Annie Elizabeth Storey, Liverpool, Lancs.
    Died: 7 Jan 1947, Normandy Campaign, Germany, aged 20.
    Buried: Hamburg Cemetery, 1A, K, 2
    Commemorated: **Not listed on 7 DWR WW2 Memorial.**
    DWR Enlistment Book: OVER 36, page 173.
"FATHER, IN THY GRACIOUS KEEPING LEAVE WE NOW OUR LOVED ONE SLEEPING"

WALKER, John, 3189550 LCpl, 1/7th DWR.
Son of Thomas and Marion Walker, husband of Elizabeth King Walker, Jedburgh, Scotland.
    Died: 3 Feb 1947, aged 24.
    Buried: Jedborough (Castlewood) Cemetery, 2, 877.
    Commemorated: **Not listed on 7 DWR WW2 Memorial.**
    DWR Enlistment Book: UNDER 34, page 133.
"DEATH IS BUT A PATH THAT MUST BE TROD IF MAN WOULD EVER PASS TO GOD"

2/7th DWR (115 RAC).

SPANTON, George Samuel, 4620178 LCpl, 2/7th DWR (115 Regt RAC).
    Died: 23 Aug 1944, aged 27.
    Buried: Washington Cemetery, K 98.
    Commemorated: **Not listed on 7 DWR WW2 Memorial.**
    Barclay History RoH, Page 377.
    DWR Enlistment Book: TED 20, page 18.

HERITAGE AND LEGACY

Following the Second World War the two Territorial Army battalions returned to the United Kingdom in 1946. The 5th Battalion left Lubbecke, as a cadre, on 1st June, 1946, and their original three Anti-Tank gun Batteries (370, 372 and 373) were placed in suspended animation on the same date. On 1st May, 1947, the 5th Battalion became 578 (Mobile) Heavy Anti Aircraft Regiment RA (TA), Headquarters at St Paul's Street, Huddersfield. After a number of changes of title and role, the Battalion reverted to the infantry role on 1st May, 1957, Q Battery, 382 Medium Regiment RA (TA) being split, volunteers from that Battery becoming 5th/7th Battalion (West Riding) (TA), Headquarters at St Paul's Street, Huddersfield.

The 7th Battalion also returned to the United Kingdom in 1946 and was placed into suspended animation. It was reformed on 2nd April, 1947, Headquarters at Milnsbridge, later moving to Wellesley House, Longwood, Huddersfield. On 20th May, 1957, the battalion was amalgamated with the 5th Battalion, becoming 5/7th Battalion (West Riding) (TA), Headquarters at St Paul's Street, Huddersfield.

In July, 1961, the TA was again reorganized, the 5/7th Battalion being re-titled the West Riding Battalion. until 1967, when the West Riding Battalion was reduced to Cadre Strength, under the administrative control of the Yorkshire Volunteers, which had been formed on 1st April 1967, Headquarters in York. The Halifax Company and Keighley detachment became C Company of the 3rd Battalion the Yorkshire Volunteers.

On 1st April, 1971, the original Yorkshire Volunteer Battalion was redesignated as 1st Battalion, when the 2nd and 3rd Battalions of the Yorkshire Volunteers were raised. The 3rd Battalion, Headquarters in Huddersfield, incorporated the cadre from the former West Riding Battalion (Huddersfield) and the Keighley detachment, formerly C Company, Yorkshire Volunteers, transferred to 3rd Battalion.

On 4th April, 1992 the 3rd Battalion the Yorkshire Volunteers was amalgamated with the 4th Battalion, raised in South Yorkshire on 1st January, 1988, Headquarters at Endcliffe Hall, Sheffield.

On 25th April, 1993, the Yorkshire Volunteers was disbanded, the 3/4th Battalion Yorkshire Volunteers becoming 3rd Battalion the Duke of Wellington's Regiment (West Riding), Headquarters at Endcliffe Hall, Sheffield.

On 1st July, 1999, 3 DWR were amalgamated into the East and West Riding Regiment, Headquarters in Pontefract.

On 6th June, 2006, the remaining infantry battalions in Yorkshire were amalgamated into The Yorkshire Regiment. The Territorial units being amalgamated into the 4th Battalion, The Yorkshire Regiment.

In April, 2023, the Yorkshire Regiment was granted the title Royal Yorkshire Regiment by King Charles III.

HUDDERSFIELD DRILL HALL

The heritage of the campaign lives on, this commemorative plaque records the strong bond between the crew of the British Railways ferry, TSS Duke of York, and is proudly on display in the Officers' Mess in Huddersfield Drill Hall (now a Reserve Army Centre and home to Corunna Company of the 4th Battalion (Reserve Army) of the Yorkshire Regiment. The plaque records the actions in which the vessel was involved: Operations Aerial, Jubilee, Starkey and Neptune/Overlord, as well as its change of name in honour of the 'Dukes' Battalion taken off the beaches in its first active service mission at St Valery in June 1940:

The plaque reads: Presented by British Railways to commemorate the rescue of the 2/7th Battalion The Duke of Wellington's Regiment from France after their last stand at St Valery-En-Caux by the SS 'Duke of York' later renamed 'HMS Duke of Wellington' June 1940.

Scott Flaving

SOTTEVILLE-sur-MER

On 11th June, 2023 a Commemorative Stele was erected and unveiled in Sotteville-sur-Mer by the inhabitants of the Community of Communes around St Valery en Caux:

Memorial erected in the Espace Communal at La Bergerie, Sotteville-sur-Mer, unveiled at 1100 hrs on 11th June, 2023.

In memory of the 65 fallen
French Cavalrymen, Chasseurs Alpins
and English Soldiers
of the 2/7th Duke of Wellington's Regiment
on the plain of Sotteville-sur-Mer
June 11 and 12, 1940
Lest We Forget

Scott Flaving, 2023

ACKNOWLEDGEMENTS

As this book was not First World War oriented, I tackled this one, covering those members of the Regiment commemorated on the four remaining memorials in the Huddersfield Drill Hall, on my own. However, a great many people helped in various ways over a protracted period of time and are due my gratitude and also thanks on behalf of those for whom this book was written - the soldiers who fought in the war; families of the fallen; the Trustees of the Drill Hall; the wider Regimental family, who may come across this book, and members of the public who have an interest in the period, the locality or the history.

First and foremost I must thank Derek Alexander, of Valence House Museum, for his continued interest, support and great patience in agreeing to continue to work hard and diligently to publish these books for us.

To Michael Green, my co-author in the preceding books in this series, for his work on the Volunteer Service Companies, in particular, and the Boer War in general and for supporting my own research into this conflict. Between us we have amassed enough material to produce another book...

Richard Harvey, in Huddersfield, and Major (Retired) Hervé Savary, in France, both of whom gave their time to look though the final draft and iron out some problems with dates, spellings and typos, all of which had passed me by on my frequent checks. Any remaining errors are all my own.

Finally, my thanks to Major (Ret'd) Stephen Armitage for kindly agreeing to write the foreword explaining the origins of this part of the trilogy.

Further reading:

Author	Title	Publisher	Printer	Date	Description	ISBN No
Archives Team: Edited	The Journal of the Duke of Wellington's Regiment - The Iron Duke	DWR	Various	1925 >	thousands pp, editorials, portraits, plates, maps, letters	dwr.org.uk
Barclay C N	The History of the Duke of Wellington's Regiment, 1919 to 1952	Regtl Council	William Clowes and Sons Ltd	1953	398 pp, plates, maps	dwr.org.uk
Brereton J M Savory A C S	The History of the Duke of Wellington's Regiment (West Riding) 1702 - 1992	RHQ DWR	Amadeus Press, Huddersfield	1993	446 pp, portraits, plates, maps	0-9521552 0-6 dwr.org.uk
Podmore A J	The Duke of Wellington's Regiment (West Riding) - The Volunteer & Territorial Battalions 1859 - 1999	RHQ DWR	R Holroyd Print, Halifax	1999	318 pp, plate, maps	dwr.org.uk
Edited	Langcliffe - Glimpses of a Dales Village	Langcliffe 2K		2000		No longer in print

The Iron Duke editions are available on-line, listed by edition number and year (for example 001-1925). These can be viewed or downloaded free of charge and are accessed through the Regimental Website – dwr.org.uk – family history research page.

There is a basic Index to this series which will help you select the editions containing articles and items of relevance to your interest.

The other books are no longer in print although copies of the three Regimental Histories have been digitised and can be obtained through the Regimental Website, dwr.org.uk, family history page.

The Langcliffe Village book is available at Skipton Library.

www.ingramcontent.com/pod-product-compliance
Lightning Source LLC
Chambersburg PA
CBHW042019090526
44590CB00029B/4331